STUDIES IN HISTORY, ECONOMICS AND
PUBLIC LAW

Edited by the
FACULTY OF POLITICAL SCIENCE
OF COLUMBIA UNIVERSITY

NUMBER 447

THE IMPEACHMENT OF GOVERNOR WILLIAM SULZER

BY

JACOB ALEXIS FRIEDMAN

The Impeachment

OF

Governor William Sulzer

BY

JACOB ALEXIS FRIEDMAN

AMS PRESS
NEW YORK

COLUMBIA UNIVERSITY
STUDIES IN THE
SOCIAL SCIENCES

447

The Series was formerly known as *Studies in History,
Economics and Public Law.*

Reprinted with the permission of Columbia University Press
From the edition of 1939, New York
First AMS EDITION published 1968
Manufactured in the United States of America

Library of Congress Catalogue Card Number: 68-58575

AMS PRESS, INC.
New York, N.Y. 10003

To
B. J. F.

TABLE OF CONTENTS

take the stand—Final pleas of defense counsel—Concluding arguments of the prosecution—Court questions scope of article four—Public vote on the impeachment articles—Division of the court—Conviction and removal—Sulzer's attack on the verdict.

CHAPTER VII

Press comments on the verdict—Up-state sentiment—Sulzer's reception on the East Side—His revelations in the *Mail* interview—McCall's rejoinder—Sulzer's campaign for the Assembly—Statement of Murphy—The Delmonico conference—The Fusion victory in New York—Sulzer's "vindication"—The John Doe inquiry—Sulzer's removal upheld by the courts—Back in the Assembly—Race for the Governorship—The 1914 state elections—General observations.

INTRODUCTION

To this day the name William Sulzer evokes in the public mind the memory of an independent governor " railroaded " out of office by a revengeful boss, of an altruistic and devoted friend of the people and champion of good government frustrated by a corrupt and vindictive machine. However convincing the testimony against the deposed executive, there are still those who feel that the case was prejudged, that the evidence somehow was manufactured. Now, as then, the political aspects of the case receive most attention. Many still look upon him as a martyr and view his disgrace as a striking illustration of the power of " invisible government."

The purpose of this study is to reconstruct, through the medium of public documents, official investigations, memoirs, and contemporary newspapers and periodicals, the events that culminated in Sulzer's impeachment by the Legislature, to analyze the evidence against the accused governor and the testimony adduced at the trial, and to trace the repercussions of his conviction. The author has attempted to assemble all the available records, organize the material into a logical sequence, and subject it to a critical appraisal. Sulzer's term of office, brief though it was, was probably the most sensational and tragic in the history of the state. His impeachment is an incident in a remarkable political struggle and occupies an important place in the annals of New York, not only because of its constitutional aspects but also because of the insight it furnishes into the workings of practical politics. The aim throughout has been to preserve an attitude of complete impartiality and to present all the pertinent facts with scrupulous objectivity. Such deductions as are made and such opinions as are expressed are based, the author feels, on indisputable evidence alone. If Sulzer does not emerge from these pages with much credit, little more can be said of the other actors in that sordid drama.

Despite the importance of the case and the widespread interest it aroused, there is a surprising paucity of reliable material and the facts recorded are of only fragmentary nature. The few accounts published are frankly partisan, being almost wholly anti-Tammany, and are incomplete and distorted.[1] Indignant and denunciatory, almost all writers accept unquestioningly Sulzer's version of the incidents that led to his break with Murphy and the legislative leaders and base their narratives almost solely on the statements issued by him after the trial. The author realizes that politics is, to a considerable extent, " an inside story " and that there are secret springs of conduct that cannot always be explored. Much that went on behind the scenes will probably never be known. The impulses behind public expressions are ofttimes obscure and why public men should act in one way rather than another is frequently a matter of conjecture. It is a truism that there is something about high public office that seems to make men over in a way that even the shrewdest cannot always understand. What makes the task in this instance more difficult is the baffling personality of Sulzer himself. Even to his contemporaries he was something of a mystery. " In many respects," wrote an Albany staff correspondent, " William Sulzer is an enigma. The more you study him at close range the less apparently you can define his thoughts, fathom his motives and comprehend the purport of his sayings." [2]

1 *Tammany's Treason* is the product of Jay W. Forrest, an independent Albany Democrat, and James Malcolm, a political reporter on the *Knickerbocker Press*, an Albany newspaper, which was looked upon as Sulzer's organ at the time of the impeachment. The collaborators were rabid Sulzer partisans and reprint without qualification many of the misstatements that were circulated by Sulzer and his friends during his fight with Murphy. The historical value of the book is for that reason nil. In their introduction the authors state that their object is to make plain "the underground or hidden causes" of the "political lynching" of a governor who "refused to do the bidding of the boss." This is equally true of Samuel Bell Thomas' *The Boss or the Governor.*

2 *Evening Sun,* July 21, 1913.

In conclusion the author acknowledges his profound gratitude to Professor David Saville Muzzey, of Columbia University, to whose inspiring guidance and scholarship this work owes whatever merit it possesses. Sincere thanks are also extended to Professors Evarts B. Green, Schuyler C. Wallace, and Samuel McKee, Jr. for their valuable suggestions.

J. A. F.

NEW YORK CITY,
SEPTEMBER 7, 1938.

CHAPTER I

SULZER'S RISE TO THE GOVERNORSHIP

" Plain Bill " Sulzer spent almost all of his active life in politics, from the day when in 1884, his eloquence was enlisted as " cart tail " orator in the service of Grover Cleveland's campaign for the presidency, until his tragic débacle in 1913, when he was ousted from the governorship of New York State. His rise and fall from power constitute one of the most absorbing chapters in the political annals of New York.

He was born in Elizabeth, New Jersey, on March 18, 1863.[1] His father was German and his mother of Scotch-Irish descent. His early life was spent on a farm and he received his elementary education in a country school. When he was still a boy, his family moved to the City of New York, settling on the lower East Side. His parents hoped to make him a Presbyterian minister and so, while working in a store, he attended night classes at Cooper Union. There he entered a debating society where he was soon recognized as a forceful and energetic speaker. He attracted the attention of John Reilly, Tammany leader of the old Fourteenth Assembly district in which he resided. Acting on his advice, young Sulzer studied law [2] and on reaching his majority, was admitted to the bar. He took an early interest in politics and even before becoming a lawyer, he came to be known on the East Side as " Reilly's boy spellbinder." [3] Reilly made his protégé a member of the Tammany Hall General Committee for the district and sent him on the stump. Sulzer won a reputation as a stellar cam-

1 There are brief biographical sketches of Sulzer by George W. Blake in *Sulzer's Short Speeches*, (New York, 1912), and by Edgar L. Murlin in *Public Papers of Governor Sulzer*, 1913.

2 He attended lectures in Columbia College Law School and also studied law in the office of Parrish and Pendleton.

3 *Times,* October 18, 1913.

paign orator and he rendered effective party service in each successive election.[4]

In 1889 Sulzer obtained his reward. At the request of his sponsor, he received the nomination for the Assembly, and, running as a " Jeffersonian Democrat," was elected by a large majority. Though only twenty-seven at the time, he did not remain in the background in Albany and rose rapidly to a position of prominence among the members of his party. He took himself and his duties seriously and applied himself to his legislative responsibilities with remarkable intensity. Through the influence of Tammany Hall he was placed upon the Committee on General Laws, an unusual honor for a new member.[5] He obeyed orders unhesitatingly, with the result that he was renominated and reelected in 1890. He was held in high regard by Richard Croker, then leader of Tammany Hall, and was considered so dependable, that the organization permitted him to introduce several measures which tended to enhance his popularity with his constituents. Sulzer was returned to the Assembly in 1891 and 1892, and when returned once more in 1893, was the unanimous choice of the Democratic majority for the post of Speaker,[6] the youngest man up to that time to hold the office.[7] As presiding officer of the Assembly, he showed a disposition to serve the party machine and appeared to be a ready tool of Croker.[8] He reduced the usual representation of the minority on the committees, almost all of which he put under the control of Tammany Hall and Kings County Democrats.[9] The Legislature of that year is reported to have been most scandalously partisan and its effect

4 *Tribune,* January 3, 1893.

5 New York State, Assembly Journal, 1890, Vol. I, p. 52. For Sulzer's other committee assignments see the New York State Legislative Manual, 1890-94.

6 Assembly Journal, 1893, Vol. I, p. 7.

7 *Tribune,* January 3, 1893.

8 *Ibid.,* January 7, 1893.

9 *Ibid.,* January 10, 1893.

was to end the Democratic party's rule in Albany until 1910. The New York *Evening Post* says: " The session of 1893 was remarkable for the number of pet measures that were rushed through, for incompetent committees, for ' snap ' hearings, for strangled measures, for the surreptitious, tricky, jamming of ' ripper bills ' with graft as the goal, and with Speaker Sulzer frankly, naively, and unquestioningly obeying every nod and beck of the Croker-Sheehan-Murphy triumvirate. . . . The Legislature represented a small group of political bosses, and it served the machine they constructed." [10] The New York *World,* with somewhat more forbearance, remarked, " On the whole its record is not essentially better or worse than that of its predecessors for some years past. It was machine-ridden. . . . The Legislature has done the will of the bosses with a shameful but by no means unprecedented servility." [11] Sulzer himself publicly acknowledged that " all legislation came from Tammany Hall and was dictated by that great statesman, Richard Croker." [12] This frank acknowledgment is particularly revealing in view of his latter-day contention that his public career had been wholly free from Tammany influence and that he had won his way solely by serving his constituents.

Sulzer bore a striking physical resemblance to Henry Clay and was commonly known about the Assembly Chamber as " Henry Clay Sulzer." [13] He had Clay's steep forehead, high cheek bones, large mouth, and deep-set eyes; also the same tall, loose-jointed figure.[14] Proud of the likeness, he studiously

10 October 16, 1912, John Temple Graves, on the other hand, writes: " Under his [Sulzer's] speakership, New York enjoyed the lowest tax rate and the most economical budget in 47 years and the cleanest and the shortest session of the Legislature in 51 years."—*Cosmopolitan,* Vol. 53 (July, 1912), pp. 248-49, " William Sulzer—Democrat."

11 Editorial, April 21, 1893.

12 *Tribune,* April 25, 1893.

13 *Ibid.,* January 2, 1893.

14 A vivid description of Sulzer, given by James Creelman, is quoted in the *Outlook,* Vol. 103 (January 11, 1913), p. 51.

set out to enhance it by growing a long forelock and training it to fall over his forehead in the Clay manner.[15] He is described as looking like " an intensified and exaggerated Henry Clay," as Clay " might have been had his features kept on developing in the way they were going." [16] He further cultivated the resemblance by theatrical emphasis of voice and gesture, which made him a frequent butt of newspaper ridicule.[17] Even in his dress he sought to achieve a theatrical effect and was usually made up to portray the part of " a statesman of the people." [18] Sulzer's pose was ever that of the reformer. He began it in the Legislature and continued it throughout his political career. Among the measures he sponsored in the Assembly were those which called for the abolition of imprisonment for debt, the limitation of the hours of labor, state care of the insane, conservation of natural resources, free lectures for workingmen, and ballot reform.[19] Nothing apparently was too small to escape the attention of Assemblyman Sulzer where the comfort, convenience, or welfare of the people was concerned. To some he appeared to be, while he was still climbing, a fearless defender of the weak against the strong, a champion of popular rights, and a born leader of progressivism; [20] to others he was

15 Henry Morgenthau, *All in a Lifetime*, (New York, 1922), p. 155.

16 *Current Literature*, Vol. 53 (November, 1912), p. 513, " Palladium of our Liberties."

17 Henry F. Pringle remarks that newspaper reporters looked upon him (Sulzer) as " very much of an ass."—*Alfred E. Smith*, (New York, 1927), p. 169.

18 Morgenthau gives the following description of Sulzer as he appeared to him one day in his office during the 1912 campaign: " His coat was of one pattern, and his vest of another. His baggy trousers were of a third. The gray sombrero was rather dingy; his linen just a trifle soiled. Familiar as I was with Sulzer's poses, through our acquaintance, I mentally noted the skill of the morning's costume, in dressing the part of 'a friend of the people.' "—*Supra*, pp. 155-56.

19 A complete summary of Sulzer's record in the Assembly may be found in *Sulzer's Short Speeches*, pp. 19-21; also in E. Vale Blake, *History of the Tammany Society*, (New York, 1901), p. 175.

20 *Tribune*, August 27, 1906; *Evening Post*, October 3, 1912.

simply a vain and empty demagogue, a cheap, professional politician.[21]

Having shown himself to be a faithful organization man, the rising young statesman was promoted to Washington. In the fall of 1894, he won the nomination for Congress from the Tenth District, probably the most cosmopolitan in the United States, located in the heart of Manhattan's East Side, inhabited at first largely by Irish and Germans, later predominantly by Jews. Although that year witnessed a Republican victory, Sulzer carried the district, one of the three in New York City won by the Democratic party.[22] Upon the death of Reilly, Sulzer became virtually leader of the district. Though not a native of the East Side, he knew intimately, from long residence, the lives and thoughts of the people, and enjoyed an unwavering confidence which enabled him to retain his seat for nine successive terms, notwithstanding the adversities of the Democratic party.[23] His enormous popularity made him one of the most successful vote-getters in the state and he repeatedly ran ahead of his ticket.[24]

In Washington the " young Henry Clay of the East Side " was at first looked upon as something of a joke.[25] This attitude seemed to persist even after years of unbroken political success. Because of his effervescence, he was sometimes called " Seltzer " and was often referred to in Congress as " the Siphon of Debate." [26] His brass-band methods and Fourth-of-July ora-

21 See *Harper's Weekly*, Vol. 58 (August 23, 1913), p. 25, " The Dr. Cook of Politics," by Norman Hapgood.

22 *New York Red Book*, 1913, p. 35.

23 Sulzer contended that his nomination every two years did not come as a favor from Tammany. In 1898 Croker sought to prevent his renomination, but so strong was the personal machine Sulzer had built up that he was able to seize the nomination over Croker's head.—*Times*, October 18, 1913.

24 A study of Sulzer's remarkable vote-getting record appears in the *New York Critic*, April 15, 1912; quoted in *Sulzer's Short Speeches*, pp. 24-26.

25 *Times*, August 18, 1913.

26 *Tribune*, July 29, 1910.

tory stamped him as a demagogue. He was adept in all the devices of popularity and was endowed with all the bombastic qualities of the typical spellbinder. Even in an interview with newspaper men he would orate. One reporter gives the following pen picture of him in action: " Sulzer never sat down at all. He strode on long, thin legs, back and forth across a space about four feet wide, spouting words, gesturing with upraised hand or clenched quivering fist as he exuded oratory, as a spellbinder exudes to a group of yokels about the town pump. For fully fifteen minutes he declaimed thus: ' I want to say to you, and through you to all the people of the State of New York, that my nomination is not a personal triumph, but a vindication of the slogan, " Let the people rule." ' " [27] Another reporter once observed, " William Sulzer, the man, is hard to reach. To get at the real Sulzer you have to wade through, not a mass of red tape and ceremony or a retinue of lackeys, but an exasperating bog of bombast and ' hifalutin ' oratory, best summed up in the effective slang word ' bunk '." [28]

Sulzer's eloquence bubbled forth at the slightest pressure. Speaking on his bill calling on the government to keep the Statue of Liberty in New York harbor lit every night in the year, he indignantly asked, " Why is it that after all this time this light must go out? Is liberty dead? I hope not. I am a friend of liberty here and everywhere. As a citizen of this Republic, I take a just pride in the grandeur of Liberty Enlightening the World and for all it typifies here and symbolizes to people in other lands. I would not darken its effulgent light, but I would make it burn brighter and brighter as the years come and go. It stands at the gates of America, a magnificent altar to man's faith in liberty, whose light should penetrate the darkness of tyranny throughout the world and guide men from oppression to our hospitable shores of freedom." [29] On another

27 *Evening Post,* October 4, 1912.
28 *Ibid.*
29 *Sulzer's Short Speeches,* pp. 38-39.

occasion he fearlessly proclaimed his faith in republican institutions. " I take my stand with the people against empire,
and in favor of the perpetuity of the republic," he said. " Ours
is the great republic, the beacon light of the world, the refuge
of the oppressed of every clime, the home for the downtrodden
of every land, and it is the imperative duty of those who are
here and enjoying the inestimable blessings of our free institutions to see to it that the government of Jefferson, of Jackson, and of Lincoln does not perish from the earth." [30] He
unequivocally declared himself " a man of the people." When
asked to define the term, he gave the enlightening reply, " A
man of the people is one who loves his fellow man, and who is
in sympathy with his hopes, his aims, his aspirations. He is
the man who gets up in the morning and works hard all day
and feels that he has earned his day's wages if he has done
one man a good turn." [31]

Sulzer professed to be the friend of all humanity and
champion of universal liberty. He earnestly pleaded the cause
of the Cuban insurgents in Congress and strongly advocated
American recognition of Cuban independence.[32] He introduced
a resolution extending sympathy " to the liberty-loving and
patriotic Boers of South Africa " and demanded that the sale
of munitions of war here for English use in South Africa be
stopped.[33] He denounced Russia for the outrages against the
Jews, and proposed a resolution of protest.[34] He introduced a
resolution congratulating the people of China on the establishment of a republic.[35] " When it comes to preserving our liberties," said a Washington correspondent, " William is a whole

30 *Ibid.*, p. 94.

31 *Times,* October 4, 1912.

32 *Tribune,* April 8, 1898. See also Joseph E. Wisan, *The Cuban Crisis
as Reflected in the New York Press,* (New York, 1934), p. 257.

33 *Tribune,* February 12, 1901. The entire address, entitled " Justice for
the Boers," is reprinted in William Sulzer, *Life and Speeches, 1898-1916.*

34 *Ibid.*

35 *Congressional Record,* 62nd Cong., 2nd Session, Vol. 48, Part I, p. 634.

canning factory. He can scent an outrage on those liberties all the way from the Capitol to the White House, or vice versa, as the case may be. . . . It makes no difference what the outrage on our liberties may be. The whole boundless universe is Bill's. He lets go at the Czar and at King Leopold with equal vigor and with equal output. He is a little brother to the oppressed of all the world. ' Our ' to him means all nations, all creeds, all colors and all conditions. He is for the universal conglomeration of man." [36] Another newspaper man wrote similarly, " From the tall, thin, pyrotechnical figure of the impassioned Congressman a dithyramb was always to be expected when any issue that arose could be construed as an assault upon popular liberty. Freedom shrieked in that spare, restless figure with the keen blue eyes, the Napoleonic lock with a charter to rove at large over his forehead, the singular likeness to Henry Clay when the great Pacificator was young. He was accused of bombast, and certain it was that the moment he scented an invasion of the people's privilege in any quarter he launched into an amazing oration. Oratory is the breath of his nostrils. The pose is the man. He confutes objections with what has been compared to an avalanche of speech. His opponent releases a verbal deluge upon himself. . . . He gyrates and brandishes and fulminates when roused to action." [37] The inimitable Mr. Dooley had a great admiration for his old friend Bill and was moved to praise for " a man who has to blow his nose ivry time he thinks iv th' troubles iv ithers." Said Mr. Dooley with his matchless wit : " It's always been a great relief to me whin bowed down undher th' yoke iv oppressyon to know that ol' Bill was weepin' or runnin' f'r office or makin' some other sacrifice f'r me. He has always been a frind iv th' people. He has lavished his sobs on thim an' has ast nawthin' in return but their votes. While he was in Washin'ton

36 *Current Literature*, Vol. 53 (November, 1912), p. 513, " Palladium of our Liberties."

37 Philadelphia *Public Ledger*, quoted in the *Literary Digest*, Vol. 45 (November 30, 1912), p. 1031.

no poor man ivir called on Bill an' came away empty handed. He always clutched in his emacyated fin a bag iv sunflower seeds an' a copy iv Bill's last appeal f'r humanity." [38] Norman Hapgood once dubbed him " The Dr. Cook of Politics." " He never in his life went to work quietly to do good, without seeking noisy acclaim," he writes. " He never stood up for his opinion against his immediate advantage. He never relied upon reason, but placed his trust in pose and rhetoric. He had no element of superiority, and yet the people trusted him. He posed and screamed, and the people took him at his word. . . . Sulzer has never done an unpopular thing that I know of. He never had any morality except to seek cheap success at any cost." [39]

While Sulzer may have been all that, an examination of his legislative record discloses that he was an advocate of many good causes. He grew steadily in reputation during his nine successive terms in Congress where he identified himself with progressive legislation and worked for industrial and social reform. He was a forceful debater and took a close interest in the proceedings on the floor of the House. He favored the establishment of a Bureau of Corporations to secure the better enforcement of the anti-trust law. He was always an ardent pleader for the cause of labor and introduced a bill for the creation of an independent Department of Labor.[40] He showed his devotion to progressive principles by introducing a resolution to amend the constitution so as to permit the election of United States Senators by direct vote of the people. He advocated the income tax amendment to the Federal constitution and favored the publicity of campaign contributions. He was author of a bill in Congress for an eight-hour work day. He supported the establishment of a parcel post; championed the revival of the merchant marine; and supported the move-

38 *Times,* August 31, 1913.
39 *Harper's Weekly,* Vol. 58 (August 23, 1913), p. 25.
40 *Congressional Record,* 62nd Cong., 2nd Session, Vol. 48, Part V, p. 4364.

ment for the conservation of natural resources.[41] After the
elections of 1910, which returned a Democratic majority to
the House of Representatives, Sulzer became chairman of the
important Foreign Relations Committee, a post in which he
was praised by Woodrow Wilson as showing " capacity and
discretion of a very fine sort." [42] In this office he strongly
opposed American intervention in Mexico and used his influence to prevent the despatch of troops across the border. He
sought to expose by means of committee hearings " the true
story " of how the United States acquired the right to build
the Panama Canal. He led the fight for the abrogation of the
treaty of 1832 between the United States and Russia because
of the latter's refusal to recognize American passports borne
by Jews. His resolution passed the House almost unanimously
and the treaty was abrogated.[43] Sulzer also played an active
part in national politics. He was a delegate to the Democratic
national convention in 1896, and in the ensuing campaign
was one of the few enthusiastic supporters in the East of
William Jennings Bryan for president, whom he regarded as a
" bulwark against the centralization of wealth and power." [44]
He continued to represent New York at every national convention through 1912.

Until his election as governor, Sulzer's public career was a
curious mixture of apparent independence and diffident subservience to party mandates. A combination of independent and
machine politician, he was a subject of debate even among the
rank and file of his own party. Sulzer himself always sought
to convey the impression of freedom from party dictates. In a
recent interview with the author, he boasted that he held his

41 A complete summary of Sulzer's Congressional career may be found
in his *Short Speeches*.

42 *Times,* October 4, 1912.

43 *Congressional Record,* 62nd Cong., 2nd Session, Vol. 48, Part I, p. 353.
A complete summary of Sulzer's record as chairman of the Foreign Relations Committee is given in *Ibid.*, Part XII, appendix, pp. 819-21.

44 *Tribune,* July 24, 1896.

district practically single-handed. During his Congressional career, it is said, Tammany twice tried to shelve him, but he won in spite of the organization, owing to the confidence and loyalty of his constituents.[45] Yet Sulzer did call Tammany " the greatest vehicle " for the accomplishment of the good of the people.[46] In view of his virulent denunciation of Tammany during the latter part of his career, this eloquent eulogy of his makes interesting reading: " The men who, in season and out of season, continually denounce Tammany and Democracy, who denounce its leaders, who revile it and prophecy all evil concerning it, know not of what they talk. Its organization is thoroughly, simply and absolutely Democratic . . . Chronic fault-finding is unfair, sweeping denunciation is unwarranted. . . . Tammany is Democracy. Tammany needs no defense from any man. It needs no eulogy but its own history, its own record, and its own indefatigable efforts for its principles and the people. That record and that history speak in trumpet tones to the world more eloquently than words of mine. Read its history, read what it has done for the people in many a struggle, and for the Democratic party, ere you judge it and condemn. . . . Tammany will go on and on forever—to its truer and grander destiny." [47]

His rapid political rise naturally stimulated his ambitions and he aspired to the governorship. Sulzer announced his candidacy for the first time in 1896 but Tammany rejected him.[48] He tried again in 1898 with no more success, Boss Croker openly ridiculing his ambition.[49] Despite the disregard shown by the organization leaders, he persistently pursued the gubernatorial nomination and was at hand at every state convention to press

45 Jay W. Forrest and James Malcolm, *Tammany's Treason*, (Albany, 1913), p. 21.

46 From a public address quoted in the *Tribune*, October 18, 1913.

47 From a speech delivered in Tammany Hall, February 13, 1902, reprinted in pamphlet form and included in *Life and Speeches*.

48 *Tribune*, September 17, 18, 1896.

49 Forrest and Malcolm, *supra*, p. 20.

his claims. He was urged as head of the state ticket in 1906 by several prominent party leaders who were friendly toward him, and that year a campaign committee opened headquarters in Buffalo to support the Sulzer boom.[50] Although his name evoked tremendous enthusiasm in the convention, he was again turned down, in favor of William Randolph Hearst, the personal choice of Charles F. Murphy, Croker's successor as leader of Tammany Hall.[51] Two years later his efforts were equally fruitless. His supporters urged his name even more eagerly in 1910, when the factional fight in the Republican party seemed to assure Democratic success. The convention nominated, however, John A. Dix, chairman of the Democratic State Committee, who, though affiliated with the anti-machine Democrats, was supported by Murphy.[52] Sulzer was said to have been so disappointed at his failure to receive the nomination that he was uncertain " whether he would continue to maintain even the appearance of friendly relations with Tammany which had so often deceived and repudiated him." [53]

Political conditions in 1912 favored Sulzer's nomination. Governor Dix, from whom independent Democrats had hoped for a reform administration, had proved to be utterly subservient to the party machine and consequently had lost up-state support.[54] Under his weak and compliant administration Tammany had extended its control beyond the confines of New York City.[55] Most of the Democratic leaders of the state went on record as opposing a second term.[56] The party's presidential candidate, Woodrow Wilson, also exerted his influence against

50 *Tribune*, September 18, 1906.

51 *Ibid.*, September 27, 1906.

52 Roscoe C. E. Brown, *Political and Governmental History of the State of New York*, (Syracuse, 1922), Vol. IV, pp. 187-88.

53 Forrest and Malcolm, *supra*, p. 22.

54 *Ibid.*, p. 25.

55 For a detailed description of the strengthening of Tammany's hold on the state government during Dix's administration, see *Ibid.*, pp. 23-26.

56 *Times*, October 2, 1912.

his renomination, demanding a " free and unbossed " convention.[57] The Republicans nominated Job E. Hedges, prominent attorney, as governor and the Progressive party selected Oscar S. Straus, well-known Jewish philanthropist and former member of Roosevelt's cabinet. Straus's nomination brightened Sulzer's chances and made him a favorite from the start. The need was for an available candidate who could hold intact the normal Jewish vote against Straus.[58] This, it was felt, Sulzer could do owing to his effective espousal of Jewish rights in Congress, particularly because of the prominent part he had taken in the abrogation of our treaty with Russia.[59] He would also, it was reasoned, not only carry the normal Democratic vote but, because of his reputation as an advocate of political and social reform, at the same time draw the support of the large number of independents who might be inclined to support the Progressive ticket.[60] The public considered him as one of the most respectable of the Tammany adherents; from the Tammany viewpoint he was " safe." [61] And so the name of Congressman Sulzer was put forward for governor at the state convention in Syracuse on October 3, 1912 as the only possible compromise between Tammany and the up-state Democratic reformers. In popularity he was unquestionably the strongest candidate in a field which included also Governor Dix, Supreme Court Justices Victor J. Dowling and James W. Gerard, and Martin H. Glynn, Albany newspaper publisher and state comptroller during the first administration of Governor Hughes. The overwhelming majority of Democratic county chairmen were reported as being for him.[62] Though undoubted master of

57 Roscoe C. E. Brown, *supra*, p. 223.

58 Oscar S. Straus, *Under Four Administrations*, (New York, 1922), p. 320.

59 To attract the Jewish voters, the Sulzer campaign slogan was, " Non-Jewish but pro-Jewish."—Morgenthau, *op. cit.*, p. 157.

60 *Ibid.*

61 *Ibid.*, p. 156.

62 *Times,* October 2, 1912.

the convention, Tammany leader Murphy declined to indicate
publicly whom he favored. Yielding to the up-state opposition,
he reluctantly abandoned Dix and had his name withdrawn at
the end of the third ballot. He refused, however, to commit
himself on any of the other candidates, even going so far as
personally to abstain from voting.[63] After a conference with
his board of advisers, he turned the delegates " loose," giving
the word that he would let them vote as they pleased.[64] Supported by most of the independents and part of the New York
City delegation, Sulzer received the nomination on the fourth
ballot, at the hands of what appeared to be an " unbossed "
convention. The choice was a popular one, as evidenced by the
tumult of enthusiasm that followed the announcement.[65] Glynn,
maker of the " keynote " speech in the convention, was nominated for lieutenant-governor without opposition.[66] The platform of the party was decidedly progressive, providing for
advanced social and industrial reforms and a statewide direct
primary law.[67]

The prevailing opinion that the Democratic state convention
was " unbossed " was only an illusion. Despite the Tammany
pretence that it was uncontrolled, it was from the start manipu-
lated by Murphy.[68] " The convention," wrote one of the delegates, " was absolutely in the hands of Murphy; and the freedom of the delegates mere stage-play." [69] It was with Tammany
support that Alton B. Parker was selected as permanent chairman, against the vain opposition of the independent element.[70]

63 *World*, October 3, 1912.

64 *Ibid.*

65 *Ibid.*

66 *Evening Post*, October 3, 1912. Glynn was considered an independent
Democrat. Yet, according to Jay W. Forrest, he was throughout the con-
vention in close and confidential communication with Murphy and other
Tammany leaders.—*Tammany's Treason*, p. 34.

67 *Times*, October 3, 1912.

68 Henry Morgenthau, *op. cit.*, p. 157.

69 Quoted in *Evening Post*, editorial, October 7, 1912.

70 Roscoe C. E. Brown, *op. cit.*, p. 224.

Sulzer's nomination, it was widely rumored, had been arranged beforehand by Murphy, Patrick E. McCabe, Democratic boss of Albany, and Norman E. Mack, New York member of the Democratic National Committee.[71] While Murphy seemed unwilling to express any preference in public, he is reported to have passed the word among the delegates, shortly before the fourth ballot was taken, to watch how " Packy " McCabe voted and to follow his lead.[72] McCabe gave his vote to Sulzer. State Senator Robert F. Wagner cast the solid vote of New York County for him, thus making his nomination certain.[73] When asked, after the convention, whether he was satisfied with the result, Murphy evasively replied, " It was an open convention. As a Democrat I ought to be." [74]

George W. Blake, political reporter and close confidant of Sulzer, testified to the author that Sulzer received advance information of his nomination from Murphy himself. Yet, when interviewed at his hotel immediately after the convention, he pretended that the nomination had come to him as a surprise. " This nomination came to me when I least expected to get it," he asserted.[75] He had had no intention of entering the state campaign, he went on to say, but had been persuaded to leave Washington by the importunities of political friends. Every one knew how relentlessly he had pursued the nomination for sixteen years, yet he stated, " I did not care whether the convention nominated me or not." [76] Asked why he wanted to be governor, he replied, " I hope to put the government back into the hands of the people," and added that he was " very confident " Murphy would help him attain that laudable purpose.[77]

71 *Tribune*, October 18, 1913.
72 *Evening Post*, October 7, 1912.
73 *World*, October 3, 1912.
74 *Times*, October 3, 1912.
75 *Evening World*, October 4, 1912.
76 *Ibid.*
77 *Times*, October 4, 1912.

He pledged himself to be governor " in fact as well as in name." " While I believe in party organization, I shall not accept orders from anybody," he challengingly declared. " And if the people of New York make me their Governor, they can rest assured I shall be the Governor and the Executive office will be in the Capitol." [78] At the official notification ceremonies, held at the National Democratic Club in New York City on October 10, 1912, after pointing with pride to his life, vision, and affection for the people, he affirmed himself the candidate of a " free and unfettered convention of independent delegates," and again pledged his faith that if he was elected, the Executive office would be in Albany and nowhere else. " I am free, without entanglements, and shall remain free . . . William Sulzer never had a boss, and his only master is himself," he declared with emphasis.[79] Tammany Hall leader Murphy, it is reported, heard the boast with a smile.[80]

The consensus of opinion among Democrats was that Sulzer would make a strong candidate, and his choice, despite his Tammany background, was widely approved among reformers. Woodrow Wilson expressed his gratification in the following statement: " The freedom of action and of choice which the convention exercised must afford every Democrat real satisfaction. In choosing a candidate, it named a man whose reputation for integrity and independence is unquestionable, a man of high principle, devoted to the public interest. . . . He certainly deserves the suffrages of independent men of every caste." [81] William G. McAdoo, of the National Campaign Committee, found his nomination " personally gratifying " and asserted that Sulzer " in every way measures up to the standards which the Progressive Democracy demands of its candi-

78 *Evening World*, October 4, 1912.

79 From Sulzer's speech of acceptance, included in his *Miscellaneous*, Vol. I.

80 *Times*, October 11, 1912.

81 *Evening Post*, October 3, 1912.

dates." [82] William J. Bryan praised him enthusiastically, saying he might well be called " a man of the people." [83] William R. Hearst expressed similar sentiments, declaring he had " the correct Democratic conception of the words ' the people '." [84] The " Empire State Democracy," organized through the efforts of Thomas Mott Osborne and Senator Franklin D. Roosevelt to war on Tammany Hall, withdrew its own state ticket and pledged its support to Sulzer, satisfied that he was " the clear choice " of the convention and had been nominated " without any aid from Tammany Hall." [85] The New York *World* hailed Sulzer as the representative of " progressive Democracy," without a stain on his record, as one who had never been " subservient to a corrupt boss or a corrupt corporation." [86] The New York *Times* urged every Democrat to vote for him unhesitatingly, praising his courage, integrity, and political record, confident he would administer the office of governor " with ability, with independence, with good sense, and with good results to the State." [87]

Some skeptics here and there, however, recalling his record of approved regularity and subservience to the machine, questioned the sincerity of his insurgency. The New York *Tribune* called Sulzer a Tammany " sub-boss " and " a steadfast advocate of Tammany methods and Tammany theories of government." Recalling that he worked a lifetime in the service of Croker and Murphy, it wanted to know on what matter, vital to Tammany, he had ever shown his independence.[88] The New York *Evening Post* viewed Sulzer's nomination as " a bitter disappointment." The convention, it declared, " has chosen a man who in no wise measures up to the needs of the hour, or

82 *Times*, October 4, 1912.
83 *Evening Post,* October 10, 1912.
84 *Times*, October 17, 1912.
85 *World,* October 5, 1912.
86 Editorial, October 4, 1912.
87 Editorial, October 4, 1912.
88 Editorial, October 9, 1912.

to the needs of the office. . . . Sulzer is the Murphy candidate; he could not have been chosen save by Murphy's full approval. However independent he may have been at times, he is and has been essentially a part of Tammany Hall, against whose infamies he has never taken up arms. Nor is there the slightest reason to believe that, if elected, he will really cut loose from the influences which have made him what he is and kept him in public life." Expediency rather than fitness, it felt, dictated his choice. " The Democrats nominated a man who throughout his career has been a joke—the butt of ridicule. . . . It would be difficult even in the friendliest spirit to speak of his past career and avoid the use of the word demagogue." [89] William Barnes, chairman of the Republican State Committee, took the nomination as a jest, and, in view of Sulzer's much vaunted independence, thought it would be interesting to recall his career at Albany as Speaker of the Assembly.[90] Oscar S. Straus pointedly inquired, " Will a man who has for thirty years been aligned with Tammany Hall and received all of his preferment at its hands be able to free himself from the clutch of the Tiger?" [91] And Richard Croker, from Liverpool, England, gave this statement respecting Sulzer's " independence " declaration: " There is not a man in Tammany who came to me for advice oftener or looked for political favor more than William Sulzer." [92]

Sulzer made his campaign largely on the " boss " issue, repeatedly affirming that he had never been " the puppet " of any man, and would be solely " the people's Governor." [93] In an interview with newspaper reporters he emphatically asserted, " I am my own master. The only boss I have ever had is the man under my own hat. If I am elected Governor, I pledge

89 Editorial, October 3, 1912.

90 *Times,* October 4, 1912.

91 *Ibid.*

92 *World,* November 8, 1912.

93 *Times,* October 31, 1912.

the people that I will be the Governor. No man and no faction will ever make me do anything that is not absolutely right or for the best interests of all the people of this State." [94] Similar professions of independence appeared in almost every one of his campaign speeches.[95] Inasmuch as Sulzer had been a Wigwam stalwart for so many years, it was but natural that the real bosses of the party should view his boasts of independence as part of his characteristic campaign manner, as part of the usual pre-election flapdoodle disseminated for the benefit of " the peepul." [96] Shrewd observers of the political scene received his protestations that he was his own master with frank disbelief, preparing for a kind of theatrical encounter between Sulzer and Murphy, " the former to chase the latter with ' the cheap numerosity of a stage army,' and to strike at him with a tin sword, the two thereafter to get together and ' do business ' amicably." [97]

The division among the Republicans gave Sulzer the election. He received 649,559 votes to 444,105 for Hedges and 393,183 for Straus, the remaining 80,368 votes being scattered among the minor parties. The official record shows, therefore, that the popular majority against Sulzer was 268,097.[98] Despite his boast that he had been elected governor by the largest majority ever given a candidate for that office, he polled a smaller vote than had John A. Dix two years previously,[99] and actually received the smallest vote of any Democratic candidate for governor in fourteen years.[100] He ran slightly behind Wilson in the state and obtained considerably fewer

94 *Sun*, October 7, 1912.

95 See *Times*, October 17, 19, 20, 22, 23, 31, 1912.

96 See, for example, the *Literary Digest*, Vol. 45 (November 30, 1912), p. 1030.

97 *Nation*, editorial, Vol. 96 (January 9, 1913), pp. 27-28, "New Governor."

98 New York State, Manual of the Legislature, 1913, pp. 668-69.

99 Dix obtained 689,700 votes when he ran for governor in 1910.

100 *World*, editorial December 31, 1912.

votes than Glynn, the candidate for lieutenant-governor.[101] The split in the Republican ranks also gave Tammany Hall control of both branches of the Legislature by overwhelming majorities, New York City sending an almost solid delegation to Albany. In the Senate the Democrats filled thirty-three of the fifty-one seats (Republicans seventeen, Progressives one), while in the Assembly the party won an even larger majority, securing one hundred and three out of the one hundred and fifty seats (Republicans forty-three, Progressives four).[102] The reform elements viewed Sulzer's election as marking the beginning of an era of social and political reform.[103]

That all was not well between Sulzer and Tammany became apparent soon after the election. On December 21, 1912 the United Democracy celebrated its victory at the Waldorf-Astoria Hotel with a testimonial dinner given in honor of the Governor-elect. A marked feature was the absence of several of the party leaders. Most conspicuous among those was Murphy who, though invited, stayed away without offering any written or verbal apology. The explanation given was that he had been kept at home by the unexpected arrival of some visitors, but the real reason for the Tammany chieftain's failure to appear at the dinner was that one of the invited guests was Bryan.[104] Murphy evidently was still unable to forgive Bryan for his harsh denunciation of the New York delegation and Tammany Hall in particular at the Baltimore national convention.[105] Governor Dix was also absent from the festivities, and it was recalled that in a speech before the City Club a few nights before, Sulzer had taken a thrust at the extravagance of the Dix administration, while pledging himself to a policy of retrenchment and economy.[106]

101 Manual of the Legislature, 1913, p. 665; p. 671.

102 *Ibid.*, pp. 526-28; pp. 568-73.

103 *Review of Reviews*, Vol. 46 (December, 1912), p. 654, "What Happened in New York."

104 *Tribune*, December 22, 1912.

105 *World*, editorial, December 23, 1912.

106 *Tribune*, December 20, 1912.

Sulzer's inauguration in Albany on the first of January was marked by ostentatious simplicity, as befitted the induction into office of the " People's Governor." With Jeffersonian precedent, he walked the half mile from the Executive Mansion to the Capitol, followed by a jubilant and boisterous throng, to whom the new Governor was still just " plain Bill." [107] He was attired in an ordinary business suit and soft fedora, in striking contrast with the frock coat and high silk hat worn by Dix, and kept chewing on the end of a cigar.[108] The military parade, which formerly added pomp to the inaugural ceremonies, was omitted at his own request. The Tammany braves were not so conspicuous as they had been two years before. The absence of Murphy was a portent of disappointment to the politicians and office-seekers and provoked considerable comment.[109] The Boss was represented, however, by several of his district leaders, by Thomas F. Smith, secretary of Tammany Hall, and by John H. McCooey, Democratic leader of Brooklyn.[110] Governor Dix made a short address in which he transferred the responsibilities and cares of his office to the new incumbent. There might have been a faint suggestion of sarcasm when he told his successor that he had his sympathy.[111] Sulzer's inaugural address was brief and simple. The note of triumph at the realization of his lifelong ambition was sounded in the phrase, " The hour has struck, and the task of administrative reform is mine." He made no reference to the outgoing Governor. The inaugural was recognized by many as a reiteration of the best passages of his campaign speeches. He repeated that he had no boss save his conscience and intended to have

107 *Ibid.*, January 2, 1913.

108 *World,* January 2, 1913.

109 Murphy was away, it was explained, either because he did not wish to embarrass Sulzer at the very outset of the administration with his presence or because he was peeved at having received a formal, not a personal, invitation to attend the inaugural ceremonies.—*World,* January 1, 1913.

110 *Times,* January 1, 1913.

111 *Tribune,* January 2, 1913.

none. " Grateful to the people who have honored me with their suffrages, I enter upon the performance of the duties of the office without a promise, except my pledge to all the people to serve them faithfully and honestly and to the best of my ability. I am free, without entanglements, and shall remain free. No influence controls me but the dictates of my conscience and my determination to do my duty, day in and day out, as I see the right, regardless of consequences. In the future, as in the past, I will walk the street called straight, and without fear and without favor I shall execute the laws justly and impartially—with malice toward none." He dedicated himself to the maintenance of representative and democratic institutions, promised an economical and business-like administration and " progressive reforms along constructive and constitutional lines." He " resolved to shirk no responsibility; to work for the welfare of the people; to correct every existing abuse; to abolish useless offices and wherever possible consolidate bureaus and commissions to secure greater economy and more efficiency; to uproot official corruption and to raise higher the standard of official integrity; to simplify the methods of orderly administration." [112] The Governor repeated the speech shortly afterward from the steps of the Capitol to a large crowd that had been unable to make its way into the Assembly Chamber.[113] He rechristened the Executive Mansion the " People's House," and invited even the humblest citizen to its doors.[114]

In his first message to the Legislature, delivered on the day he took office, he outlined his program as Governor. The message was notable for its advocacy of progressive measures. He urged the immediate ratification of the proposed amendment providing for the direct election of United States Senators, taking occasion to reaffirm his faith in popular government. "If the people cannot be trusted," he reminded his

112 *Public Papers of Governor Sulzer,* 1913, pp. 5-8, *passim.*

113 *World,* January 1, 1913.

114 Morgenthau, *op. cit.,* p. 165.

listeners, " then our government is a failure, and the free institutions of the fathers doomed." [115] He advocated direct primaries, woman suffrage, conservation of natural resources, and extension of the merit system. His program of social legislation included a scheme of minimum wages, workmen's compensation, further restrictions on child labor, the establishment of legal safety standards in factories to guard against the accidents and diseases of industry, and the reorganization of the Department of Labor with more power to investigate conditions and enforce the law.[116] Both houses of the Legislature were organized by Tammany. Alfred E. Smith was elected Speaker of the Assembly and Aaron J. Levy leader of the Democratic majority. Robert F. Wagner became President pro tempore of the Senate. Tammany also assumed control of all important committees.[117]

115 *Public Papers of Governor Sulzer*, p. 26.

116 The entire message appears in *Ibid.*, pp. 21-39.

117 Assembly Journal, 136th Session, 1913, Vol. I, pp. 8, 27-32; Senate Journal, 136th Session, 1913, Vol. I, pp. 9, 15-17.

CHAPTER II
GOVERNMENT BY INVESTIGATION

EVEN to the most casual observer it was evident that Sulzer's gubernatorial career would be a stormy one. Much of what he had said during the campaign was not taken seriously, but when he assumed office, he almost immediately asserted his independence of Tammany Hall. On the day after his inauguration, he solemnly proclaimed himself the leader of the Democratic party of the state and declared that he refused to recognize any one's authority to dictate to him. He made this remarkable declaration to a group of press representatives with whom he was discussing his plans for the investigation and reorganization of the state departments. In reply to a question of one of the correspondents, who was evidently seeking to test his relations with Murphy, as to whether the proposed investigation had the consent of the Tammany leader, he said he would settle the question once and for all, and dictated the following statement: " I am the Democratic leader of the State of New York. The people decreed it at the polls and I stand on the verdict. I cannot succeed in doing what I want to do as Governor unless I am the leader. If any Democrat wants to challenge that, let him come out in the open and the people will decide." He would not countenance any secret deals or confidential conferences. If Murphy wanted to see him, he said, he would have to do so in the Executive Chamber and his advice would receive no greater consideration than that of any one else. " There will be no secrecy about anything I do," he pledged. " Everything in this administration will be open and above board." [1] Independents throughout the state heard Sulzer's defiance of the " invisible government " with genuine

[NOTE.—All newspaper references in this and subsequent chapters, unless otherwise indicated, are taken from the newspapers of the year 1913.]

1 *Times,* January 3.

gratification and acclaimed his courage.[2] Although Democratic politicians and legislators were reported to be filled with consternation,[3] publicly neither Murphy nor any of the other party bosses took up the gauntlet. Murphy felt apparently that he could hold the Governor in check through his control of the Legislature, inasmuch as a Tammany man headed almost every important committee in the Assembly and Senate.

Sulzer sought at once to embody his independent position in practical measures of reform by directing an investigation of the state administrative departments, with a view to running down charges of waste and graft, reducing expenditures, abolishing useless jobs, and raising the standards of official integrity. No influence would be allowed to prevent the disclosure of wrongdoing, he warned, and any such revelations would result in the immediate punishment of the offenders. He also expressed his determination to bring about the enactment of necessary administrative reforms and, while disclaiming any intention of interfering with the Legislature, he plainly intimated that if its members failed to cooperate with him, he would submit his cause to the decision of the people.[4] But whatever fears of detrimental disclosures Tammany officeholders might have entertained must have quickly given way to a feeling of reassurance when the personnel of the Committee of Inquiry was announced.[5] As its head the Governor designated John N. Carlisle, of Watertown, independent Democrat and long an aggressive opponent of Tammany. The other members appointed were John H. Delaney, of Brooklyn, and H. Gordon Lynn, of New York, both Tammany men. The selection of Delaney and Lynn aroused doubts in the minds of independents as to whether the proposed investigation was to be " on the level," even though in naming them, Sulzer

2 *World*, January 3.

3 *Ibid*.

4 *Times*, January 4.

5 *Public Papers of Governor Sulzer*, p. 652.

paid high tribute to their sincerity and ability as investigators.[6] Delaney, business manager of the *Morning Telegraph,* was regarded as one of Murphy's most intimate friends,[7] and Lynn was characterized by Raymond B. Fosdick, former Commissioner of Accounts in New York City, as " one of Murphy's right hand men." [8] The bill appropriating the funds to defray the expenses of the committee passed the Assembly by a unanimous vote [9] and in the Senate was approved by a party vote of twenty-nine to eleven, the Republicans voting in the negative.[10] And so Sulzer began his march to hoped-for fame as a reform Governor.

The first visit of Murphy to Albany after Sulzer's assumption of office was on January 12, but only in his capacity as presidential elector. Along with others he attended the Governor's reception and talked with Sulzer, but denied to inquisitive newspaper correspondents that politics had any place in their conversation.[11] The Tammany chieftain unobtrusively lingered in the capital several days, discussing patronage in his hotel suite with members of the Legislature and Democratic county leaders, and when he returned, gave no indication of any friction between himself and the Governor. He appeared to be well satisfied with his visit to Albany and one Tammany man acknowledged that he had been able to " put across a few things." [12] He refused to comment openly on the question of the leadership of the Democratic party, and when asked to define his attitude toward the new Governor, he smiled and

6 *World.* January 3.

7 *Ibid.*

8 *Ibid.*, February 10.

9 Journal of the Assembly of the State of New York, 136th Session, 1913, Vol. I, p. 114.

10 New York State Senate Journal, 136th Session, 1913, Vol. I, p. 45. The Republican legislators presumably feared exposure of irregularities during the years of Republican state control.—*World,* January 8.

11 *Times,* January 13.

12 *Ibid.*, January 16.

blandly replied, " I'm with Governor Sulzer to do anything to make his administration a success." [13] To shrewd political observers this evasive response sounded unconvincing, and one newspaper cartoonist, with prophetic vision, portrayed a frigid meeting between Sulzer and Murphy, bearing the legend, " Albany Weather Report: Chilly—Likely to be Colder." [14] To intimates Murphy made it plain that he still regarded Sulzer as a loyal follower of Tammany Hall, despite his independent bearing, and that he expected no trouble with him. He described newspaper versions of the Governor's attitude toward Tammany as "newspaper guff," adding, " Sulzer is all right." [15]

Sulzer soon had the opportunity of proving the sincerity of his public professions of independence of boss control and whole-hearted devotion to the public interest. This opportunity came with the selection of a successor to William R. Willcox as chairman of the Public Service Commission of the first district, whose term was to expire on February 1. The New York City authorities sent the Governor a letter, signed by Mayor Gaynor and all but two members of the Board of Estimate and Apportionment, urging the reappointment of Willcox, or at least his retention, until the signing of the contracts between the city and the Interborough and Brooklyn Rapid Transit Companies, which had been drawn up after two years of negotiation. The letter held that the loss of his expert knowledge at a time when the proposed operating contracts were still pending would be " a public misfortune." [16] Ex-Mayor Seth Low joined in the demand on the Governor not to defeat the consummation of the contracts by replacing Willcox, who was friendly to the so-called " dual " subway plan, with some one who might be unfriendly to it and thereby throw the entire situation into confusion.[17] An impressive pro-

13 *Ibid.*, January 18.
14 *Ibid.*
15 *World,* January 15.
16 *Times*, January 9.
17 *Ibid.,* January 24.

test against any Executive action that might jeopardize the subway plan was also presented to Governor Sulzer on January 31 by a large delegation of New Yorkers representing numerous civic bodies. In addressing them the Governor stated that his " mind was open " and that he was still " seeking light." [18] It was no secret, however, that a systematic campaign to influence his mind was being waged by the advocates of municipal operation of the subways, who opposed the reappointment of Willcox. At the head of this group was William Randolph Hearst, who was reported to have proposed several candidates for the post, including Clarence J. Shearn, his attorney, John Temple Graves, one of his editors, and John Purroy Mitchel, President of the Board of Aldermen.[19] Rumor had it that in accordance with Sulzer's ante-election pledges, Hearst would have a say in filling the vacancy on the Public Service Commission.[20] While Sulzer was naturally reluctant to break with Hearst and thereby forfeit his powerful newspaper support, he was also ambitious to succeed himself in Albany two years hence and possibly become the state's favorite son for the Presidential nomination in 1916. He therefore could not afford to antagonize Tammany, which would be sure to deny him a renomination if he failed to appoint an organization Democrat.[21] To yield to Hearst's insistence that a municipal operation

18 *Ibid.*, February 1.

19 *World*, January 22. In a recent interview with the author, Sulzer stated that Hearst himself wanted the job of Public Service Commissioner.

20 *Times*, January 22. This report was denied by the Executive office. With regard to Shearn's current visit to Albany, it was explained that he had called only to bring to the Governor's attention some of the inequalities of the subway contracts.—*World*, January 25.

21 This is borne out by the following incident described by Henry Morgenthau in his autobiography: " One day he [Sulzer] telephoned me to come up at once to his rooms in the Waldorf-Astoria. He had a matter of great importance to discuss, he said, and we could talk it over at luncheon. When I arrived, I found him in great excitement. 'The powers,' he exclaimed, meaning Tammany, 'are trying to force me to appoint a certain man chairman of the Public Service Commission, and I am refusing to do it because I don't think it a proper appointment. But they are getting very angry

advocate be chosen, moreover, meant the overturn of the subway plan, a responsibility Sulzer was not prepared to take, for Democratic leaders feared the effect the failure of the negotiations might have on the approaching elections in New York City. How then, in naming a Public Service Commissioner, he could give satisfaction to both Murphy and Hearst was the awkward dilemma Sulzer faced. Unofficial information from Albany conveyed the impression for a time that no change in the personnel of the Commission would be made until the signing of the contracts,[22] but the Governor finally bowed to political expediency. On the third of February, after a hurried visit to New York,[23] which he obviously wished to keep secret,[24] he sent to the Senate the nomination of Edward E. McCall, Tammany Justice of the Supreme Court.[25] Immediate confirmation followed, without even the formality of reference to a committee, by a straight party vote of twenty-five to ten.[26] In vain did the Republican floor leader, Elon R. Brown, suggest that the people of New York first be given an opportunity of expressing their views on the selection and that rumors of Tammany influence be investigated.[27]

In giving his reasons for the selection of Justice McCall, Sulzer eloquently praised his ability and independence of char-

about it, and I don't know what to do.' I told him there was only one thing he could do and that was to continue to refuse to appoint him. ' But,' complained Sulzer, ' it means my political death if I don't name him!' "—*All in a Lifetime*, p. 166.

22 *World*, February 3.

23 *Ibid.*

24 His visit, Sulzer explained the next day, was to make a personal appeal to McCall to accept appointment.—*Ibid.*, February 4. Actually, it was to confer with Murphy, as he himself subsequently admitted. See p. 249.

25 *Public Papers of Governor Sulzer*, p. 511. He sent in, at the same time, the nomination of Devoe P. Hodson, a former city judge of Buffalo, as Public Service Commissioner for the second district, despite earlier reports that Carlisle would be chosen. Hodson was the choice of William H. Fitzpatrick, Murphy's lieutenant in western New York.—*World*, February 4.

26 Senate Journal, 1913, Vol. II, p. 45.

27 *Times*, February 4.

acter and expressed his implicit confidence in McCall's determination to do what was right. He further stated that McCall
had been persuaded to resign from the bench and take the
appointment at " great sacrifice " and only after much urging.
He wound up his statement with the unequivocal assertion that
he had made the selection entirely on his own initiative. " Mr.
Murphy," he said, " made no recommendation to me, directly
or indirectly, of any applicant or any candidate for this
office." [28] McCall, too, insisted that the matter of his appointment was from the beginning one solely between the Governor
and himself.[29] Murphy declared himself " pleased " with the
designation and likewise denied having made any recommendations to the Governor.[30]

In spite of Sulzer's repeated denials, the rumor that McCall
was Murphy's choice persisted. Tammany legislators made
scant concealment of their gratification. The promptness with
which the nomination was approved and the exceptionally
laudatory comments about McCall made by the organization's
spokesmen in the Senate, Wagner and Frawley, strengthened
the suspicion of Tammany influence.[31] Anti-Tammany Democrats, who had encouraged the Governor in his independent
stand, failed to discern in the nominee any special qualifications
for the office [32] and were chagrined at what they frankly described as " the surrender of the Governor to Murphy and his
financial allies." [33] The New York *World,* a staunch admirer

28 *Times*, February 4.

29 *World,* February 4.

30 *Times*, February 4.

31 See *World*, February 4.

32 McCall himself confessed that he was completely ignorant of his new
duties. " As to the work on which I am to enter," he said, " my mind is more
than open, it is blank ! . . . All I know about the rapid transit problem is
what the average man knows." — *World*, Feb. 4. Yet Sulzer called him
"peculiarly qualified." McCall delayed the signing of the subway contracts
but after study accepted them without change.

33 *World*, February 4. Norman Hapgood records a conversation he had
with a man high up in Tammany Hall, early in February, 1913, in which he

of the Governor, sorrowfully acknowledged that in appointing
a man " affiliated with the inside clique of Tammany Hall,"
Sulzer had done the very thing his worst political enemy would
have wished him to do. " At a time when he should have shown
his strength and his leadership he has surrendered to Fourteenth Street. . . . In naming him Governor Sulzer has shaken
the fine promise of independence that he built up after his
inauguration." [34] The New York *Times* denounced McCall's
selection as " a spectaculer, cynical, impudent display of Mr.
Murphy's arbitrary power " and declared that " Mr. Sulzer's
leadership has vanished with the first occasion he had to show
it." [35] Sulzer made haste to reassure his progressive friends
that he was still free from boss control, and at a dinner given
in his honor by the Lotos Club in New York City on February
8, the first public function he attended after taking office, he
renewed his pledge of independence in the administration of
state affairs. " Long ago," he declared, " I made a vow to the
people that if I became Governor no influence would control me
but the dictates of my conscience and my determination to do
my duty, day in and day out, as I see the right. Have no fear,
I shall stick to that." [36]

In the meantime the Committee of Inquiry, which Sulzer
had appointed, began its public hearings in the Capitol. It first
directed its attention to alleged abuses in the office of the
Adjutant-General and reopened the case of the purchase of
Albany property from the First National Bank of which ex-
Governor Dix was formerly vice-president, for a new arsenal.
Testimony was received contending that the purchase of the
site was contrary to the advice of the Attorney-General and

quotes him as saying that Sulzer appointed McCall at Tammany's behest
and that Sulzer got " his " in the form of campaign funds.—*Harper's Weekly*,
Vol. 58 (October 11, 1913), p. 24, " The Tammany Plot."

34 Editorial, February 4.

35 Editorial, February 5.

36 *Public Papers of Governor Sulzer*, p. 1252.

had been disapproved by the State Armory Commission.[37] As a result of the inquiry steps were immediately taken to recover the money paid.[38] The committee also launched an investigation of the contracts granted in connection with the restoration then in progress of the Capitol Building, which had been partially destroyed by fire two years before. A vigorous blow at the old spoils system was struck when it was decided that all further repair work be stopped and that competitive bidding be invited for its completion. Under the current arrangement the contractors received a profit of ten per cent of the amount expended, the materials being furnished by the state. Stirred by reports of exorbitant profits, Sulzer announced the appointment of John A. Hennessy, a New York newspaper man, to serve as Executive Auditor, a position suggested by the inquiry, to exercise a check on unwarranted expenditures.[39] " If the people knew what I know about some of the things that have been going on here for years they would stand aghast," he exclaimed.[40] Hennessy's investigation of the State Architect's office revealed such gross irregularities in connection with the electrical and other contracts that the work had already cost twice the original estimate. Among the abuses discovered by him were the changing of specifications after contracts had been awarded, the employment of inspectors who were inexperienced and irresponsible, the padding of payrolls at the request of politicians and legislators, tremendous overcharges for work done, and charges even for work not done at all, so as to swell the total cost.[41] He found the State Architect, Herman W. Hoefer, an organization man whom Sulzer had reappointed at the beginning of his term, neither by training nor ability competent to fulfill his duties, and recommended his immediate

37 *Public Papers of Governor Sulzer*, p. 601.

38 *Ibid.*, pp. 602-3.

39 *Ibid.*, p. 501.

40 *Times*, January 23.

41 Hennessy's complete report appears in the *Public Papers of Governor Sulzer*, pp. 944-61.

removal.[42] Hoefer's forced resignation followed. Friends of the Governor pointed to the removal of the State Architect as first proof that Sulzer dared to uncover crookedness and corruption in a department headed by a Tammany man. This act of courage, they said, resulted in bitter hostility on the part of Tammany leaders toward the Governor for what they regarded as political " treason." [43]

The Committee of Inquiry continued its activities with an investigation of the State Prison Department where differences developed between the head of the department, Colonel Joseph F. Scott, a prominent penologist who had been appointed by Governor Dix, and the new administration. The trouble was said to be due in the first instance to Scott's refusal to accede to the Governor's request to remove George W. Benham as warden of Auburn Prison and appoint in his place Charles F. Rattigan, a Democratic state committeeman, chief lieutenant of Murphy's old-time political foe, Thomas Mott Osborne, who had given Sulzer strong support in his campaign.[44] With the summoning of the State Prisons Superintendent before the Governor's Committee of Inquiry, many believed, the first real clash between Sulzer and the Democratic organization was likely to come.[45] The Governor's graft hunters were said to have received instructions to "get something" on Scott in order to force his retirement.[46] Scott, on the other hand, contending that his record was clear, challenged the investigators to go through his department rigorously.[47] He had the support not

42 Sulzer had reappointed Hoefer despite the objection made at the time by the American Institute of Architects that his experience was utterly inadequate for the position.

43 Samuel Bell Thomas, *The Boss or the Governor*, (New York, 1914), p. 99.

44 *World*, January 9. Benham, who was a Republican and in charge of Auburn Prison for about nine years, was described by Scott as the ablest man in the state prison service.—*Ibid.*

45 *Times*, February 12.

46 *World*, February 13.

47 *Ibid.*

only of independent Democrats, except for the small Osborne faction, but also of Tammany, which certainly was not prepared to help Sulzer pay off political debts to its own enemies.[48] A canvass of the Senators, to whom the name of any successor to Scott would have to be submitted for confirmation, showed them to a man to be out of sympathy with Sulzer in his fight with the Superintendent of Prisons. They felt the latter was entirely in the right in refusing to comply with the Governor's peremptory demand to provide a job for one of his henchmen, even at the risk of his own removal from office.[49] Thus far Sulzer had avoided a break with the organization. All his appointments had been acceptable to the Tammany leader and his up-state lieutenants, with the possible exception of Carlisle, head of the Committee of Inquiry, and a certain Milton E. Gibbs, Rochester lawyer and independent Democrat, whose nomination for State Hospital Commissioner had been unanimously rejected by the Senate as unfit, after an adverse report by the finance committee.[50]

Though not recommending Scott's dismissal, the Governor's investigators in their report made ten specific charges of neglect against the Prisons Superintendent which, in their opinion, "required explanation and if possible, justification." [51] Scott's friends contended that the committee's report had been "cooked up" in order to furnish Sulzer with grounds for forcing his retirement.[52] Accusing the committee of bias, Colonel Scott notified the Governor that he would not resign under fire and that he was determined to fight it out.[53] He refused to comply with the Governor's request to appear before him, but sent a letter instead in which he made a general denial to the charges served upon him and defended his management

48 *Times,* March 5.

49 *Ibid.*

50 Senate Journal, 1913, Vol. II, Appendix I, p. 107.

51 *Public Papers of Governor Sulzer,* pp. 835-41.

52 *World,* March 10.

53 *Times,* March 12.

of the state prisons.[54] His removal, which became almost inevitable from the moment he declined to accommodate the Governor in the Rattigan matter, followed on March 13. The reasons assigned by Sulzer were that he was " inefficient, incompetent, derelict and neglectful of duty." [55] In a public statement, following his dismissal, Scott declared, " In no way do they [the charges] blind the public eye to the fact that my removal is for personal, political reasons of the Governor." [56] Until a successor was confirmed, the Governor himself was in charge of the Prison Department, according to an opinion rendered by the Attorney-General,[57] and the way was now opened for the replacement of the warden of Auburn Prison. As had been predicted, the summary action of Sulzer created a hostile feeling among the Tammany element in the Legislature and left no room for doubt that an open break was impending. The Senate freely criticized him for making the prison system of the state " a football of politics " [58] and, without a dissenting vote, adopted a resolution of censure introduced by Senator John F. Murtaugh, an up-state Democrat not allied with Tammany. The resolution called Scott's removal " unjust and unfair " and requested the Governor to allow Scott a hearing before " an impartial tribunal " on the charges preferred against him.[59] Sulzer ignored the Senate's wishes and the very same day sent in the nomination of Judge John B. Riley, of Plattsburg, as Superintendent of Prisons.[60] Seeking evidently to vindicate his dismissal of Scott, Sulzer, on March 14, appointed George W. Blake, a New York newspaper man and close per-

54 *World*, March 14.

55 *Public Papers of Governor Sulzer*, p. 848.

56 *World*, March 14.

57 Annual Report of the Attorney-General of the State of New York, 1913, Vol. II, pp. 150-52.

58 *World*, March 14.

59 Senate Journal, 1913, Vol. I, p. 575.

60 *Ibid.*, Vol. II, Appendix I, p. 106.

sonal friend, as special commissioner to investigate the management and affairs of all the penal institutions of the state.[61]

Still another victim of the investigation conducted by the Committee of Inquiry was the State Superintendent of Highways, C. Gordon Reel. After receiving charges of extravagance, fraud, and political favoritism in connection with highway contracts and repairs, but before a formal report on the department had been submitted, Sulzer announced the dismissal of Reel from office with the statement, " There must be no more waste, no more graft, and no more incompetency in building and maintaining good roads in this State." [62] He made it clear at the same time that there would be no construction on new road work until the completion of the inquiry, and that if any basis was found in the charge that men prominent in politics had been interested in highway construction, a more searching investigation would be made. This warning was followed by the appointment of Hennessy as special commissioner to examine and investigate the State Highway Department.[63] In his letter to the Superintendent, Sulzer notified him that he was being removed " in the interest of the public service and general welfare." [64] Reel's defense was that inasmuch as the Highway Commission included two others besides himself, it was manifestly unfair to hold him alone responsible for any transgressions.[65] He denied that he had refused to aid the committee in its investigation of his department and accused it of being out " to get his scalp." [66] As viewed by Tammany,

61 *Public Papers of Governor Sulzer*, p. 855.

62 *Ibid.*, p. 833.

63 *Ibid.*, p. 916.

64 *Ibid.*, p. 834.

65 The State Highway Commission at that time was composed of the State Superintendent of Highways, Superintendent of Public Works, and State Engineer and Surveyor.—Legislative Manual, 1913, pp. 442-43.

66 *Times*, March 11.

Reel's dismissal was simply another "stage play" for the benefit of the newspapers.[67]

At the time of the removal a rumor was circulated about the Capitol to the effect that Tammany leader Murphy had asked the Governor to name his close friend and partner in the contracting business, ex-Alderman James E. Gaffney, as Reel's successor. The rumor was coupled with the report that Murphy had approved Reel's removal on the assurance that a good Tammany man would be named in his place.[68] Murphy's persistence on behalf of Gaffney, it was added, had taken the form of threats that the Governor's reforms and appointments would be held up by the Legislature, unless the demand were complied with, and that the Governor was determined to resist the pressure even at the risk of a conflict with the organization.[69] Stung by this report, Murphy broke his usual silence and in the first statement of any length that he made since the inauguration of Sulzer categorically denied that he had ever suggested the name of Gaffney as Superintendent of Highways or for any other position. "If I knew that Governor Sulzer had offered a place to Mr. Gaffney," he answered, "I would advise Mr. Gaffney to decline it. I am certain that if Governor Sulzer is questioned about this he will answer as I have answered." [70] Murphy was said to be inclined at first to pay no attention to reports emanating from Albany of an impending break between him and the Governor but his long-suffering patience had become exhausted at the story that he was eager to lay his hands on the fifty million dollar appropriation for highway improvement by having his business associate made head of the department. What irritated the Tammany leader

67 *World*, March 18. Sulzer later admitted that he had no proof of corruption against Reel when he removed him, but simply thought him "incompetent" and "a fool."—*Times*, January 22, 1914.

68 *Times*, March 11.

69 A few days later it was added that the chief's ultimatum had been, "Gaffney or war."—*World*, March 17.

70 *Times*, March 12.

even more, according to those close to him, was the suspicion that Sulzer himself had inspired the story, and that if this were confirmed, a break between them would most certainly follow.[71]

A question that naturally arose was why the Governor, if so strongly prejudiced against Gaffney, had earlier in his administration appointed him chairman of a group of non-partisan " experts " to investigate the whole subject of road construction and advise the Governor on highway matters.[72] Sulzer had had only words of praise for Gaffney at that time and evidently had seen nothing wrong in putting an intimate friend of Murphy at the head of so important a board, notwithstanding disclosures linking some of the Democratic leaders with scandals in the Highway Department.[73] According to a correspondent of the New York *Times,* only a day before the report was handed to newspaper men that Murphy was plotting to force Gaffney's nomination, a close friend of the Governor had told him that Sulzer regarded Gaffney as a good man to head the department but that he understood him not to be a candidate.[74]

Sulzer had nothing to say in answer to Murphy's explicit denial that he had made any request for Gaffney's appointment, but following it, a somewhat revised version of the original story emanated from the Governor's office. This time it was not that Murphy had urged the appointment but simply that " Mr. Murphy must have known of the use of Mr. Gaffney's name," and that a number of legislators had warned the Governor that unless the man appointed to succeed Reel was acceptable to the organization, his constructive legislation was doomed

71 *Ibid.,* March 18.

72 *Public Papers of Governor Sulzer,* p. 529.

73 " Mr. Gaffney is a big and experienced contractor," said Sulzer. " I had a long talk with him and was astonished to learn how much he knows about good roads and road building. He will prove a valuable member of the board."—*World,* February 25.

74 *Times,* March 13.

to defeat.[75] The statement, which was anonymous, sought to convey the impression that there was trouble between the Executive Chamber and Tammany Hall and implied that Murphy was responsible for the Legislature's delay in enacting the Governor's program. " The game is to see what the Governor will do; to make him show his hand on appointments. Well, Mr. Murphy will wait a long time if that is his purpose," the statement read.[76] In commenting on the widely circulated rumors of coming war, Lieutenant-Governor Glynn, regarded as an independent Democrat, declared that there was no foundation whatever for the Governor's apprehension that his program of reform was being held up. " If the Governor is looking for a fight," he was reported to have remarked with a laugh, " I am afraid he will have to manufacture it himself. I am going to tell the Governor that his constructive legislation is in no danger and that this sort of talk will do neither him nor the party any good." [77] The feeling that if war did come it would have to be of Sulzer's own making was shared by other party members, who publicly scoffed at any suggestion of a row with the Governor. Tammany legislative leaders avowed their friendliness toward the Governor, denying reports that any attempt was contemplated to hold up administrative measures, and expressed their determination to give him all he asked for.[78] Thus far no legislation proposed had been considered too radical for the legislators and his appointments had not been altogether displeasing to the organization. It was no secret, however, that Sulzer was not well liked by the Tammany element in the Legislature, who suspected him of trying to build up an independent organization in order to further his own political ambitions.

Several days after the story of the alleged break between the Governor and the Boss had been circulated, an " emissary "

75 *Ibid.*
76 *Ibid.*
77 *Ibid.*
78 *World*, March 13.

of the latter, no less a person than Gaffney himself, called upon Sulzer at the Waldorf Hotel in New York in a supposed effort to patch up the differences between the two men. Two versions of the conference appeared. Gaffney explained that he had called simply to assure the Governor that he was not a candidate for the state highway job and that his business interests would make it impossible for him to accept the appointment, even if it were offered him. He ridiculed the suggestion that Murphy had sent any ultimatum to Sulzer on his behalf.[79] The Governor said nothing for publication, but his advisers reported that he had told Gaffney with emphasis that he would not submit to Tammany dictation, would never send in the name of any man having the indorsement of Murphy, and was determined to "have it out" with him.[80] That night both Sulzer and Murphy attended the annual dinner of the Friendly Sons of St. Patrick in the Hotel Astor, but exchanged no greeting, though seated not far from each other.[81]

That trouble was brewing was plainly to be seen in Murphy's refusal to attend a dinner given to Sulzer by his East Side friends in the Café Boulevard, New York, on March 18 to celebrate his fiftieth birthday, notwithstanding earlier assurances that he would attend.[82] Practically all prominent organization leaders boycotted what was to have been a family affair. At the dinner Henry Morgenthau, head of the Finance Committee of the Democratic National Committee, urged the guest of honor to stand firm in his resolution to be the Governor, not "the agent of undisclosed principals who hide themselves from public view." Seeking apparently to stiffen Sulzer in his fight with Tammany, he warned him that his one master was "enlightened public opinion" and that unless he led in the fight for good government, the people would find a new leader.[83]

79 *Times*, March 18.
80 *World*, March 18.
81 *Times*, March 18.
82 *Ibid.*, March 17.
83 Henry Morgenthau, *op. cit.*, p. 169.

Sulzer met the challenge and in his reply reasserted his earlier pledge " to do the right," without regard to political or personal consequences.[84]

The very next day an announcement was issued from Tammany Hall to the effect that Sulzer and Murphy had secretly met in Delmonico's Restaurant [85] the afternoon after the St. Patrick dinner and, after a long talk, had patched up the differences which threatened to make them enemies and had come to a definite understanding over patronage.[86] The alleged meeting was said to have been arranged by a number of Tammany leaders. When shown the story in the newspapers, Sulzer made the laconic comment, " Nothing to it," and refused to say anything more.[87] The report was insistent, however, that it was Sulzer who had done the " backing down " and that the meeting could not be regarded otherwise than as a victory for the Tammany chief. The fact that United States Senator James A. O'Gorman called upon Sulzer at his hotel, just before the alleged meeting, was considered to be of some political significance, although neither of them would discuss the nature of their conference.[88] Murphy, with his usual urbanity, asserted that he knew of no war between the Governor and himself and likewise denied the report of the meeting.[89] Although Sulzer disavowed the " peace conference " with Murphy and continued his belligerent talk, it was intimated at the Capitol that he was not really seeking a quarrel with the Democratic organization. "I'm at war with no man," was the way the Governor put it, when questioned about his relations with Murphy.[90] He was represented as desir-

84 *Public Papers of Governor Sulzer*, p. 1285.

85 Delmonico's was a fashionable restaurant on Fifth Avenue, in New York City, where Murphy was accustomed to hold his private political consultations.

86 *World*, March 19.

87 *Times*, March 19.

88 *Ibid.*, March 20.

89 *Ibid.*

90 *World*, March 20.

ing merely to be let alone in the performance of his duties and to be allowed to carry through his program of reform. He even recognized, it was said, the propriety of giving consideration to recommendations made by Tammany Hall where patronage in New York County was concerned, but reserved absolute independence in the distribution of patronage in other sections of the state.[91] By dealing directly with the heads of the county organizations, Sulzer hoped to limit Tammany's influence in the matter of appointments to the City of New York, weaken Murphy's leadership up-state, and thereby loosen his hold on the Legislature.

A large part of the public assumed an attitude of skepticism and asked whether there really was a single genuine issue between Governor Sulzer and Boss Murphy. Even the shrewdest correspondents at Albany confessed they were puzzled as to whether the fight was on the level or simply a comic opera war. Despite the manifestoes of independence that continued to come forth from the Executive Chamber in ever-increasing volume and ever-growing belligerency, the doubt persisted as to whether the Governor had actually made up his mind to defy Murphy. " Governor Sulzer is lost in a fog of uncertainty," wrote the *World*. " New York is not sure of him. The Legislature is not sure of him. The State does not know whether he is leader or follower. It has yet to find evidence that he has a definite programme of principles to which he is determined to adhere, whatever the cost may be." [92] Three months after his solemn announcement that the leadership of the Democratic party and the Governorship would thenceforth be combined in one person, it was evident that Sulzer was still without a substantial following among anti-Tammany men. The hesitation of the reform element in rallying behind Sulzer arose not only on account of his long record of obedience to Tammany and his unconcealed vanity and ambition, but also

91 *Times*, March 20.
92 Editorial, April 12.

on account of the distrust of his fundamental honesty, and uncertainty as to whether he possessed the mental grasp and moral equipment to take up the challenge. " Is the Governor altogether sincere? Will he, when the time comes, back up his theatrical words by matter-of-fact deeds? " asked one editor.[93] It was doubtful, too, whether the members of the Democratic majority in either branch of the Legislature, if forced to choose between the controlling leadership and that of Sulzer, would take their stand with the latter. This attitude was probably induced more by the lack of confidence in the Governor's qualifications for leadership and in the sincerity of his intentions than by Tammany dictation.

Another circumstance that caused independent Democrats to hold aloof from the Governor was the keen disappointment that came to them early in his administration, when he showed his apparent servility to Murphy in filling the vacancies on the Public Service Commissions. They were displeased, moreover, with his evident intention of combating Tammany with the discredited methods of the professional politician. They urged him to strike out for real independence by naming to all offices under his control straight-out anti-Tammany men, defying the organization to do its worst, and appealing to the people for support should Tammany resort to reprisals.[94] But the Governor was said to frown on the suggestion and assert his faith in the adequacy of his county autonomy plan for the emancipation of up-state Democracy from Tammany domination. Intimate friends wanted him to sever all relations with the regular Democratic organization and make an open declaration of war on Murphy, pointing out that his plan for the dispensation of patronage did not go far enough in breaking the power of the party machine, because the majority of the county bosses would not be likely to recommend anyone for appointment who had not first received Murphy's approval.[95] On

93 The *Nation*, Vol. 96 (March 20, 1913), p. 276.
94 *World*, March 17.
95 *Ibid.*, March 25.

March 24 a group of prominent independent Democrats visited Sulzer at the " People's House " to advise him that the time was ripe for a concerted attack on Tammany.[96] The following day came Sulzer's public " proclamation of political emancipation." The occasion was the annual dinner of the Democratic Editorial Association of the state. In a speech which bristled with assaults on " invisible government," he formally reiterated that he was the party leader. He recalled that he was the candidate of a free and open convention, had entered office without a single promise, and then added, amid prolonged cheering: " I have never been an agent, and I never will be. No man, no party and no organization can make me a rubber stamp. I am the Governor. Let no man doubt that." [97] While no mention was made of Tammany or Murphy, it was obvious whom he had in mind. He also spoke of the deplorable conditions in state affairs he found on taking office, told of his efforts to accomplish administrative reforms, and took occasion to repudiate any personal ambition. " In the performance of my duty," he averred, " I have no friends to reward; no enemies to punish; no ambition to gratify; no machine to strengthen; no organization to build up." [98]

Sulzer's supporters hoped he would be able to create the semblance of a genuine fight between an independent Governor and a Tammany-controlled Legislature, convincing enough to win him the sympathy of the people. Thus far the plan had failed because of the willingness of the lawmakers to enact the bills recommended by him, contrary to the reports of his spokesmen that the organization was holding up his legislative program. With a municipal campaign to be fought out in New York in the fall, Tammany seemed eager to build up a record of reform legislation and avoid an open fight. In the latter part of March the Governor's Committee of Inquiry ended its

96 *Times*, March 25.

97 *Public Papers of Governor Sulzer*, p. 1292.

98 *Ibid.*, p. 1297.

hearings and in the voluminous report it submitted condemned
the wasteful conduct of the state's administrative machinery,
asserting that the government's business and financial affairs
were being conducted " without system, extravagantly and with
adverse and divided responsibility, which would bring ruin
to any business not having the resources of the State." [99] It proposed a number of reforms designed to remedy those defects
and put the administration of the state departments on a sound
and constructive business basis.[100] Five bills embodying its
recommendations were drawn up and introduced into the Legislature. The first bill created a State Board of Efficiency and
Economy, headed by a Commissioner, with broad powers of
investigation and authority to recommend to the Governor and
heads of departments improvements in administration. The
second created a State Board of Estimate, made up of nine
members including the Governor, Lieutenant-Governor, State
Comptroller, Attorney-General, Commissioner of Efficiency
and Economy, Senate and Assembly leaders, as well as the
chairmen of the Finance Committees of both houses, to meet
annually for the purpose of preparing the state budget. The
third bill established a State Board of Contract and Supply
as a central purchasing agency for all supplies needed by state
departments and institutions. The two remaining bills contained amendments to the executive law conferring on the
State Comptroller fuller powers of audit over all state expenditures.[101] Despite Sulzer's talk of a Tammany plot to hold up
all legislation in order to compel him to come to an understanding with Murphy regarding patronage, the Legislature
passed the most important of his governmental reform bills
without serious opposition. A number of other administrative
reforms were enacted by the Legislature at the suggestion of
the Governor, among which were the establishment of a State

99 The entire report of the committee appears in *Ibid.*, pp. 653-770.
100 *Ibid.*, pp. 770-76.
101 *Ibid.*, pp. 435-38.

Highway Department with a single responsible head, to take the place of the Old Highway Commission, the reorganization of the State Health Department with extensive new agencies to exercise thorough supervision over health and sanitation,[102] and the enactment of an extensive body of legislation for the betterment of factory conditions. The last series of bills, prepared by the Legislative Factory Investigating Commission since 1911 under the chairmanship of Senator Wagner, included the reorganization of the State Labor Department and the creation of an industrial board with broad powers of investigation and authority to make regulations respecting tenement house labor, stricter regulation of the employment of women and children in industry, increased protection against fire hazards and industrial accidents, and the general improvement of working conditions.[103]

Sulzer caused to be introduced several other progressive measures. In a special message sent to the Legislature on January 13, he urged the repeal of the charter granted during the Hughes administration to the Long Sault Development Company, authorizing it to generate electric power at the Long Sault Rapids in the St. Lawrence River. He emphatically declared that the state's natural resources belonged to the people and that as " trustees of future generations " the government should prevent their exploitation by private interests. He also called attention to an opinion of the Attorney-General that the grant was unconstitutional and void because it was a private bill granting an exclusive privilege.[104] Bills carrying out the recommendation were subsequently passed by the two houses of the Legislature [105] and signed by the Governor.[106]

102 *Public Papers of Governor Sulzer*, pp. 466-68.

103 *Ibid.*, pp. 439-40.

104 *Ibid.*, pp. 40-45.

105 Senate Journal, 1913, Vol. I, p. 663; Assembly Journal, 1913, Vol. III, p. 3353.

106 *Public Papers of Governor Sulzer*, pp. 459-60.

Early in the session (January 27) Sulzer also sent to the Legislature a special message urging the enactment of remedial legislation to prohibit certain alleged abuses on the Stock Exchange.[107] Several bills designed to carry out his recommendations were introduced by Stephen J. Stilwell, chairman of the Senate Codes Committee, and by Aaron J. Levy, majority leader of the Assembly. The governing board of the New York Stock Exchange assured Sulzer of its willingness to cooperate with him in fixing the highest standards of trading,[108] but registered strong objection to any radical changes that might upset legitimate business, especially condemning proposed bills calling for the incorporation of the Exchanges and limiting the rate of interest on call loans to fifteen per cent.[109] Of the nine so-called Wall Street measures presented in the Legislature, six were passed and signed, those making more stringent the law against bucket shops and " wash sales," providing a penalty for the manipulation of quotations on securities, prohibiting brokers from trading against customers' orders, forbidding brokers to do business while in an insolvent condition or to hypothecate customers' securities, and preventing fictitious transactions and the issuance of false statements.[110] The bill limiting call loan rates died in committee and another, doubling the tax on stock transfers, was withdrawn by the Governor himself, after he was persuaded that the burden was unjustified and oppressive.[111] The proposal which aroused the greatest opposition in financial circles, the one compelling all Exchanges dealing in securities to incorporate, after having

107 *Ibid.*, pp. 55-69.

108 The board did make a move to reform the Exchange from within by adopting a number of rules intended to prevent manipulation and reckless trading.—*Times*, February 6.

109 *Ibid.*, February 27.

110 Legislative Record and Index, 1913, pp. 68-69, 276-77.

111 *Times*, March 11.

passed the Assembly, was killed in the Senate following an adverse report of the Judiciary Committee.[112]

An incident that produced political repercussions was Sulzer's signing of the Jackson Full Crew bill, which prescribed the minimum number of employees in the operation of certain trains.[113] The railroad companies bitterly opposed the measure, and in an open letter, published in leading newspapers throughout the state, had urged the people to demand that Sulzer veto the bill and leave the subject to be dealt with, as heretofore, by the Public Service Commissions.[114] The presidents of the principal railroads in the state personally appeared before Sulzer a few days before he signed the bill, importuning him to follow the example of Governors Hughes and Dix and veto the proposal.[115] They characterized the increase in train crews as an unnecessary expenditure of about two million dollars a year, which in the last analysis would have to be borne by the traveling public and shippers. Notwithstanding the vehement protest of the railroad officials, Sulzer put " the man above the dollar," and in his memorandum accompanying his approval of the measure declared he was more interested in the conservation of human life than in the conservation of railroad dividends.[116] The Governor's signing of the bill stirred the report that he had done so in fulfillment of ante-election pledges secretly made to John V. Fitzgerald, legislative representative of the Brotherhood of Railroad Trainmen in New York State. The basis of this report was a circular letter, marked confidential, which was purported to have been sent by Fitzgerald on the eve of the 1912 election to officers and members of the Brotherhood for

112 Legislative Record and Index, 1913, p. 299.

113 *Public Papers of Governor Sulzer*, pp. 424-28.

114 See, for example, *Times*, March 29.

115 Hughes and Dix had vetoed similar measures on the ground that the Public Service Commissions had ample power to order an increased number of trainmen, an opinion Sulzer challenged. — *Public Papers of Governor Sulzer*, pp. 1109-14.

116 *Ibid.*, p. 1128.

the purpose of making votes for Sulzer. In this letter, reprinted in the New York *Times*,[117] Sulzer was alleged to have told Fitzgerald that if elected he would not only sign the full crew bill but would also aid in securing its passage through the Legislature. " I would come out openly for the bill," Sulzer was quoted as saying, " but if I did, the railroads would spend a barrel of money to defeat me." The signing of the bill was followed by the introduction of a resolution by Senator Elon R. Brown, leader of the Republican minority, asking the Judiciary Committee to inquire whether the Governor, because of his alleged conduct, had not rendered himself ineligible for office.[118] The resolution was referred to the committee without protest.[119] The charge drew from Sulzer a prompt and vigorous denial. To correspondents who asked him whether he had anything to say concerning the Brown resolution, he angrily replied, " Why, that resolution is rot. You don't suppose a matter like that can intimidate me." [120] He went on to accuse the chairman of the Republican State Committee, William Barnes, with not only instigating but actually dictating the resolution. He denounced Barnes as being part of the " invisible government " and warned him to stay away from the Capitol. He indignantly denied having made campaign pledges to anyone except the people, adding that even if he had, as a candidate, promised to sign the bill, it would have been " all right." He dismissed the incident with the comment, " It's all

117 April 5.

118 Senate Journal, 1913, Vol. I, pp. 1063-64. A secret pledge such as the one Sulzer was accused of having made was, of course, not only improper but also unconstitutional. The constitution requires the Governor to swear, before entering upon his duties, that he had not made any promises or offered any valuable consideration to influence votes.

119 The proposed inquiry was shut off by the Democrats, who could scarcely be expected to aid the Republicans make political capital out of the affair, especially after it was discovered that almost a majority of the members of both houses had promised before election to vote for the bill.— *World*, April 29.

120 *Times*, April 3.

a trick of Barnes, Brown and the railroads." [121] Fitzgerald was summoned to the Executive Chamber and after the meeting Sulzer informed newspaper men that he had obtained from him a denial of the authenticity of the letter, as well as a statement to the effect that the Governor had never made any promises that would have justified him in sending out such a letter.[122] Senator Brown in his retort refuted the charge that Barnes had inspired his resolution and condemned Sulzer's view that it would have been proper to make a secret promise. " Is this treating public office as a public trust? " he pointedly asked.[123] As for Barnes, he simply laughed at Sulzer's challenge and facetiously remarked that he would thereafter transfer his visits from the Capitol to the " People's House." [124]

His signing of the full crew bill, according to Sulzer, arrayed against him the railroads and other corporate interests, as well as the newspapers under their control. To this day Sulzer is convinced that they plotted his political destruction in revenge and spent huge sums of money to bring about his subsequent impeachment and removal from office.[125] In a public statement issued after his conviction, he declared: " The three things that led up to my removal were my fight for direct primaries, the graft investigations and not the least by any means my signing of the full crew bill which gave me the enmity of the great railroad corporations." [126]

121 *Ibid.*

122 *Ibid.*

123 *Ibid.*, April 8. This incident marked the beginning of a protracted quarrel between Governor Sulzer and Senator Brown in the course of which the latter charged the Governor with mental unsoundness and the Governor, in turn, characterized Brown as a "political fossil of the Paleozoic age."— *Tribune*, May 3.

124 *Times*, April 3.

125 In an interview with the author, Sulzer alleged that on the eve of his impeachment, the New York Central Railroad sent to Albany $300,000, charged to "construction," presumably for purposes of bribery.

126 Forrest and Malcolm, *op. cit.*, p. 183.

While there were few differences over legislation, the issue which did threaten to force a deadlock between the Governor and the Legislature was patronage. The dispute began soon after Sulzer entered office, becoming increasingly bitter as the breach widened, and continued to the day of the impeachment, with the result that the administration of state affairs was often thrown into confusion and chaos. With a safe majority at its command in the Senate, the Democratic organization was always in a position to block any objectionable nominations. The strength of the Governor had twice been tried out, each time with the same result. The first time was when the upper house refused to confirm Gibbs for a place on the State Hospital Commission, after an unfavorable committee report.[127] The more important test came when Sulzer removed Colonel Scott as State Superintendent of Prisons. In this instance too the vote of the Senate was unanimous against the Governor. Some of Sulzer's friends advised that without regard to the wishes of the Tammany machine, he select men of outstanding reputation and flawless record, send the entire list to the Senate at once, and defy it to hold up appointments of such character. Instead, he showed a disposition to bargain and compromise and was said to be willing even to give Tammany the larger share of appointments on condition that a few of the more important places go to independent leaders up-state. He agreed, according to reports, to appoint organization men to the Supreme Court vacancies in New York City, provided Tammany placed no obstacles in the way of his appointees to other offices. In order to cajole the Tammany-controlled Senate, Sulzer's plan was to withhold nominations to the bench to the last and send in his own names one at a time, waiting in each case for confirmation before submitting the next.[128] This policy, dictated seemingly by suspicion, angered the Senate leaders and they agreed not to report favorably on a single appointment

127 Senate Journal, 1913, Vol. II, p. 107.
128 *Times*, April 18.

until his entire list had been submitted. Rather than risk defeat for his nominees, Sulzer allowed several important posts to remain vacant or continue to be filled by men whose terms had expired, but whose places he would like to give to those of his own selection. Among the important posts waiting to be filled were two up-state Public Service Commissioners, head of the new Labor Department, Commissioner of Efficiency and Economy, Health Commissioner, State Architect, and member of the Hospital Commission.

Sulzer was anxious to break the deadlock in the Senate over appointments and mutual friends were reported as trying to arrange the terms of a *modus vivendi.* " If he [Murphy] is willing to do the right thing by the Governor, the Governor is willing to do the right thing by him," was the way one of Sulzer's confidants put it.[129] That the mediators outside of the Legislature had evidently succeeded in arranging a working agreement between Sulzer and Murphy became apparent when the list of long-delayed appointments was finally submitted to the Senate on April 21.[130] It included John N. Carlisle as Commissioner of Highways, John Mitchell as Commissioner of Labor, John H. Delaney as Commissioner of Efficiency and Economy, and Eugene A. Philbin, a Democrat of independent leanings, and Bartow S. Weeks, a member of Tammany Hall, as Justices of the Supreme Court for the First District.[131] Both judicial appointees were favored by organization leaders [132] and were confirmed within a few days.[133] Delaney too was

129 *Ibid.,* March 29.

130 An unconfirmed report was printed in the *World* (April 15) that Sulzer, Murphy, and McCall had conferred for three hours after the Jefferson Day Dinner at the Waldorf-Astoria Hotel on April 13, and that a decision had been reached as to Supreme Court Judgeships. McCall emphatically denied the report of such a conference, saying, " That story is absolutely false."

131 Senate Journal, 1913, Vol. II, Appendix I, pp. 130-31. Sulzer held back the nominations for the Public Service positions, evidently as a means of forcing action on his other appointments.

132 *Times,* April 22.

133 Senate Journal, *supra,* p. 133.

persona grata and although Carlisle was an avowed anti-Tammany Democrat, no serious opposition was expected to be put in his way. The only appointment about whose confirmation there was any doubt was that of Mitchell, former President of the United Mine Workers of America, a personal selection of the Governor. Tammany preferred to have in the enlarged Labor Department, with its increased patronage, one whose party regularity could not be questioned.[134] The announcement of these selections, particularly of Carlisle and Mitchell, cheered the independent Democratic element which saw in them an indication of Sulzer's determination to follow his own course.[135] But Tammany politicians and legislators also took comfort out of the list, interpreting it as " peace offerings " to Murphy and as marking the approach of an era of better feeling between the Governor and the Democratic organization.[136] They were especially pleased with the naming of Delaney, close political henchman and personal friend of Murphy, as head of the Efficiency and Economy Department with its great supervisory power over state appropriations and expenditures.[137] The Democratic leaders in the Senate agreed not to offer any objection to the names submitted by Sulzer except Mitchell as Labor Commissioner and Riley, whose appointment as Superintendent of Prisons was still awaiting confirmation, but to defer a favorable report until all the Governor's nominations had been sent in. This policy was adopted in order to guard against any departure from the understanding that the two vacancies on the Public Service Commission would be filled by good party men. Failure to do so, it was understood, would be followed by reprisals.[138]

134 *Times*, April 22.

135 *World*, April 22.

136 *Times*, April 22.

137 Sulzer subsequently explained that his appointment of Delaney was the result of "a deal" with Murphy, whereby the latter would approve Carlisle as Highway Commissioner in return.—*Ibid.*, January 22, 1914.

138 *Ibid.*, April 23.

The Senate confirmed the nomination of Carlisle and Delaney [139] but rejected Mitchell and Riley by a straight party vote the day before adjournment.[140] Both had been adversely reported by the Finance Committee, Mitchell ostensibly because of his short residence in the state, and Riley because he was deemed unfit.[141] Angered by the Senate's action, Sulzer sent in as substitute nomination for Superintendent of Prisons Riley's law partner, George S. Weed, of Plattsburg.[142] The very next day Sulzer withdrew Weed's name, owing to the hostility indicated, and on the last day of the session nominated Herman Ridder, editor and proprietor of the New York *Staats-Zeitung*, whom the Senate promptly confirmed on motion of Senator Wagner.[143] Two weeks after the adjournment of the Legislature, Ridder notified Sulzer that for business reasons he was unable to accept the office.[144] This opened the way to a recess appointment and on May 26 Sulzer again named Riley as Superintendent of Prisons, despite his earlier rejection by the Senate.[145] While there was no doubt of the Governor's legal power to make a recess appointment, in view of Ridder's failure to qualify, the naming of a man once rejected by the Senate was clearly an evasion, if not a violation, of the constitution.[146]

139 Senate Journal, *op. cit.*, p. 139.

140 *Ibid.*, pp. 142-43. No action was taken on the nomination of Eugene M. Strouss, a Rochester Democrat allied with the anti-Tammany faction, for State Hospital Commissioner.

141 *World*, April 22.

142 Senate Journal, *supra*, p. 144. Sulzer added the name of Lewis F. Pilcher, of Brooklyn, for the position of State Architect to fill the vacancy caused by the resignation of Hoefer. Pilcher was backed by McCooey, Democratic boss of Brooklyn, although the Governor called him a " Sulzer Democrat."—*World*, May 3.

143 Senate Journal, *supra*, p. 146.

144 *World*, May 17.

145 *Public Papers of Governor Sulzer*, p. 511.

146 According to section 39 of the Public Officers Law, where a vacancy exists or occurs while the Senate is not in session, the Governor has the power to fill such vacancy by appointment for a term which shall expire at

Sulzer resorted to similarly doubtful tactics in behalf of Mitchell. He waited until the Legislature adjourned its regular session and during the recess again announced his appointment as Commissioner of Labor,[147] notwithstanding the fact that he had already twice been rejected by the Senate.[148] Attorney-General Carmody declared the appointment illegal, maintaining that the Governor had no power of appointment in cases where the term of office expired before the recess of the Legislature.[149] Sulzer insisted, however, that Mitchell was Labor Commissioner *de facto* and expressed confidence that the courts would confirm his right to the office.[150] The Attorney-General's opinion that the Governor had exceeded his authority was upheld by Supreme Court Justice Alden Chester in denying Mitchell's application for a writ of mandamus to compel the State Comptroller to issue a warrant for the payment of his salary, as a matter of law and not in the exercise of discretion.[151] The Court of Appeals, to which the case went for a final determination of the law, sustained the decision of the lower court, holding that when a vacancy occurred after the term had expired, the Governor had no authority to make an appointment without the Senate's concurrence.[152] The Labor Department remained without a head until the Legislature

the end of twenty days from the commencement of the next meeting of the Senate.—See Annual Report of the Attorney-General, 1913, Vol. II, p. 357.

147 *Public Papers of Governor Sulzer*, p. 514.

148 On May 2 the Senate notified the Governor of its refusal to confirm the nomination. On May 3 Sulzer again nominated Mitchell. The Senate at once acted adversely upon the nomination and adjourned sine die.

149 Annual Report of the Attorney-General, *supra*, pp. 355-59.

150 *Times*, May 29. The Governor's contention was that John Williams, former Labor Commissioner, did not send in his resignation until May 16, 1913, although his term of office had expired at the end of 1912.

151 *The People ex rel. John Mitchell, Relator, v. William Sohmer, as Comptroller of the State of New York, Defendant.* Miscellaneous Reports, Vol. 81, pp. 293-98.

152 Court of Appeals, State of New York, Vol. 209, pp. 151-167. The decision affirmed the order of the Appellate Division of the Supreme Court (157 Appellate Division 923).

reconvened in extra session, when Sulzer offered as his next choice for Commissioner James M. Lynch, of Syracuse, president of the International Typographical Union.[153] His name too was held up in the Senate, and the dispute over appointments for Labor Commissioner, as well as for Superintendent of Prisons, had not reached a conclusion when the Governor was impeached.[154]

In the meantime Sulzer's graft investigators were busy unearthing evidences of official wrongdoing. After completing his inquiry into the State Architect's office, John A. Hennessy was appointed to investigate the construction of state highways.[155] Shortly before the adjournment of the Legislature, Sulzer made public a series of reports submitted to him by George W. Blake, special commissioner to investigate prisons and reformatories, in which sweeping charges of fraud and corruption in the administration of state prisons were made. In a preliminary report on the Great Meadow Prison at Comstock, Blake wrote that a conservative estimate would fix the loss to the state " through carelessness or graft " in the construction of the buildings at that institution at $500,000.[156] Nor had any attempt, he said, been made to conceal the wrongdoing. " It is so brazen and conspicuous that even the most unobserving visitor to the prison building must observe it," he reported. " For more than two years this prison building job has been used to rob the State." He alleged the existence of " a prison ring " forged for the purpose of stealing the people's money, including the State Architect, his representatives at the prison, and the Superintendent of Prisons, through whose hands bills passed for inferior work or for work not

153 Senate Journal, 1913, Vol. II, Ext. Session, Appendix II, p. 85.

154 Governor Glynn, Sulzer's successor, renominated Lynch, whom the Senate promptly confirmed.—Senate Journal, *supra*, p. 175.

155 *Public Papers of Governor Sulzer*, p. 915.

156 *Ibid.*, p. 857. As the prison was only partly completed and only $1,100,000 had been spent for construction work, it would appear from Blake's report that almost half the money had been squandered or stolen.

done at all. He recommended that further construction be stopped and suggested that steps be taken to institute criminal proceedings against those directly or indirectly connected with the work.[157] The report was fortified with affidavits from " experts " swearing that the grounds on which the buildings were erected were wholly unsuitable and that neither material nor workmanship came up to the specifications demanded.[158] Blake's findings with respect to conditions in Sing Sing Prison were unqualified in condemnation of responsible officials. " The prison," he asserted, " is remarkable because of the lack of any cohesive or well-poised plan of government. It is so slipshod and incompetent as to breed the suspicion at first glance that the purpose is to cover up dishonest methods by a brazen show of innocent carelessness." He reported favoritism, gross immorality among the inmates, filth, and " criminal carelessness if not down-right grafting " in the commissary department. He accused Warden Kennedy of unbusiness-like management that caused the state to lose thousands of dollars " in a way that points directly to graft." He also censured former Superintendent Scott for failing to correct existing evils or of ever making a single suggestion of value for the improvement of the prison system, despite his reputation as a penologist. He found no evidence that he was " either competent, conscientious or industrious." [159] Similar conditions were found to prevail in Auburn Prison.[160] In a supplementary report on conditions in the Great Meadow Prison, Blake brought to light new facts regarding the construction of the buildings which indicated that the contract for the work was let under conditions that

157 *Ibid.*, pp. 856-63, *passim.*

158 *Ibid.*, pp. 863-66.

159 *Ibid.*, pp. 898-914, *passim.* Warden Kennedy emphatically denied ever accepting a dollar of graft and demanded an immediate grand jury investigation into the charges. He contended that Blake had disregarded fair play and pronounced certain features of the report as " characteristic of dramatic methods."—*Times*, May 13.

160 *Public Papers of Governor Sulzer*, pp. 867-85.

pointed to " a conspiracy to rob the State." Gross incompe-
tence and systematic falsification of the books, with graft
hidden somewhere in the juggling of the figures, were among
the charges made. His conclusion was: " Lack of system and
the waste of public money in experiments are the most conspicuous features of the prison management." [161]

161 *Ibid.*, pp. 885-97, *passim.*

CHAPTER III
SULZER'S CAMPAIGN FOR DIRECT PRIMARIES

THE Governor's clash with the Democratic organization reached its climax in his determination to secure the enactment of a statewide direct primary law. While the two had had encounters over legislation and patronage, up to that point there had been no open rupture. Now all rules of maneuvering were flung aside. It was not so much the idea of the direct primary itself as Sulzer's insistence on his own particular brand of reform and the tactics he employed in his fight on its behalf that precipitated the final break. In his first message to the Legislature, Sulzer made no specific recommendations, simply calling for the adoption of such amendments to the existing law as would simplify the procedure of the direct primary system and make it more effective.[1] Nor did he, during the first few months of the session, give any indication of what kind of primary bill he sought, except to say that he favored the best that could be written.[2]

On February 17, a bill embodying the Democratic organization's program for election reform, drafted under the supervision of the legislative leaders, was introduced by Senator George A. Blauvelt.[3] It contained a number of provisions intended to reduce the expense of the primary and election machinery, proposed an increase in the time allowed for filing independent designations for the primaries, and a reduction in the number of signatures required for independent nominations. The bill did not, however, extend the application of the direct primary principle beyond existing limits, and left the state convention as the sole means of nominating state offi-

1 *Public Papers of Governor Sulzer*, p. 28.

2 *Times*, January 21.

3 Senate Journal, Vol. I, p. 295. Similar legislation in the lower house was proposed by Assemblyman Patrie.

cials.[4] For about two months the Blauvelt bill was debated back and forth in the two houses without a word from the Governor against it. Then came his falling out with Murphy, and simultaneously arose his interest in direct primaries. Independent Democrats among his advisers began urging him to take a vigorous stand for the adoption of a thoroughgoing direct primary law, statewide in scope, and to compel the Legislature to go on record before adjournment. Accordingly, on April 10, as the regular session was already drawing to a close, Sulzer sent a special message to the Legislature in which he outlined his recommendations for reform. He quoted from the platforms of the three leading parties of 1912 to remind the legislators that they were all " irrevocably " bound to enact legislation for electoral reform and a statewide direct primary system.[5] He expressed the belief that if people were qualified to elect their officials, they were competent also to nominate them, and that if it was wise to permit them to name the candidates for some offices, it was wise to trust them with the power to nominate for all offices. He proposed, therefore, the complete abolition of the convention system and the inclusion of all state offices under the operation of the direct primaries. Other recommendations included the elimination of the party emblem from primary ballots, the prohibition of the use of party funds in primary elections, the framing of party platforms by a party council composed of members of the state committee and candidates for state offices, a reduction in the number of names required on a nominating petition, and publicity of all expenses incurred in connection with candidacies for nomination.[6] Those reforms, he believed, would destroy the corrupt

4 For a detailed analysis of the Blauvelt bill and other proposals pertaining to direct primaries, introduced during the 1913 session, see the *Report of the Committee on Legislation of the Citizens Union*, pp. 13-18.

5 *Public Papers of Governor Sulzer*, p. 103. The Democratic platform of 1912 with respect to direct primaries was not very explicit. It simply promised to " perfect and simplify " the existing law.

6 *Ibid.*, p. 105.

political influences which had usurped the powers of government. " The changes which I advocate in our primary law are in harmony with the spirit of the times and of democratic institutions," he asserted. " They aim to restore to the people rights and privileges which have been usurped by the few, for the benefit of invisible interests which aim to control governmental officials, to pass laws, and to violate laws with impunity. To these invisible powers I am now, always have been, and always will be opposed." [7] A partisan debate followed the reading of the message in the Senate. Senator Salant, leader of the Progressives, expressed his gratification that the Governor had become one of them on primary legislation.[8] Senator Brown called attention to the fact that early in the session he had introduced a primary bill embodying practically all the reforms mentioned by the Governor, save the abolition of the state convention.[9] The Democratic leaders expressed their determination to retain the state nominating convention and ventured the prediction that the Blauvelt bill would be the only one that would be sent to the Governor for approval.[10]

Sulzer followed up his special message to the Legislature with a speech in the Executive Chamber the next day, where he presided at a conference called to discuss election reforms. " That message is my platform on this legislation," he declared with emphasis. The election amendments he suggested would be enacted before the first of January, he said, or he would " know the reason why," a significant warning that if the Legislature failed him, there would be an extra session.[11] The

7 *Ibid.*, p. 106.

8 The Salant-Schaap bill, introduced early in the session, was drawn along the lines of a bill advocated by former Governor Charles E. Hughes. Although the Citizens Union pronounced it the best direct primary bill before the Legislature, it never emerged from the Judiciary Committee.

9 The Brown-Vert bill, introduced February 28.—Senate Journal, Vol. I, p. 466; Assembly Journal, Vol. I, p. 775.

10 *Times*, April 11.

11 *Ibid.*, April 12.

conference was not attended by any state or county leaders of the Democratic party. Among those present were such Democrats who for years had been at odds with the organization, and a scattering of independent Republicans and Progressives who happened to be interested in the question of direct primaries. Sulzer made it plain to his new political friends that he had embarked on a fight to the finish with Murphy in order to demonstrate to the people that he was, in fact as well as in name, leader of the party. He also appointed a " war board " to work out the details of a direct primary law to be presented to the Legislature, by which he hoped to make his claims good.[12] Bills incorporating the recommendations made by Sulzer in his special message were introduced by Senator McKnight, on April 21, and by Assemblyman Eisner, the following day, into their respective houses.[13]

The presentation of the Governor's bill to the Legislature drew his fight with the Democratic organization into the open, with the likelihood that the question as to who was the actual leader of the party would be conclusively settled. Tammany viewed Sulzer's direct primary fight as a pure sham, prompted solely by considerations of personal vengeance against the bosses with whom he had fallen out. Critics of the Governor pointed out that it was only after he had quarreled with the boss over patronage and a break between them seemed inevitable that he began his agitation for the abolition of the state convention. They could not be persuaded to believe that a man with his political record was actuated by the single desire to promote democratic legislation, but saw in his action an effort to build up his political fortunes which were shattered with his attempt to destroy Murphy's power. If the state convention were to go, he might succeed in overcoming the opposition of the party leaders and secure his renomination in 1914. Perhaps the success of Woodrow Wilson would be his if he assailed the

12 *Ibid.*

13 Senate Journal, Vol. II, p. 1490; Assembly Journal, Vol. III, p. 2746.

bosses in New York as Wilson had assailed them in New Jersey. To such men Sulzer appeared to be engaged in the purely selfish work of aggrandizing himself at the risk of disrupting the party to which he owed every political preferment that had ever come to him.

The legislators treated Sulzer's claims to party leadership with undisguised scorn and hurled their defiance at him by passing the Blauvelt bill by an overwhelming vote. Although Sulzer had made it perfectly plain that he was opposed to the organization measure because it did not appreciably change the prevailing primary system, it went through the Senate on April 16 by a vote of thirty-one to fifteen.[14] It was approved in the Assembly the following week by an even more impressive majority, the final vote recording one hundred and four members in its favor and only twenty-one opposed, a few of the "ayes" reserving the right to vote for a more drastic primary bill should the opportunity come.[15] Several far-reaching amendments, proposed on behalf of the Republican minority by Assemblyman Harold J. Hinman, were rejected without debate. Sulzer accepted the challenge and promptly returned the Blauvelt bill to the Legislature with a veto message which fairly bristled with invective. He branded it "a fraud," "a miserable makeshift," "a mere patchwork," "wholly fraudulent," and "a glaring breach of the pledged faith of every member of the Legislature." He denounced the slight amendments made to the existing law as designed simply to deceive the voters and in no sense constituting a real and honest direct primary law. He contrasted the many shortcomings of the Blauvelt bill with his own, which he described as embracing "an honest, a sincere, a comprehensive, and a practical plan" for genuine reform, that would restore political power to the people and destroy "the disgraceful secret alliances between big business interests and crooked and corrupt politics." His was a

14 Senate Journal, Vol. II, p. 1399.
15 Assembly Journal, Vol. III, p. 2773.

nonpartisan measure, he declared, for whose enactment every member of the Legislature was " solemnly bound in honor by the highest moral and political obligations " to vote. He indignantly refused to be a party to the betrayal of the people with false pretenses. " No political party can make me a political hypocrite," was his parting challenge.[16]

Sulzer's vitriolic veto message aroused anger and amazement in the Legislature and it was openly predicted that his own primary bill would be beaten in retaliation. Senator Wagner found the tone of the message " decidedly offensive " and, speaking for the Democratic majority, asked whether their disagreement with the Governor over the details of one of his reforms was sufficient reason for being branded as false and dishonorable. " I think," he declared, " the members of the majority feel badly hurt when, having succeeded in passing all the legislation advocated by the Governor in the belief that it is in the interest of reform, in the end, because we refuse to be stampeded, we meet with characterizations such as have been used by the Governor in connection with our action. To be called fraudulent and dishonorable men causes pain and disappointment to us all." [17] The Republican members of the Legislature, including seventeen Senators and forty-two Assemblymen, many of whom had voted against the Blauvelt bill, issued a formal statement on April 25 declaring their willingness to accept the Sulzer primary bill except the provision for the abolition of the state convention, which, they maintained, would be contrary to their party platform. This condition Sulzer would not even consider, preferring to risk the entire measure than accept any sort of compromise. " Neither the crossing of a ' t ' or the dotting of an ' i ' nor the changing of the simplest language in the bill will be tolerated," he declared. " My bill or nothing. That is the slogan." [18] From

16 *Public Papers of Governor Sulzer*, pp. 190-96, *passim*.

17 *Times*, April 30.

18 *World*, April 30.

that point on, therefore, the Republican machine made common cause with the Democratic organization.

Sulzer lost no time in organizing his campaign to arouse sentiment in behalf of his measure throughout the state. Once having made up his mind to use the direct nominations issue as a weapon in his fight on Tammany, he solicited the support of prominent Progressives and independent Republicans who wanted to dethrone William Barnes as chairman of the Republican State Committee. Hundreds of letters and telegrams were broadcast calling upon newspaper editors, labor unions, granges, boards of trade, and civic bodies of all kinds to pass resolutions endorsing his bill.[19] Learning that the legislative leaders had received orders to block all the bills he desired passed before the final adjournment, he decided to apply the lash in his primary fight. He summoned the chairmen of the Democratic County Committees to the Executive Chamber on April 26, fifty-one of the sixty-two responding, to declare openly whether they were for him or against him in his effort to obtain the enactment of a statewide primary law. He issued a sharp warning that he would expel from the party every Democrat who opposed him. " If any Democrat in this State is against the Democratic State platform, that man is no true Democrat, and as the Democratic Governor of the State I shall do everything in my power to drive that recreant Democrat out of the Democratic party," he threatened. " Rest assured that in this struggle those who help me will win my gratitude; that those who oppose me will merit condemnation. If he is with me, I will be with him. If he is against me, mark well what I say, I shall be against him. He must either be a party to driving me out of public life, or I must be a party to driving him out of the Democratic party." [20] His explicit ultimatum to the county chairmen was to line up their representatives in the Legislature in support of " this honest, this just, this fair,

19 *Ibid.*, April 26.

20 *Public Papers of Governor Sulzer*, pp. 1312-15.

this nonpartisan State-wide direct primary bill " or he would line up the people against them.[21] That the Governor's warning was apparently taken to heart was shown by the immediate adoption of resolutions endorsing his bill and recommending its passage, adverse votes being cast by only two chairmen who had some " scruples " about interfering with the work of the Legislature.[22] This meeting was preliminary to a crowded public hearing held by the Senate Judiciary Committee on the Governor's bill at which the Sulzer zealots gave a noisy demonstration of their enthusiasm.[23] Sulzer disappointed his critics by not appearing in person, but there were large numbers of his followers present who excoriated the legislators for " political dishonor." Those included independent Democrats who were unsuccessful candidates for office or who were holding office under the Sulzer administration, Progressives who made the direct primary one of their cardinal principles, and a few Republicans. The burden of the arguments advanced in favor of the bill was that it would make public officials and party organizations more responsive to popular will.[24]

The Governor's address to the Democratic county chairmen created widespread resentment among Tammany men. Senator Blauvelt issued a formal statement condemning Sulzer's declared intention of driving out of the party any man who refused to support his bill as " radically unjust and unfair." He earnestly defended the right of legislators to exercise their honest and independent judgment, " uninfluenced by partisan selfishness, a judgment wholly as honest as the Governor could form." He also questioned the wisdom of several salient features of the Governor's bill, particularly the abolition of state conventions which, he maintained, would give New York City a decided advantage over up-state districts in nominating

21 *Ibid.*, p. 1317.
22 *Times*, April 27.
23 *World*, April 27.
24 *Ibid.*

candidates for state offices.[25] Alfred E. Smith, Speaker of the Assembly, felt that the fate of the Governor's proposal depended ultimately on whether the legislators found any demand for it among their constituents. Personally, he said, he had discovered no sentiment in its favor. He doubted whether the existing primary law had yet been given " a fair trial " and challenged Sulzer's interpretation of the party's platform. A statewide primary bill, he maintained, was not one which would abolish the state convention but one which would apply to all parts of the state.[26] John H. McCooey, Democratic leader of Kings County, likewise evidenced no alarm over the Governor's threat. He pointed out that up-state Democrats were opposed to his plan because the abolition of the state convention might make it possible for urban centers with a large population, like New York and Buffalo, to combine to control the state. In passing, he took occasion to explode the notion that the Legislature was being run by political bosses. " This talk that the Legislature is ruled by the bosses is all buncombe," he exclaimed indignantly. " It is no more controlled by the bosses than is the Executive of this State." [27] Legislative leaders condemned Sulzer's peremptory demands as entirely out of accord with his anti-boss declarations. " No boss ever resorted to such unscrupulous methods to attain his purpose," was the bitter comment.[28] Their answer was to lay plans for the quick assassination of his pet bill. A caucus of Democratic Senators on the night of April 28 bound themselves to oppose the measure. No vote was reached in the caucus of the Democratic Assemblymen, but those who attended expressed the belief that it did not stand a chance.[29]

Sulzer was unable to overcome the silent strength of the party leaders and, as anticipated, his direct nominations bill

25 *Ibid.*, April 28.
26 *Times*, April 28.
27 *Ibid.*
28 *Ibid.*, April 29.
29 *Ibid.*

met the overwhelming defeat in the Legislature which it almost seemed to invite by its radical character. His threat to call the Legislature back in extra session unless his bill was passed did not have the calculated effect. On April 30 the McKnight bill was beaten in the Senate beyond hope of resuscitation. Forty-two votes were cast against it and eight votes, two of which were furnished by Republicans, were all that its advocates could muster in its favor.[30] During the four-hour debate that preceded the final vote the Governor was freely denounced for the dictatorial methods he had adopted to compel the adoption of his bill. The merits of the proposed legislation were lost sight of as member after member stood up to censure the campaign of intimidation and cajolery carried on in the Executive Chamber during the preceding weeks and to announce their refusal to be politically excommunicated because they would not yield to the views of one man.[31] Senator Brown, who led the debate, warned that the Governor's bill " would throw the State government into the hands of the demagogues." [32] Senator John F. Murtaugh, a Democrat with independent leanings, branded Sulzer as " a political Tamerlane," erecting a pyramid of the heads of decapitated Democrats who happened to disagree with him.[33] Senator Wagner charged him with bad faith in not making his views on primary legislation known while the Blauvelt bill was in course of preparation. Had Sulzer shown an interest in the question earlier in the session, harmonious action might have been achieved, he felt. He charged Sulzer with using his office for " self-advertisement " and seeking front page publicity, and accused him of " ingratitude " to the party that had made him.[34] He urged his colleagues not to

30 Senate Journal, Vol. II, p. 1825.

31 Legislators who had gone to see Sulzer on behalf of their local legislation carried away the impression that unless they voted for his primary bill, they need expect no favor at his hands.

32 *Times*, May 1.

33 *Ibid.*

34 *World*, May 1.

be browbeaten, but to stand up against the Governor's threats. He also read a letter signed by Chester C. Platt, secretary to Governor Sulzer, alleged to have been sent to state officials, peremptorily summoning them to appear at the hearing on the McKnight bill. " You are holding a lucrative office under the present administration. You are expected to be present and if possible speak for the bill," the letter admonished.[35] Following the example of the upper house, the Assembly on May 1, after a five-hour debate, defeated the Governor's measure (the Eisner bill) by a vote of ninety-three to forty-seven, despite the active lobbying of several office-holders, presumably at Sulzer's behest.[36] A number of amendments proposed by minority leader Hinman were rejected prior to the final vote. On every side Sulzer was bitterly denounced for his coercive methods. Even independent Democrats freely joined in the denunciation, enraged at being fought with the very weapons of the bosses in the name of emancipation from boss rule.[37] The Legislature completed its defiance of the Governor by hurriedly repassing the Blauvelt bill before adjournment on May 3.[38] Except for the fact that it conceded a few more points to the reform spirit, the second Blauvelt bill was the same as the one so caustically vetoed by Sulzer once before. As the regular session neared its close, the legislative and executive branches of the state government were in undisguised war. The Governor was openly derided, his emergency messages urging the adoption of several measures still pending ignored, his nominations rejected with scant ceremony. " The State Capitol to-day [May 2] resembled a Balkan war map," wrote one newspaper correspondent.[39]

35 *Times*, May 1. Platt pronounced the letter " bogus."—*Ibid.*, May 2.

36 Assembly Journal, Vol. III, p. 3300.

37 *Times*, May 2.

38 Senate Journal, Vol. II, p. 2099; Assembly Journal, Vol. III, p. 3301.

39 *World*, May 3.

Sulzer's comment on the defeat of his bill was: "The bill was not beaten on its merits. It was defeated solely by the party lash and the bipartisan caucus combination, dictated by agencies outside the Capitol." [40] But not disheartened, he declared, "The battle for direct primaries has just begun. The fight will go on until the cause of the people triumphs." [41] He reiterated his determination to summon the Legislature in extra session and announced his intention of stumping the state during the intervening period in an effort so to stir public sentiment as to compel the passage of his bill. He expressed his intention of visiting the district of every legislator who had aided in the nefarious work of repudiating the party's platform and of laying the matter directly before his constituents. He made it plain too that he would fight the bosses with their own weapons and would use the patronage power of his office to make reprisals against the leaders who opposed him by ousting every one of their protégés in the state service who was not protected by civil service regulations. Appointments would go only to those who sided with him against the organization.[42] An unprecedented publicity campaign was launched from the Executive Chamber and prosecuted with the greatest vigor. In every direction the Governor brought to bear all the pressure at his disposal. The general opinion in Albany was that Sulzer had burned all his bridges behind him and that thenceforth there would be open warfare with Tammany. His friends had pronounced him ready to stake his entire political future on his attempt to put through a primary bill that would sound "the death knell of boss power." [43] The issue raised in the direct primary fight was one in which no quarter could be given. Sulzer had definitely set out to break Murphy. Political observers, however, were of the opinion that direct nominations

40 *Ibid.*, May 2.
41 *Times*, May 2.
42 *Ibid.*
43 *Ibid.*, April 29.

on the Sulzer pattern did not have a chance and predicted that his efforts in its behalf would be fruitless. Inasmuch as the organization had set itself sternly against the abolition of the state convention, it was doubtful whether any one of the Democratic legislators could be persuaded to change his vote. Nor were the Republicans inclined to support a bill of such far-reaching character.[44] It was absurd for Sulzer to hope to win over the Republican party to a measure which a Republican Governor, Charles E. Hughes, had in vain tried to put on the statute books.[45]

Sulzer hoped to obtain the sympathy of all good men in his fight against Tammany but not all good men were convinced that the primary issue was a fit cause for such warfare. He might have found more general support were there not so much doubt about the wisdom of the proposed primary law. Many earnest and public-spirited reformers who approved the principle of the direct primary deplored some of the changes Sulzer would make in the electoral machinery, particularly the abolition of the state convention. The state convention, they held, was a time-honored institution valuable for the formulation of party principles and policies, and, if composed of delegates chosen by the enrolled voters, could become a thoroughly representative body. While the direct primary system might work well in the political subdivisions of the

44 William Barnes promised the support of the Republican legislators provided the state convention were retained but Sulzer's reply was that the wiping out of the state convention was the essence of his bill. — *Times,* May 18.

45 In 1909 and again in 1910 Hughes had appealed for the passage of the so-called Hinman-Green Direct Nominations bill, but both efforts were blocked by a bipartisan combination in the Legislature. Hughes called a special session but despite the weight of Theodore Roosevelt's influence, the bill was again decisively beaten by the cooperation of the Democratic organization and machine Republicans. Roosevelt openly accused Barnes of being in personal communication with the legislators in an effort to defeat the proposed primary legislation. See Roosevelt's testimony in *Barnes vs. Roosevelt,* Vol. I, p. 19; also Benjamin P. DeWitt, *The Progressive Movement,* (New York, 1915), p. 63.

state, it was also argued, it would be a mistake to apply it to the nomination of state officials and judges of the Court of Appeals. Some of the objections voiced were that no man could be nominated for high state office unless he had a powerful party organization or a large campaign fund behind him; that nominees, if there were several candidates, might be chosen by minority groups; and that, in view of the fact that it was virtually impossible for the people generally to acquaint themselves with the qualifications of candidates for the bench, it was improbable that the nomination of judges by direct popular vote would insure an able and independent judiciary.[46] What reason was there to suppose, Sulzer's critics asked, that the abolition of the whole party machinery of government would actually destroy the power of the professional politicians or secure the designation of better men for office? Even under the convention system the people had a way of making their will felt, whenever they had any to express, as shown by the nomination for Governor of such men as Cleveland and Hughes. Granting that the party system had its defects, was the resort to the direct nominations principle the solution of every political problem? Sulzer sought to make a moral issue out of the direct primaries, but, as the *Times* pointed out, there was " no inherent morality or immorality either in the caucus and convention, or in the committee designation and the direct primary, no evil that cannot be cast out if the people will take the trouble to do it." [47]

On May 8 Governor Sulzer issued a proclamation summoning the Legislature to meet in an extra session on June 16, in order to resubmit the direct nominations bill that had been contemptuously rejected in the closing days of the regular session.[48] He issued the call the day after a conference held in the Executive Chamber by advocates of his measure. It was a

46 *Times*, May 5.

47 Editorial, May 20.

48 *Public Papers of Governor Sulzer*, p. 16.

picturesque gathering of social, political, and moral uplifters of all sorts who had gathered to restore government to the people. The audience was composed largely of men who either held office or hoped to hold office under the Sulzer administration, disgruntled Democrats outside the organization fold, a handful of Republicans, a large representation of clergymen, and a sprinkling of suffragettes.[49] Every county in the state was represented. The conference was well staged, the Governor dramatically entering the packed Chamber from his private office a half hour late, " with long stride and statesmanlike pose," amidst loud applause, the audience rising to welcome him.[50] In his address Sulzer reiterated his threat to use the patronage of his office to punish those who opposed him and reward those who would help him. He even intimated that he would employ his veto power against lawmakers who were against his bill. After denouncing the action of the legislators of the two machines who had combined to defeat his bill, he reaffirmed his belief that a direct primary law would still be written on the statute books, despite the skepticism of practical politicians.[51] After a flood of oratory, a campaign committee of one hundred was appointed, composed of twenty-five anti-Tammany Democrats, twenty-five Republicans, twenty-five Progressives, and twenty-five without party affiliations. An imposing array of prominent names headed the list, including William Randolph Hearst,[52] Herbert H. Lehman, George W. Perkins, District Attorney Charles S. Whitman, John Purroy Mitchel, Caleb H. Strong, Ralph Pulitzer, and Vincent Astor. Smaller committees, likewise nonpartisan, were appointed to

49 *World*, May 8.

50 *Times*, May 8.

51 *Ibid.*

52 Many persons believed that Sulzer's direct primary fight was prompted very largely by a desire to regain the political friendship of Hearst, whom Sulzer once violently abused, and the support of his newspapers. As evidence they called attention to the appointment of Hearst himself, of Hearst's private secretary, and of Hearst's counsel, Clarence J. Shearn, to Sulzer's campaign committee.—*Ibid.*

direct publicity and lead the fight in the various counties, particularly in those districts whose representatives voted against the bill. A Committee of Ways and Means, headed by Henry Morgenthau, was charged with the duty of raising funds to defray the necessary expenses of the campaign " for restoring to the people their rights." [53] The list of recruits to the Governor's cause included ex-President Theodore Roosevelt who announced his intention of supporting Sulzer in his fight for primary reform and called on all Progressives to do likewise. In a letter to the members of his party, written on May 12, he denounced both the Republican and Democratic parties as parties of " privilege " and " reaction." [54] Endorsing the Sulzer bill, he wrote in the *Review of Reviews:* " The envenomed opposition of both the Murphy and Barnes machines to it is of itself sufficient proof that it is emphatically in the interest of the people as a whole." [55]

That Sulzer meant every word of his ultimatum to the Democratic county chairmen that unless they rallied to his support, he would starve them of all patronage soon became apparent. The first announcement of the tactics that were to be employed came on May 16, when the publicity bureau of Sulzer's campaign committee declared that the Governor had recognized Daniel J. Dugan, a member of his direct primary committee, as the Democratic leader of Albany County, in place of Patrick E. McCabe, Senate clerk and one of Murphy's up-state satellites.[56] The same course, the committee's statement declared, would be pursued in every up-state county where political patronage had hitherto been at the disposal of the Tammany boss's henchmen.[57] All department heads whom the Governor could control through his power of removal were told to weed out organization men in order to make room for those recom-

53 *Ibid.*
54 *World*, May 13.
55 June, 1913, Vol. 47, p. 686.
56 *World*, May 17.
57 *Ibid.*

mended by party leaders friendly to him. Contractors on Capitol repair work were notified by Sulzer that certain McCabe men were to be dismissed and that those selected to fill their places were not to receive appointment until approved by him personally.[58] Duncan W. Peck, Superintendent of Public Works, in control of jobs on the Barge Canal, made it clear that, in obedience to the wishes of Sulzer, he would name only Sulzer partisans.[59] In the State Highway Department, already under the control of a Sulzer appointee, John N. Carlisle, hundreds of positions were taken from men loyal to the organization and bestowed on those recommended by party leaders who had ranged themselves on Sulzer's side.[60] To the Executive Chamber streamed a steady procession of disgruntled Democrats who seized on the current fight between the Governor and the organization to " break in " and get even with those who had kept them out of power.[61]

Opponents of the Governor vehemently charged him with attempting to wreck the Democratic organization and build up a personal machine by his use of patronage, while masquerading as a reformer.[62] Public office, they declared, had become a private asset with him, and loyalty to himself was thenceforth evidently to be the supreme test of fitness for places in the public service.[63] In many instances, it was said, appointments were being made without regard to merit, and civil service rules were being changed more frequently than ever before to meet the political exigencies of the Governor's fight.[64] The policy of wholesale decapitation of Democratic officeholders was inaugurated by Sulzer, it was also charged, in obedience

58 *Ibid.*, April 30.
59 *Ibid.*, May 16.
60 *Times*, June 12.
61 *Ibid.*, July 20.
62 *World*, August 4.
63 *Telegraph*, July 1.
64 *Times*, July 20.

to the orders of Hearst. As proof was quoted the following remark made by one of Hearst's lieutenants on a visit to Albany: " We have never felt sure whether the Governor really is with us. His loyalty and sincerity from now on will be measured not by what he says in his speeches but by the number of heads of Murphy's henchmen which drop into the basket." [65]

Sulzer also brought his veto power into play. He killed a considerable number of thirty-day bills left with him by the Legislature, his displeasure falling most heavily on measures introduced by Tammany members. He cut out more than three million dollars from appropriation and supply bills, disallowing many new positions in the office of the state comptroller, secretary of state, and various boards and commissions.[66] He rejected the Blauvelt bill for a second time and for the same reasons.[67] He disapproved the McClelland bill providing for a referendum on June 3 on the question whether a state convention be held to revise the constitution, to meet the following April. The measure had been denounced by the Republicans and Progressives as a purely political scheme intended to make fusion in New York City difficult and thus aid Tammany in the approaching municipal election.[68] The Governor apparently took no notice of the political significance of the measure for, in his veto memorandum, he gave as his sole reason that there was insufficient time to prepare the adequate machinery for the special election. The Democratic party pledge to summon a constitutional convention would just as well be kept, he said, if the convention were held a year later.[69] Another measure he

65 *Ibid.* In his *Imperial Hearst*, (New York, 1936), Ferdinand Lundberg writes that during the administration of Sulzer, Hearst exercised "enormous influence" in Albany. "Sulzer was a Hearst puppet," he states, "with Hearst financing his campaigns and receiving appropriately valuable favors." (pp. 251-52).

66 Bills vetoed, with accompanying memoranda, are given in *Public Papers of Governor Sulzer*, pp. 217-411.

67 *Ibid.*, p. 268.

68 *Times*, May 15.

69 *Public Papers of Governor Sulzer*, pp. 231-33.

refused to sign was the Foley-Wagner workmen's compensation bill, which had the endorsement of the state superintendent of insurance.[70] He also vetoed the Murtaugh hydro-electric bill which authorized the establishment of a state plant on the Mohawk River for the generation and sale of electricity to Albany and surrounding area. While in sympathy with the general purposes of the bill, Sulzer explained in his veto memorandum, he doubted its constitutionality, expressed the fear that it might cripple the efficiency of the Barge Canal, and asserted that the St. Lawrence was a more desirable site for the development of hydro-electric power.[71] This veto was the signal for a bitter attack upon Sulzer by Lieutenant-Governor Glynn, who had been chief sponsor of the bill and most instrumental in securing its passage. Having been repeatedly assured by Sulzer of his support, he found the veto utterly " unexplainable and indefensible." He accused Sulzer of insincerity and rank hypocrisy. " Governor Sulzer brags about being a friend of the people," he wrote. " When he vetoed this bill he was an enemy of the people and a friend of the corporations. Talk is cheap. Actions tell where a man stands." The Democratic state platform, he added, committed the Governor to this bill as much as it did to direct primaries. " Evidently only such portions of the state platform are binding upon the Governor as suit his whims or the pocket-books of his corporation friends." He openly attributed the veto to the influence of the public utilities, particularly of Samuel Beardsley, attorney for the power interests, who had supported Sulzer's nomination for Governor.[72] Friends of Glynn also saw in the disapproval of the hydro-electric bill retaliation for his refusal to support

70 *Ibid.*, pp. 248-52. The State Federation of Labor opposed the Foley bill because it continued the monopoly enjoyed by the casualty companies in this field of insurance. Organized labor favored the Murtaugh-Jackson bill which would establish a state insurance fund.—*Times*, May 4.

71 *Public Papers of Governor Sulzer*, pp. 295-99.

72 *Times*, May 29.

Sulzer's efforts to force his direct primary bill through the Legislature, though Sulzer denied it.[73]

The Governor likewise used his power of veto, it was reported, in order to canvass support for his bill among members of the Legislature. Several lawmakers who called upon him to discuss local legislation were plainly told that unless they would vote for his measure, he would veto their proposals, irrespective of their merits. Senator James A. Emerson, Republican, testified, for example, that when he came to the Governor to request favorable action on a bill providing for the construction of a state highway in his district, he was answered, " I will sign that bill if you will vote for my primary bill." [74] He was also reported as having threatened members of the Legislature to remove their friends from office unless they supported his primary views.[75] Such coercive methods were bitterly condemned by Senator Wagner as " radically unfair and improper." The Senators, he maintained, were quite as conscientious as the Governor in the performance of their public duty, " though perhaps not as spectacular," and would courageously withstand his dictation when they believed him to be wrong.[76]

On May 18 Sulzer left Albany for his " swing around the circle," accompanied by a retinue of stenographers, secretaries, newspaper correspondents, and members of his campaign committee, confident that the people would be aroused to such a pitch of enthusiasm that the Legislature in extra session would not dare to reject his reform bill again.[77] That same day appeared a special article in the New York *World,* in which he flung a direct challenge to Murphy and Barnes and appealed to the public to rally to his call for war. He denounced the Democratic legislators for their " glaring betrayal of the people's

73 *World*, May 29.

74 *Times*, May 18.

75 *Ibid.*, May 19.

76 *Ibid.*

77 *Ibid.*, May 18.

trust" in violating the campaign pledge for party reform. He characterized the party chieftains as bosses who were in politics "for plunder," whose political activities could not stand "the searchlight of publicity," who held the Legislature "in the hollow of their hands," and who had "bartered the public interests." [78] This latest blast forced Tammany to abandon its policy of treating the Governor's utterances with contemptuous silence. After a conference with Tammany leaders, Senator Wagner issued a statement in which he emphatically disputed Sulzer's interpretation of the party's platform. Speaking authoritatively as chairman of the committee on resolutions at the Syracuse convention, he denied that the Democratic party had ever committed itself to the abolition of the state convention. The term "statewide" as used in the platform, he maintained, simply contemplated a primary law that would have a uniform application throughout the state, and was not intended to cover state as well as local offices.[79] He accused Sulzer of deliberately disregarding the truth in this matter, and challenged him to defend the merits of his particular bill instead of making general statements that could be applied to any direct primary bill. He branded as "absolutely untrue" the assertion that Murphy and Barnes held the Legislature "in the hollow of their hands," avowing that the only dictation the members had to withstand was the dictation of the Governor. He rebuked Sulzer for attempting to discredit the integrity of members of the Legislature, asserting that they had passed more progressive and beneficial legislation than any previous Legislature in the history of the state. As for Sulzer's solicitude for the party platform, he declared, he himself had seen fit to veto measures passed in compliance with platform pledges, such as the calling

78 May 18.

79 Wagner's interpretation of the platform was the one commonly accepted at the time it was drawn up. An editorial appearing in the *World* on October 3, 1912, denounced the plank on direct primaries as "fraudulent" on the ground that it "left the state nominating convention untouched."

of a constitutional convention and the workmen's compensation bill.[80]

Sulzer opened his direct primary campaign in Buffalo on May 19, where he spoke at meetings held either under Progressive auspices or managed by the Conners faction of the Erie Democratic organization which was trying to dethrone Fitzpatrick, a Murphy lieutenant.[81] In his thrice repeated speech he appealed for popular support against boss rule. He emphatically asserted that not only had the convention system proved itself inadequate to carry out the wishes of the people, but had become an instrumentality through which the powers of government were " prostituted and brought under the dominion of unscrupulous men." " Political conventions must go. Disgraceful secret alliances between special privilege and crooked politics must cease," he exclaimed. If the people, he said, were competent to elect public officials, they were competent to nominate them. " The spirit of true Democracy is summed up in the slogan, ' Let the people rule.' They cannot rule until they obtain a successful method of nominating the candidates of all political parties." It was impossible, he claimed, to have both direct primaries and state conventions. After summing up the features of his own bill, he affirmed, " I am convinced that every member of the Legislature is solemnly bound in honor, and by the highest moral and political obligations, to vote for its enactment; and those who fail to do so will be forced to yield to public opinion." And toward the close of the speech came this significant passage: " Let us keep the faith. That is where I stand, and I will stand there to the end. If any Democrat is against me in my determination to keep Democratic faith, I must of necessity be against him . . . and as the

80 *World*, May 19.

81 It is interesting to note that when Governor Hughes was fighting for direct primaries, Conners bitterly fought for the continuance of the existing system.—*Times*, May 20. It was quite evident that Sulzer's support among Democratic politicians was prompted less by any widespread desire for reform than by the greed for patronage and power.

Democratic Governor of the State I shall do everything in my power to drive that recreant Democrat out of the councils of the Democratic party." [82] A strong battery of speakers supported Sulzer, including Clarence J. Shearn, Hearst's counsel, John Mitchell, labor leader, and a number of local advocates of the direct primary.[83]

Sulzer did not confine his efforts to making speeches. Prior to his departure, he made it clear to office-seekers that the county would not get " a look in " on patronage unless its legislators came to the support of his bill. " Not another job will go to Erie County from the Executive Chamber until the legislators see fit to vote for my direct primary bill," he warned.[84] The two Senators and eight Assemblymen who had opposed Sulzer's bill made no public reply to what they privately styled " Sulzer's ravings," [85] but Fitzpatrick, leader of the local Democratic organization, was more outspoken. The Governor's invasion of his bailiwick, he announced, would not change a single vote in the Erie delegation to the Legislature, despite his threat.[86] This was interpreted to mean that Murphy and his lieutenants had determined to fight it out.

The Governor and his crusading band continued their tour through territory where they received a cordial reception. He addressed large crowds in Elmira, Corning, and Schenectady, unsparing in his condemnation of the party bosses. A feature of all his speeches was the rhetorical question put to his audiences whether they wished to nominate candidates themselves or preferred to leave that function with three men : " One in New York, one in Buffalo, and one in Albany," an obvious reference to Murphy, Fitzpatrick, and Barnes.[87] A dramatic

82 *Public Papers of Governor Sulzer*, pp. 1324-33, *passim*.
83 *Times*, May 20.
84 *Ibid.*
85 *World*, May 20.
86 *Times*, May 20.
87 *Ibid.*, May 21.

episode occurred in Elmira where, in much the same manner as in his earlier speeches, Sulzer accused the delegates to state conventions of being more eager to carry out the wishes of the party leaders than of the individual party voters. He then turned to Senator Murtaugh, who was seated on the platform, and coaxingly appealed to him for his support, convinced that if Murtaugh joined the primary fight, " the backbone of the opposition would be broken." Much to his discomfiture, the Senator refused. In a vigorous speech in reply, he frankly questioned the merit of Sulzer's proposal to abolish the state convention and emphatically denied that failure to pass his particular bill would involve a breach of party faith.[88] Murtaugh's stand was bound to have a telling effect throughout the state because he was known to be an independent lawmaker. Before leaving the city, the Governor threatened to drive Murtaugh from public life.[89] Similarly, in Schenectady, he accused the local Senator, Loren H. White, of disloyalty for having voted against his bill, and virtually read him out of the party.[90] Without stint and midst lusty cheers, he continued his denunciation of the party bosses, for the first time during his campaign mentioning Barnes and Murphy by name. He referred to the former as " Boss Barnes " and to the latter as " Mr. Murphy " (with sarcasm). " It is these men," he said, " who are preventing the will of the people from being carried out by their representatives in the Legislature." He warned the Tammany leader to stay in his own county. " I think I know the Tiger's place. It should be in a cage and that's where we will put it before we get through," he confidently predicted.[91] He gave a new name to his primary bill, christening it " the People's bill," because, he explained, the people everywhere seemed to be for it, with the exception of a few bosses and some editors whose papers were controlled by the " special interests."

88 *Ibid.*
89 *Ibid.*
90 *World*, May 22.
91 *Times*, May 22.

"Who dares to challenge my bill?" he shouted. "Any one who does it is an enemy of the State, an enemy of the people, an enemy of the hopes of every one." [92] In all his campaign speeches he gave more attention to the character of the men opposing him than to the merits of his reform.

Sulzer expressed himself as greatly pleased with the first part of his tour and contended that he had received sufficient assurance of support to justify confidence in his victory.[93] Some of those who accompanied him, on the other hand, openly admitted their skepticism and doubted whether he had changed a single vote among the lawmakers in the districts he had visited.[94] While he had been warmly received and evidently continued to enjoy a large measure of personal popularity, it was problematical whether he had succeeded in arousing public sentiment or of spreading much knowledge of the virtues of the reforms he was advocating. The Governor's broadsides did not go unanswered and Tammany Hall soon started a "back-fire." Speaking before the Democratic County Committee of Richmond, Senator Wagner justified the state convention as indispensable to the development of party opinion and defended it as capable of bringing popular choices into public office. He praised the work of the Legislature and maintained that if the Legislature were to yield to the Governor's ultimatum, it would be abdicating its constitutional function and become a "mere puppet" of the Executive. Referring to Sulzer's threat to drive Senator Murtaugh from public office, he said that no boss would dare resort to such methods. "If we in the Legislature, standing courageously by our convictions, undeterred by threats or promises, and responsive to what we believe to be the will of the people, are enemies of the people, the people may well beware of its self-designated 'friends,'" he exclaimed. Senator Blauvelt, who spoke at the same meeting, char-

92 *Ibid.*
93 *Ibid.*, May 23.
94 *Ibid.*

acterized Sulzer's followers in the primary campaign as " outcasts of every party." The Governor, he said, was misleading the people. " The Sulzer bill is simply the bill of William Randolph Hearst." [95] Senator Griffin wrote an open letter to the Governor, calling him a " tyrant " who was attempting to make " abject slaves " of the legislators. " Are you," he asked, " the high priest of direct nominations with a mission from heaven to put on the rack all who do not worship at your shrine? " Asserting that Sulzer was trying to make himself party dictator, he added: " No man in civil life, no matter what his talents for depravity may be, could be half so dangerous a party boss as the Chief Executive of the State." [96]

Sulzer's next appearance on the stump was on May 28 in New York City where, it was reported, he would start the work of building up a personal organization in Tammany's own stronghold.[97] A large corps of direct primary advocates assisted him in his campaign, including District Attorney Whitman, Comptroller Prendergast, Borough President McAneny, John Purroy Mitchel, President of the Board of Aldermen, and Bainbridge Colby, Bull Moose leader. He spoke in widely separated parts of the city, addressing more than a dozen meetings, which in most cases were crowded, and from time to time aroused real enthusiasm by his belligerent assaults on Barnes, Murphy, and McCooey. He insisted that he had been forced into the fight by the bosses, but that he was quite willing " to accommodate " them. " I warn anybody who attacks me," he challenged, " that I will strip him of his hide, and tack the hide on the ceiling of the Capitol at Albany." [98] He made only passing reference to the provisions of his direct primary bill, spending most of his time castigating the lawmakers who had thus far refused to accept it. While there was

95 *Times*, May 23.
96 *World*, May 22.
97 *Times*, May 29.
98 *Ibid.*, May 31.

no doubt about the popularity of his attack on Tammany Hall and its leaders, his listeners seemed only moderately interested in the cause he had come to advocate. It could hardly be said that his campaign helped to illuminate the subject of direct primaries or make for intelligent reasoning. Tammany politicians professed to be less concerned after Sulzer's invasion of their territory than before. His campaign in the city, they pointed out exultantly, had shown unmistakable evidence of the strong influence wielded over him by Hearst. It was Hearst, they charged, who was responsible for Sulzer's failure to keep his promise to address a large meeting in Carnegie Hall, held under the auspices of the Non-partisan Direct Primary League, the reason being that the arrangements committee had declined to permit either Hearst or his attorney to speak.[99] Swiftly disillusioned as to the Governor's sincerity, Charles H. Duell, chairman of the League, declared that Sulzer's championing of the " people's cause " was in reality nothing but a clever game of politics whose purpose was a new alignment of the Democratic forces of the state under the dual leadership of Sulzer and Hearst.[100]

Before his return to Albany Sulzer declared himself greatly pleased with his campaign in the city. " The size and temper of the audiences have been gratifying," he declared. " I think the issue has taken as strong a hold here as it has up-State. I cannot but believe that concrete results will come from the fight we are making for the purpose of restoring political power to the people." [101] But if Sulzer had succeeded in making a single convert among the lawmakers of his party, those converts made no public demonstration of their repentance. On the contrary, at one of the Bronx meetings Senator Griffin told the Governor to his face that he resented his dictatorial methods.[102] And at

99 *Ibid.*, May 29.

100 *Ibid.*, May 30.

101 *Ibid.*, June 1.

102 *Ibid.*, May 29.

one of his Staten Island meetings Senator Blauvelt, who shared the platform with Sulzer, openly announced that, despite threats of retaliation, he would again vote against the Sulzer measure at the extra session.[103] The Democratic Senators and Assemblymen from Manhattan and the Bronx, who met at the Hotel Knickerbocker on June 4 to take inventory of their strength, reported that Sulzer's speeches had had no appreciable effect on public sentiment in their districts and that not a single member who had voted against the administration bill at the regular session had been persuaded to change his attitude.[104] Even those legislators who had voted for the Sulzer bill, Eisner and Gibbs, for example, condemned the Governor's methods of campaigning.[105] Senator Wagner led the attack with a warmly applauded address in which he demanded that the Governor be compelled to account for the repeated attacks he had made on state officers and members of the Legislature. " Governor Sulzer said on the stump that the State departments are honeycombed with corruption and that if the people knew the real character of the lawmakers they would organize lynching parties," he asserted. " These are only two samples of the reckless and irresponsible utterances he has made in his attempt to disrupt the Democratic party and make himself leader, using as a cloak a Direct Nominations bill which, it should be apparent by this time, the voters of this State do not want." The legislators, he declared, had a right to know who the " grafters " were and the Governor should be compelled at the extra session either to make good or retract his statements.[106] Wagner also unqualifiedly accused the Governor of a vicious and vindictive use of his veto power in the fight for his primary bill, citing specific instances, and threatened an investigation of every Assemblyman and Senator who should change his vote on the

103 *Ibid.*, May 31.
104 *World*, June 5.
105 *Ibid.*
106 *Times*, June 5.

Sulzer bill at the extra session from the negative to the affirmative.[107] He attributed Sulzer's veto of the Capital district hydroelectric bill to the importunities of Samuel A. Beardsley, Democratic leader of Oneida County and counsel for the power interests. He quoted Beardsley as having openly boasted to certain lawmakers, long before the bill was enacted, that he "had got Sulzer." [108] The price would be paid at the extra session, according to the report, when William D. Peckham, a Senator from Beardsley's district, would reverse himself and vote for Sulzer's bill. Another rumor had it that Sulzer signed a $750,000 road appropriation bill for Senator Emerson's county with the understanding that he too would vote for his bill. Wagner told also of the experience of another member of the Senate, Seth G. Heacock, who was informed by the Governor, when asked to approve a bond issue for one of the communities in his district, that the measure would not be signed unless he changed his vote. The Governor was quoted as saying, "You have a nerve to come to me with such a request after voting against my Direct Nominations bill. You needn't look to me to sign any of your bills unless you vote for my bill at the extra session." [109] "It is time the mask was torn from this hypocritical strife," Wagner declared, "and after this direct primary campaign is over we will show who is boss and who is making corrupt bargains to veto and sign legislation." [110] The Kings County Democratic Senators and Assemblymen also met to define their attitude toward Sulzer's bill and likewise decided to stand firm in their opposition.[111]

Both Barnes and McCooey issued statements in reply to the Governor's attacks upon them. They protested that Sulzer misrepresented their attitude since they were on record as

107 *World*, June 5.
108 *Times*, June 5.
109 *Ibid.*
110 *World*, June 5.
111 *Ibid.*

favoring direct nominations except for the abolition of the state convention. Barnes also took occasion to censure the Governor's coercive tactics. " I am not concerned or interested," he said, " whether the Democratic party is run by a Sulzer machine or a Murphy machine. They present a great similarity to my mind. Coercion, compulsion of support through the use or withdrawal of patronage, are the familiar notes that are struck by the patronage-made machine. I cannot believe that the people of New York enjoy the spectacle of a Governor giving and withholding patronage and executive approval of legislation for personal support of himself as ' leader ' when he is using the methods of a boss." [112]

A sixteen-page pamphlet entitled, " The Truth About Direct Primaries," condemning the bill sponsored by Governor Sulzer as faulty and unscientific, was issued by a committee of prominent Democrats, headed by National Committeeman Norman E. Mack and including several former state officeholders. Copies of the pamphlet were sent to all members of the Legislature. The committee made no personal attack upon Sulzer except to say that he appeared to be unable " to distinguish between expressions of opinion and statements of facts," and that he seemed to think that " dogmatic assertion " could be made " independent of logic or analysis." [113] It challenged Sulzer's belief that it was through the skillful manipulation of political conventions that party bosses found the greatest opportunity to carry on their nefarious work. It asserted, to the contrary, that in the handling of conventions political organizations and political leaders were " particularly sensitive to public sentiment," as evidenced by the nomination of such independent Governors as Tilden and Cleveland, not to mention Sulzer himself. It gave figures to prove that less than twenty-five per cent of those who went to the polls in November, 1912 voted in that year's primaries, and that a majority of those voting

112 *Times*, May 31.
113 *Ibid.*, June 9.

were in Greater New York. Under a simon-pure direct primary system, therefore, this vote would have been sufficient to nominate all the Democratic candidates for state office. It contended that Sulzer's proposed bill was against public policy, would hamper voting, and abolished the safeguards against fictitious independent nominations; also that the omission of party emblems was of doubtful constitutionality and " against the principles which have governed the exercise of the suffrage throughout the history of the Republic." [114] It wound up with the indignant observation that no party action had ever endorsed Sulzer's " new standard of political heresy nor confirmed his assumed power of excommunication." [115]

The last two weeks prior to the extra session found Sulzer constantly on the war path. His tour carried him through several of the larger cities up-state and ended in a whirlwind finish in New York City. He continued to assail Barnes, Murphy, and their " puppets " in the Legislature. He told of the obstacles the political bosses had been putting in his way ever since they discovered he could not be controlled. The members of the Legislature, he disclosed, were not free to vote as they pleased, for Barnes simply walks into the Senate and Assembly and tells " his automatons " what to do, while Murphy " just calls up on the telephone twice daily " to instruct his boys how " to put the Governor in a hole." [116] " Tweed was a boss," he told his audience at Glens Falls. " You remember he challenged the right of the people to have good government. With brazen audacity he defied the voters and said: ' What are you going to do about it? ' You know the answer. Have the little Boss Tweeds so soon forgotten the tragic end of big Boss Tweed? It is an old saying that history repeats itself." [117] In Catskill he again told how the bosses were trying to thwart him in

114 *Ibid.*
115 *World*, June 9.
116 *Times*, June 5.
117 *Public Papers of Governor Sulzer*, p. 1402.

his efforts to restore to the people the rights which a few had usurped for the benefit of the invisible government. " The Governor is the visible government of the State of New York," he said. " I owe my position to the people and I am going to be true to the people just so long as I am the Governor. Who is against the visible government of the State of New York as constituted by our laws? The invisible government. Who constitutes the invisible government? Why, the bosses. Two men out of ten millions of people. Just two men out of a million and a half of voters—Mr. Barnes in Albany, the Republican boss, and Mr. Murphy in Delmonico's, the Democratic boss." [118] In his speech in Rochester he once more pointedly reminded the " little Boss Tweeds " of the fate of " big Boss Tweed." [119] In urging the necessity of his primary legislation, he attributed the waste, extravagance, inefficiency, and corruption in the administration of state affairs to the fact that political power had been gradually slipping from the people.[120] Wherever he spoke he asked his listeners whether they wanted to retain the old boss system and the collective response was invariably " No! "

A meeting in Yonkers was broken up by Sulzer zealots in a riot of booing and hissing when the Westchester Senator, John F. Healy, whom the Governor had assailed in his speech as " a traitor to the people," arose to speak in his own defense.[121] Ex-President Roosevelt gave Sulzer his support in a week's speaking tour, making addresses in Buffalo, Rochester, and other large cities.[122] He attacked the bi-partisan combination in the Legislature that had beaten Sulzer's reform bill. He ridiculed the contention of the organization leaders that state conventions really recorded the will of the people, condemning

118 *Ibid.*, p. 1411.
119 *Ibid.*, p. 1431.
120 *Ibid.*, p. 1433.
121 *Times*, June 14.
122 *World*, June 11, 12.

them as " mere devices for registering the decrees of the big and the little bosses." [123] The enthusiasm he aroused seemed, however, to be more for himself than for the cause he came to advocate. Sulzer wound up his campaign for direct primaries on June 14 with several meetings in New York City, the final one taking place in Cooper Union. At none of his earlier meetings did he go so far in his arraignment of the party bosses. Several prominent Progressives likewise spoke at the Cooper Union meeting, including Oscar S. Straus and Bainbridge Colby, who presided. Also participating, for the first time in the campaign, was William R. Hearst who, in his address, contemptuously referred to Murphy as the " Hon. Charles Finance Murphy " and spoke of United States Senator Elihu Root as " I. O. U. Root." [124] Unless the Legislature supported the bill Sulzer advocated, he warned Tammany Hall, he would bolt the Democratic ticket in the fall municipal election.[125] Sulzer ended his campaign for primary reform confident that the legislators had seen a new light and certain that if they voted against the bill again, in defiance of the plain will of the people, they would simply be signing their own death warrants. He pretended to have a long list of converts to his cause.[126] Tammany was equally defiant and openly scorned his claims of great accessions of strength in both houses. Organization legislators declared they would beat the Sulzer bill even if they had to remain in session all summer. The order from Murphy was reported to be to stand pat and let the Governor do his worst, inasmuch as no further favors from him could be expected anyway.[127]

The net outcome of Sulzer's exhortations was, as the Democratic leaders had quite accurately measured it, negligible. He not only failed to bring the Legislature into line, but elicited

123 *Times*, June 11.
124 *World*, June 15.
125 *Ibid.*
126 *Times*, June 16.
127 *Ibid.*

only the most perfunctory response among the people themselves. While few disputed that Sulzer's proposed reforms
were in many respects admirable and, if enacted, would im-
prove political conditions, public opinion did not range itself
emphatically on his side. Sulzer was simply incapable of inspiring a popular uprising because the people had no great confidence in his fundamental sincerity, even when he was apparently striving for reforms in the public interest.[128] Sulzer's
whole career indicated that he was prepared to play the kind of
politics most likely to advance his own political fortunes. For
two decades he had been an obedient servant of Tammany
because that policy paid the best returns; now, for reasons of
his own, he found it expedient to adopt a different program.
Sulzer's noisy beatings of tom-toms in the front of battle
against the people's enemy, his frequently ill-judged extravagance of appeal, his naive exhibitions of egotism, were not
likely to win him the moral force of the community. " Character is, after all, the one essential in a public man," observed
one editor. " Bombastic championing of the ' people's cause,'
spectacular assaults upon bosses, even energetic work in behalf
of necessary reforms will not avail; what the people demand,
above all, is a real, honest, sincere, devoted man . . . The
popular mind seems unerringly to detect the true from the
false in its leaders." [129] " The people did not rally to the Governor because he did not talk or act like a Governor," was the
judgment of the New York *Post*. He had no dignity or self-
respect, it commented. He was loose-tongued and loud-
mouthed, boasting of what he had done and what he was going

---

128 Some time later, Lieutenant-Governor Glynn openly accused Sulzer of
faking the primary fight. Just before the direct primary campaign, he
alleged, Sulzer had asked him to go to Murphy and tell him not to pay any
attention to what he might say on the stump and to assure him that after
the campaign, he [Sulzer] and Murphy could get together and "fix up
matters to their mutual satisfaction." He refused to take the message,
Glynn added.—*World*, August 31. Sulzer made no reply to this accusation
of duplicity.

129 *World's Work*, August, 1913, Vol. 26, p. 382.

to do. " Constant violence of speech and tumultuousness of action had no success against a vicious or perverse Legislature." [130]

Just before the convening of the special session of the Legislature, a sensational statement was issued by Patrick E. McCabe, clerk of the Senate and close affiliate of Murphy, recently displaced by Sulzer as dispenser of state patronage in Albany County, in which he charged the Governor with political duplicity and dishonesty. The statement was made public with the authorization of the Democratic organization and was apparently the first step in a well-defined plan to discredit the Governor. In the capital it was looked upon as notice to Sulzer that the Tammany chieftain and the other party leaders who fought his program would no longer remain silent under the vicious attacks made upon them during the course of his primary campaign.[131] McCabe accused Sulzer of having frequently sought and obtained secret conferences with Murphy at the latter's home in New York City, while posing as a foe of the bosses on the stump. He disclosed four specific instances, telling the time and place in each case. The first two conferences were said to have taken place on February 2, when he went to New York by appointment, and on March 2, both held before the breaking point. The third meeting came on March 17. In the words of McCabe, " On the evening of March 17, Governor Sulzer attended the dinner of the Friendly Sons of St. Patrick at the Hotel Astor, made a noise in which he railed against the thing he calls ' invisible government,' and sneaked around to see Mr. Murphy the next day and spent several hours with him." [132] (This conference was reported in the newspapers at the time, but Sulzer denied it. It was confirmed, however, by Thomas F. Smith, secretary of Tammany Hall, who testified that he had himself arranged the meeting

130 July 26.
131 *Sun*, June 17.
132 *Times*, June 17.

and that Sulzer and Murphy had "buried the hatchet.")[133]
The fourth meeting was alleged to have been on April 13, after
the dinner of the National Democratic Club at the Waldorf-
Astoria Hotel. At that time the Governor, according to
McCabe, roused the Murphy household at one o'clock in the
morning, begging for an audience with the boss, which was
granted, and remained with him three hours. The Governor
was reported to have said that he had just come from Hearst's
house, where he had been abused for not urging the passage of
a direct primaries bill, and that he personally had no interest in
the matter. The Governor then urged Murphy in vain to enter
into a scheme to " deceive Hearst," offering as an inducement
to let Murphy name the two Public Service Commissioners, the
Commissioner of Labor, the State Superintendent of Prisons,
and any other positions he might select. " When this was refused he begged with tears in his eyes, but Murphy was obdurate," said McCabe.[134] " The insincerity of his personal abuse
of the Democratic leaders in the State can be proved to the
satisfaction of any fair man," he added. He called Sulzer " an
over-heated Executive with an insane political ambition," who,
like all demagogues, was basing his right to public recognition
on his interest in the poor man. For thirty years, he declared,
politics had been Sulzer's business and " that is what it is
to-day." He accused Sulzer of throwing every department of
the state into " the most abject demoralization " ever attained
by his " political antics." [135] He branded Sulzer's veto of the

133 *Ibid.*

134 *Ibid.* This meeting was mentioned in the newspapers the following day,
but was denied by Sulzer at the time. Thomas F. Smith's testimony with
regard to the April meeting was as follows: " That meeting was not as
amicable as some others had been, for Murphy accused the Governor to his
face of being an ingrate, and the Governor retaliated by saying that he
would leave the Tammany organization out in the cold so far as State
patronage was concerned. Since that time mutual friends have tried to
bring the two together, but every effort failed because Mr. Murphy said
he was through with the Governor and would have nothing more to do with
him."—*Ibid.*

135 *Ibid.*

constitutional convention measure as " the most criminal political act ever perpetrated on the party by a Democrat of any
type " and as " the work of a traitor," and condemned his veto
of the hydro-electric bill not only as a repudiation of the party
platform but also as a " surrender to the power trust." [136]

Sulzer's first comment, when shown a printed copy of
McCabe's statement, was, " I do not care to answer this until
I learn who has written it. Most of it is absolutely false." [137]
The following day, however, in a speech delivered at a direct
primary rally in Albany, he referred to McCabe as " a little
Boss Tweed," " a cats-paw," and " a squealer," and stigmatized the statement as a " screed so ridiculous " as not fit to
be dignified with a denial. He characterized it as " a libelous
manifesto, replete with statements without the slightest foundation in fact," yet made no specific denial of his alleged clandestine meetings with the Tammany boss. The whole thing, he
said, " was deliberately planned and executed by crafty enemies
of direct primaries " in order to break the force of his campaign. He expressed confidence that these attacks would not
hurt him nor would any possible personal or political consequences deter him from his determination to continue his
struggle for the enactment of a direct primary law.[138] McCabe's
statement did find corroboration, however, from Hearst who
admitted that Sulzer had visited him on the night of April 13
and that they had disagreed on that occasion. But he knew
nothing, he added, about the Governor's reported call on the
Tammany boss.[139]

136 *Sun*, June 17.

137 *Times*, June 17.

138 *Public Papers of Governor Sulzer*, pp. 1466-70, *passim*. W. Bourke
Cockran, an earlier speaker at the same gathering, apparently ignorant of
Sulzer's semi-denial of any clandestine meetings with Murphy, condoned
those meetings with the rather astonishing excuse, " You cannot blame Mr.
Sulzer for seeking power where all power lodged."—*Times*, June 18.

139 *Times*, June 18. According to a close friend of Murphy, the Governor
had assured the Tammany boss the support of Hearst and the Hearst
newspapers in the ensuing municipal campaign if only he would permit the
direct primary bill to go through.—*Tribune*, June 18.

On June 18 McCabe released a second broadside which, in its onslaught on Sulzer's integrity, was even more vitriolic than the first. He made veiled allusions to discrediting disclosures to come and repeated his accusation that Sulzer was a hypocrite. " I charge Governor Sulzer with publicly denouncing Mr. Murphy and surreptitiously calling upon him and assuring him of his everlasting loyalty and friendship, and I challenge Governor Sulzer to answer that he did or did not call upon Mr. Murphy at the times mentioned," he wrote.[140] In answer to McCabe's latest assault, Sulzer issued a prepared statement in which he again failed to make any specific reply to the charge that he had been in secret conference with Murphy and had sought to sell out Hearst and the independents who were supporting his direct primaries campaign. " For the present I shall treat that vile and villainous matter with the contempt it deserves," he declared. " Suffice it to say that I have taken my stand for good government and political righteousness, and all the mud and all the slime and all the filth they now hurl against me will not deter me in the performance of my duty as I see the right and God gives me the light. I cannot be intimidated, and I have no fear of political or personal consequences. Let every one understand that." [141]

On June 16 the special session of the Legislature convened, with the opposing forces lined up for battle. Sulzer was still confident he would win, intending to use the items he had cut out of the appropriation and supply bills as a means of forcing refractory legislators into line. The returning lawmakers, on the other hand, enraged by the attacks made upon them by the Governor during his primary campaign, were eager to throw every possible obstacle in his way and were resolved to crush his political aspirations at any price. The position of the Republicans was clearly stated by Assemblyman Hinman who, in a prepared statement, not only disputed the virtues of

140 *Times*, June 19.
141 *Ibid.*, June 20.

Sulzer's proposals for primary reform but also questioned his honesty and sincerity. He said, " Governor Sulzer's vision of the truth is somewhat clouded by vivid dreams of his further political preferment. He needs a censor. Ambitious men seem to find it difficult to be honest. The attitude of the present over-lord of all New York impels the deduction that it is ambition, not patriotism, which is leading him headlong on in his career. In his eye constantly is his own name written on the future pages of history. The public are entitled to the truth about the Governor's attitude on the subject of direct nominations. He is waging his war upon a false presentation of facts." [142]

In a special message dealing exclusively with the subject of direct primaries, Sulzer declared that he felt impelled by " a sense of public obligation " to reconvene the Legislature. He quoted from the platforms of the Republican, Progressive, and Democratic parties to prove that they were " bound by the highest political obligations " to vote for such a measure. As proof of the popularity and success of the direct primary system elsewhere, he quoted the testimony of United States Senators, Governors, and other state officials. He summed up his plea for the abolition of the state convention by saying : " These salutary changes in our primary system aim to restore to the voters of each political party the rights which have been usurped by the few, for the benefit of powers invisible, which aim to control governmental officials, to pass laws, and to violate laws with impunity. To these invisible powers I am now, always have been, and always will be opposed. No government can be free which does not allow all of its citizens to participate in the formation as well as the execution of its laws. Every other government is a mere form of despotism." He renewed his former recommendations, which did not differ essentially from the bill that the Legislature had decisively rejected at the regular session. Anything less than the program outlined, he declared, would not redeem party pledges or

142 *Tribune*, June 16.

meet the demands of the party voters. In closing, he warned:
" Let us be honest about direct primaries, and keep our pledges
to the people. At all events, as the Governor, I shall, and if
the Legislature does not, the people will know the reason
why." [143]

With the Governor's message out of the way, the fight was
on. A concerted attack was launched upon Sulzer for his extraordinary campaign tactics, not a single legislator standing up
in his defense. In the Assembly majority leader Levy ridiculed the Governor, accusing him of ignorance, not only of
his own primary bill but also of the existing primary law.
He called attention to the fact that at no time had he seen fit
to analyze the features of his bill, and that both his special
message and speeches on the stump showed him to be misin-
formed. [144] In the Senate bitter resentment against Sulzer was
expressed by Wagner, Brown, and Healy for seeking to destroy
the character of " honorable men " by an unprecedented campaign of " inference and innuendo." [145] Wagner, most outspoken of the Governor's critics, declared he would not permit
to go unchallenged what the Governor had said concerning
members in his " campaign of vilification " and repeated
Tammany's threat to investigate him. " The time has come,"
he said, " when the Senate will look more deeply into accusations that have been made against Senators and more deeply
into what has been done since the regular session. The truth
will come to light. Let us have patience and the people will
know when it has been done what promises and corrupt bar-
gains have been made to get votes for a bill the Governor is so
anxious to pass," a reference to Sulzer's reported threats to
veto local bills as a means of coercing recalcitrant legislators. [146]
Almost without exception the returning lawmakers said they

143 *Public Papers of Governor Sulzer*, pp. 117-35, *passim*.
144 *Sun*, June 17.
145 *Ibid*.
146 *Times*, June 17.

found little or no sentiment for the Governor's bill among their constituents.[147]

The Legislature was flooded with direct primary proposals. Sulzer's measure, varying only in minor details from the one defeated at the regular session, was introduced by Assemblyman Eisner and Senator McKnight. The Democratic organization's program of reform was incorporated in bills sponsored by Assemblyman Van Woert and Senator Blauvelt. Senator Brown, on behalf of the Republicans, introduced a bill which differed from the Governor's only in its retention of the state nominating convention. Prior to the hearing on the Governor's bill in the Assembly Chamber, a spectacular demonstration, in which about five hundred direct primary enthusiasts participated, was staged at the Capitol. Sulzer himself was the central figure and he received a rousing reception. He was hailed as " a leader of the plain people," one representative of the ministry even referring to him as " sent by God to lead us to victory." [148] In a passionate speech, which was greeted with enthusiastic cheering, he pledged himself never to quit his fight until it was won, despite the mud being thrown at him by " unmitigated scoundrels." " Let Mr. Murphy abuse me. I care not now," he exclaimed. " You know and I know that Mr. Murphy is the only man in the State who can beat this bill. What a spectacle! Do you realize it? One boss in the great State of New York defying the people; spurning their petitions; trampling on their rights; laughing in their faces; and like Tweed in his day, brazenly and audaciously saying: ' What are you going to do about it?' What a pitiable spectacle! Isn't it enough to bring the blush of shame to the cheek of every decent citizen in our commonwealth?" And then, alluding to the personal attacks made upon him, he declared, " No one knows better than I do how I have been threatened during this fight by the enemies of the cause. They are the enemies of the State. Behind

147 *Ibid.*
148 *Press*, June 25.

it all there is a sad story which some day when I have less to do than at present I shall tell." [149] At the crowded hearing before the Senate and Assembly Judiciary Committees little was said on the merits of Sulzer's bill but the bosses were hotly denounced and the proposed plan for direct primary reform was hailed as a panacea that would eradicate all political evils. Among the score or more of speakers were the Assistant Secretary of the Navy, Franklin D. Roosevelt, until recently a State Senator, and John Purroy Mitchel, Collector of the Port of New York. The presence of these men was said to prove President Wilson's interest in the passage of the bill.[150]

The herculean efforts put forth by Sulzer and his friends proved unavailing, however, and the bill met its second defeat by only a slightly less adverse majority than at the regular session. In the Assembly ninety-two votes were cast against it and fifty-four for it.[151] Only seven votes were gained for the bill, three of which were accounted for by the presence of members absent from the regular session. Disappointing as the outcome must have been to them, partisans of the Governor viewed Murphy's triumph as a Pyrrhic victory. The substantial support for the bill among rural Democrats, they said, clearly established the fact that outside of New York City and Buffalo, Sulzer was the recognized leader of the party.[152] Seven hours of debate preceded the vote, marked by violent denunciation of Sulzer as a " traitor " and " hypocrite." Assemblyman Louis A. Cuvillier called him " the Judas of the Democratic Party." " The Governor has fed at the public crib for twenty-five years. What right has he to complain? " he asked.[153] The defeat of the Sulzer bill in the Senate was even more decisive than in the Assembly. It was beaten by a vote of ten to thirty-eight.[154]

149 *Public Papers of Governor Sulzer*, pp. 1475-76.
150 *American*, June 24.
151 Assembly Journal, Vol. IV, pp. 35-36.
152 *Press*, June 25.
153 *World*, June 25.
154 Senate Journal, Vol. II, Appendix II, p. 69.

In the upper house too Sulzer ran the gauntlet of caustic denunciation, without a voice being raised in his behalf. Wagner angrily repudiated the charge that Murphy ruled the Legislature and warned the people to " look out for their self-designated friends." [155] The Governor's public appeal had evidently fallen on deaf ears. If there was any pronounced popular sentiment for his program of reform, it failed to manifest itself in the halls of the Legislature. Having buried Sulzer's hopes, the Assembly on June 25 approved the Blauvelt bill without debate by a party vote of seventy-seven to fifty-nine,[156] the Senate concurring, thirty-two to sixteen.[157] The Republican minority in each instance was recorded against it. Before taking a recess until July 8, the Legislature adopted a concurrent resolution, proposed by Senator George F. Thompson, providing for a legislative investigation into the Governor's alleged use of patronage and veto power in his direct primary fight, as well as into his campaign fund.[158]

Following the decisive defeat of the administration bill, rumors of peace began to circulate. Notwithstanding Sulzer's public declaration that the fight for primary reform had only " just begun," [159] the belief was expressed in quarters close to him that he was tiring of the struggle and would welcome any honorable compromise the opposition might offer.[160] The Democratic legislative leaders were reported as also ready to

155 *World*, June 25.

156 Assembly Journal, Vol. IV, p. 48.

157 Senate Journal, Vol. II, p. 70. On July 8 Sulzer again vetoed the bill for reasons similar to those stated in his former vetoes. He was " convinced," he said in his memorandum, that it did " not carry out in good faith the pledges of the leading political parties," and was " confident " that when " the opportunity " presented itself, the electors would disapprove of the bill as emphatically as he did. — *Public Papers of Governor Sulzer,* pp. 207-8.

158 Assembly Journal, Vol. IV, p. 55; Senate Journal, Vol. II, Appendix II, pp. 77-78.

159 *Press*, June 25.

160 *Times*, June 26.

join in a peace movement, fearing the effect of the internal war on Tammany's chances in the fall elections. The visit of Public Service Commissioner McCall to Albany and his long conference with Sulzer lent color to the rumors.[161] When questioned on the subject, however, Sulzer reiterated his determination to continue the warfare. " I said there would be no compromise with the bosses," he asserted. " I stand by that statement." [162]

The continuous bickering between the partisans of the Governor and the followers of the regular Democratic organization threw the administrative departments into a state of demoralization and chaos, with no prospect of the restoration of order until either Sulzer or Murphy triumphed. The Comptroller's office, headed by William Sohmer, a staunch Tammany man, tied up the work of the Highway Department, by refusing to approve the payrolls of the engineering and construction force and by delaying every contract to which technical objection might be made.[163] Payrolls of the Prison Department were likewise held up. Contracts for repair work on the Capitol were halted as a result of a disagreement among the Trustees of Public Buildings. The Public Service Commission was seriously hampered because of the refusal of the Senate to confirm the two nominees submitted by the Governor. The Department of Efficiency and Economy was crippled through lack of funds.[164]

161 *Ibid.*
162 *Press*, June 27.
163 *World*, June 26.
164 *Ibid.*, August 4.

CHAPTER IV

THE LEGISLATIVE INQUIRY

In the desperate war of extermination that followed between the Governor and Tammany leaders, Sulzer's entire political career and even his private life were canvassed for the discovery of evidence reflecting on his personal honesty and official integrity. Following the revelations of his alleged hypocrisy in his relations with Murphy, McCabe charged him with unprofessional conduct in connection with a lawsuit tried in Vermont back in 1890, in which Sulzer was counsel for one of the litigants. A copy of what purported to be a jury presentment, recommending that Sulzer be prosecuted on a charge of perjury, was made public by ex-Judge George M. Curtis, of Brooklyn, who had been associated with Sulzer in the case.[1] Sulzer indignantly branded the document as a forgery, denounced Curtis as " a liar," " a blackmailer," and " unmitigated scoundrel," and declared he would not allow himself to be drawn into a controversy designed to divert attention from the real issue, the direct primary.[2] The matter was laid at rest when the judge who presided at the Vermont trial made a statement fully vindicating Sulzer.[3] Still smarting under the charge, Sulzer accused Tammany of hiring detectives to sift scandal and gossip from every conceivable quarter in an attempt to discredit him, and challenged Murphy and " his co-conspirators " to come out in the open and produce " all the other libelous stuff " they had on him.[4] Discussing his relations with Murphy, he declared that when he first came to Albany, he wanted " to treat Mr. Murphy right," but that Murphy's demands in the matter of patronage, as in his threat of " Gaffney

1 *Times*, June 21.
2 *World*, June 22.
3 *Post*, June 23.
4 *Evening World*, June 23.

or war," and warnings not to remove Scott, Reel, Hoefer, and others made amicable relations impossible. He refused to be " part of a criminal conspiracy to loot the state." He had entered the primary fight reluctantly, he said, because he knew it would be a hard fight, and that the very men who were now denouncing him most bitterly were those who had gotten him into it. He acknowledged having met Murphy three times after becoming Governor: once in Albany, when Murphy was an elector, at which time Sulzer refused to visit him at his hotel, as Murphy insisted; then in New York, in the presence of another man, when Murphy " said things which hurt " his feelings; and the third time on April 13, when a mutual friend persuaded him to meet Murphy to see whether things couldn't be straightened out. They disagreed over patronage and direct primaries. " He [Murphy] said things I shall not repeat now," he remarked. That was their final meeting. He had a choice of resigning, surrendering, or fighting, he asserted, and he had made up his mind to fight.[5]

Sulzer's comments drew from Murphy an angry disavowal. After a conference with Smith, Wagner, Levy, McCooey, and other prominent party members, at his home at Good Ground, Long Island, he issued a statement through Thomas F. Smith, secretary of Tammany Hall, in which he made a general denial of the charges brought by Sulzer and defied him to produce proof. " Governor Sulzer is absolutely in error when he accuses me of being a party to any so-called conspiracy to discredit him," he said. He denied hiring detectives to rake his past or having had anything to do with the Vermont case. He denied having sent any messenger to Sulzer to threaten that it was " Gaffney or war," when the question of appointing a Superintendent of Highways came up, or ever having made any dishonorable propositions to him. He, furthermore, had never sought conferences with Sulzer and had always insisted on the presence of a third party when they did confer, for, as he put it,

" the Governor would not hesitate to swear my life away if he found it to his political advantage to do so." Subsequent events, he said, had confirmed his judgment.[6]

About a week later another sensation was sprung, this time from a wholly different quarter. The Governor was sued for breach of promise of marriage by a certain Miss Mignon Hopkins, a cloak model in a Philadelphia department store. In her affidavit Miss Hopkins alleged that in 1903 she became engaged to Sulzer, that he asked her at the time to keep their engagement a secret because it might interfere with his political career, that she had lived with him from time to time over a period of years, and that he had on several occasions introduced her as his wife. His marriage to another in 1908, she added, had marred her whole life and she therefore asked the court to grant her a commensurate sum in damages.[7] Sulzer contemptuously characterized the suit as merely another " frame-up." In a statement to newspaper reporters he said, " The fact is that the suit of this woman Hopkins is blackmail and more. It is instigated by my political enemies and is part of the plot of Boss Murphy and his political conspirators to discredit me because they cannot use me for their nefarious schemes to loot the State of New York." He admitted knowing Miss Hopkins years before, but emphatically denied having lived with her or ever having asked her to marry him. He admitted too that she had once before sued him for financial reparation, shortly after his marriage, and that the case had been settled out of court by a cash consideration.[8] The breach of promise suit evidently was not pressed and was soon overshadowed by charges of a more serious nature.

The next attack launched on Governor Sulzer was that outside of his official activities, he was interested in fraudulent mining companies. To this Sulzer's sole comment was, " It's a

6 *Ibid.*, June 23.
7 *Ibid.*, July 2.
8 *Ibid.*, July 3.

pure fake." [9] The charge that Sulzer was promoter of the
so-called Alaska Industrial Company had been made when he
was running for Governor. During the campaign a story was
printed in the New York *Evening Post* [10] to the effect that
Sulzer had been sued by an Alaskan missionary for $100,000
over a mining claim and had been obliged to compromise by a
cash settlement of $40,000. Sulzer denied the story at the time,
accusing his opponents of attempting to make political capital
out of a matter with which he was in no way connected. [11] He
had long since disposed of the few shares of mining stock he
held, he declared, and insisted that his connection with the
company had always been honorable. [12] So bitter was the warfare that Sulzer asked the District Attorney of New York
County, Charles S. Whitman, to begin a John Doe inquiry to
expose the persons responsible for the Vermont perjury charge
and breach of promise suit, as well as what he called " a new
conspiracy " that he believed was being plotted. [13] He accused
his political enemies of employing thugs to shadow him [14] and
even circulated reports that his life was being threatened by
the Tammany crowd. [15]

Enemies also sifted Sulzer's Congressional career and brought
to light damaging evidence of secret dealings with concession
hunters in Central America. The first broadside was fired by a
New York attorney, Joseph F. Darling, who, in an open letter
to the Governor, charged him with having used his position as
chairman of the Foreign Relations Committee to help the

9 *Sun*, July 9.

10 October 22, 1912.

11 *Post*, October 23, 1912.

12 *Times*, October 24, 1912. Officers of the Alaska Industrial Company
included Samuel I. Frankenstein, a law partner of Sulzer, Louis A. Sarecky,
Sulzer's secretary, and Charles A. Sulzer, his brother.—*Times*, October 23,
1912.

13 *Sun*, July 22.

14 *Press*, July 27.

15 *Times*, July 26.

Spriggs-Clark syndicate, in which he was personally interested, obtain a valuable concession to exploit the mineral lands in Guatemala from the " despot," Manuel Estrada Cabrera.[16] In his answer, Sulzer refuted the charges, characterizing them as " a tissue of falsehoods and exaggeration." He called Darling " a man with criminal instinct and a menace to the community." [17] About two months later the New York *Times* published a series of incriminating letters and documents which made Sulzer's caustic disavowal seem astonishing.[18] The correspondence also revealed that while a member of the Foreign Relations Committee, Sulzer was the confidential adviser of a Cuban contracting firm which was seeking the intervention of the American State Department in collecting a claim from the government of Cuba for the construction of some waterworks in the city of Cienfuegos. Sulzer's close relations with the contractors, Hugh J. Reilly and Antonio Frias, were revealed in a number of letters and telegrams that passed between them.[19] Judging from those, Sulzer used his influence in Washington to induce the Cuban government to recognize a half million dollar claim. One of his letters to Frias, written on House of Representatives stationery, read: " You can rest assured I have got everything all right. All great matters move slowly, and you must not be impatient." [20] He attended the hearings before Secretary of War Taft as the avowed friend of Reilly. From the testimony, the presumption was strong that he obtained part of the money paid by the Cuban government as a reward for his services.[21] Concerning all this, Sulzer made his characteristic observation, " There is nothing to it. It is a pure fake." [22] The following day his private secretary,

16 *Sun*, June 17.
17 *American*, June 18.
18 August 23, 24.
19 Published in the *Times*, August 23.
20 *Post*, August 23.
21 *Times*, August 23.
22 *Ibid.*

Chester C. Platt, supplemented Sulzer's denial with the statement that whatever Sulzer had done to help Reilly was done " as a matter of friendship." Sulzer, he declared, had never been financially interested in the Cuban contract.[23] An even more serious reflection on Sulzer's integrity was made in the allegation that he had likewise used his official position in Congress to help Frias in 1909 obtain a mining concession in Guatemala. (Louis A. Sarecky, Sulzer's agent, was secretary of the company with which Frias was associated.)[24] In order to aid the scheme, Sulzer was active in an effort to have coffee, Guatemala's principal export, retained on the free list in the Payne-Aldrich tariff. At the suggestion of Frias, Sulzer made a speech in the House in which he earnestly advocated closer commercial relations between the United States and the Central American countries. In arguing against the imposition of a tax on coffee, he declared, " Such a tax will be entirely for the benefit of the rich importers and against the interests of the poor consumers." [25] He also took occasion to praise the administration of President Cabrera as " wise, far-seeing, patriotic and progressive." [26] Numerous copies of the speech were reprinted in Spanish and forwarded to Guatemala.

The agency which finally set the machinery of gubernatorial impeachment into motion was the Frawley Legislative Investigating Committee. On May 2, 1913, the day before the adjournment of the regular session, a joint resolution was adopted by the Legislature, with great foresight as it later turned out, providing for the appointment of a joint legislative committee " to examine into the methods of financial administration and conduct of all institutions, societies or associations of the State, which are supported either wholly or in part by

23 *Ibid.*, August 24.

24 *Ibid.*

25 *Ibid.*

26 From a speech delivered in the House of Representatives, July 9, 1909, reprinted in Sulzer's *Miscellaneous.*

State moneys, or which report officially to the State, into the functions of any or all State departments concerned in the management, supervision or regulation of any such institutions . . . and the conduct generally of the business of all such institutions and departments, for the purpose of reporting to the next session of the Legislature such laws relating thereto as the committee may deem proper." The committee was authorized to sit after the adjournment of the Legislature, and was empowered to subpoena witnesses, to take testimony under oath, and compel the production of books and papers, " including any public record or document pertaining to the administration of any State institution or of any State department." [27]

The legislators appointed to the committee were Senator James J. Frawley (Democrat) of New York County, head of the finance committee and sponsor of the resolution, as chairman; Senators Felix J. Sanner (Democrat) of Kings County, Samuel J. Ramsperger (Democrat) of Erie County, and Elon R. Brown (Republican) of Jefferson County; [28] and Assemblymen Myron Smith (Republican) of Dutchess County, Wilson R. Yard (Democrat) of Westchester County, and La Verne P. Butts (Democrat) of Otsego County.[29] As counsel the committee engaged Eugene Lamb Richards, Tammany state committeeman from Richmond and Rockland Counties and attorney to the state conservation commission, and as secretary selected Matthew T. Horgan, Deputy Commissioner of Efficiency and Economy and confidant of Sulzer for many years. While on its face the resolution simply called for an investigation of the state departments, it was looked upon in Albany as a retaliatory measure decreed by the Democratic organization to " show up " the Sulzer administration. Appointments made by the Governor or by department heads when he controlled

27 Passed by the Senate unanimously, Senate Journal, Vol. II, pp. 2008-9; approved by the Assembly on May 3 by a vote of 137 to 8, Assembly Journal, Vol. III, pp. 3455-56.

28 Senate Journal, Vol. II, p. 2152.

29 Assembly Journal, Vol. III, p. 3622.

would obviously be a proper subject of inquiry under the terms of the resolution. To prove their contention that the creation of the committee was simply " a conspiracy " to discredit the work of the Chief Executive in stamping out corruption, friends of the Governor call attention to the fact that every one appointed to or employed by the committee was in the camp of Sulzer's enemies. Senator Frawley, they say, was present at the Delmonico conference of Tammany politicians, alleged to have been held on May 20, which conspired to " get something " on Sulzer if he did not stop his attacks on the organization and call a halt to his investigations into the highway and prison departments. " It is either Sulzer's life or ours," he is quoted as having remarked.[30] They describe him as " a fine speciman of the Tammany politician, as contemptuous of principle in politics as he was devoted to the commercial god in public affairs." [31] Senators Sanner and Ramsperger were " perfect models of Tammany ' statesmen,' " loyal henchmen respectively of McCooey, Tammany boss of Brooklyn, and of Fitzpatrick, Murphy's deputy boss in Buffalo.[32] Senator Brown was a Barnes adherent, hostile to the Governor because of some personal differences, " an excellent example of the old Tory Republican, distrustful of the people." [33] Assemblyman Smith was " a relic of the Old Guard of notorious memory which flourished in Republican politics prior to and during the administration of Governor Hughes " and always ready to help Tammany in the Assembly.[34] Assemblyman Yard, though professing to be a militant reformer prior to his election, " rushed into the arms of the boss when he arrived in Albany and remained servile ever after." [35] Assemblyman Butts also

30 Forrest and Malcolm, *op. cit.*, p. 77.

31 *Ibid.*, p. 104.

32 *Ibid.*, p. 107.

33 *Ibid.*

34 *Ibid.*, p. 104.

35 *Ibid.*

"placed himself at the disposal of Charles F. Murphy from the moment he arrived in Albany," despite the fact that he came from an independent county.[36] Horgan, who had been intimately associated with Sulzer in Washington and during his campaign for Governor, was bitterly denounced by Sulzer as "a Tammany spy" and "traitor."[37] It was Horgan, no doubt, who knew Sulzer's vulnerable points, who was most responsible for delivering him into the hands of his foes.[38]

The scope of the powers of the investigating committee was widened at the extraordinary session of the Legislature when, on June 25, a concurrent resolution introduced by Senator George F. Thompson (Republican) was adopted, instructing the committee to ascertain whether any unlawful or improper methods had been employed "by any private person or public officer to influence the votes of legislators on election or primary legislation" and "to investigate into, ascertain and report upon all expenditures made by any candidate voted for at the last preceding election by the electors of the whole State, and upon all statements filed by or on behalf of any such candidate for moneys or things of value received or paid out in aid of his election and their compliance with the present requirements of law relating thereto."[39] The Thompson resolution thus equipped the Frawley committee with the additional power to sift reports to the Governor's alleged use of patronage and veto power in his effort to win votes for his direct primary bill and specifically empowered it to delve into his campaign receipts and expenditures. The charge was made by the Sulzer adherents that Senator Thompson had been induced to offer his resolution by agents of Barnes, though Thompson

36 *Ibid.*

37 *Ibid.*, p. 108; also *World*, August 10.

38 Horgan admitted he helped to expose the Governor's past record, particularly his stock market transactions.—*World*, August 12.

39 Senate Journal, Vol. II, Appendix II, pp. 77-78. Senator Thompson took advantage of Sulzer's message to the Legislature calling for an amendment to the Corrupt Practices Act, to offer his resolution.

emphatically denied it.[40] That the legislative leaders must have had advance notice of the resolution is shown by the fact that it went through both houses unanimously and without debate.[41]

On the eve of the investigation, the legislative leaders in Albany indicated that it was no mere " fishing expedition " that they were bent on, but that they had enough information to " show the Governor in his true light to the voters." [42] The " big things on the Governor " which, they said, would come in for investigation were that he had received during his campaign numerous contributions from prominent financiers and corporations for which no proper return had been made, as required by law; that Hearst had surreptitiously helped finance Sulzer's campaign for which certain favors had been promised, and that back of Sulzer's fight against the leadership of Murphy was Hearst's ambition to become United States Senator; that Samuel Beardsley, counsel for Anthony N. Brady, had induced Sulzer to veto the hydro-electric power bill in return for a substantial campaign contribution; that the Governor tried to obtain votes for his primary bill by threatening recalcitrant Senators and Assemblymen to veto measures in which they were interested; that he approved unnecessary and extravagant appropriations as a reward to lawmakers who pledged themselves to vote for his bill and that such unwarranted expenditures amounted to about $1,500,000; and that in order to promote his fight against the Democratic organization, he had permitted the state departments to lapse into chaos and confusion by failure to fill important vacancies where the confirmation of the Senate was required.[43] Tammany men were openly prophesying that Sulzer would be " thrown out of office before October first." [44]

40 *World*, June 26.
41 Assembly Journal, Vol. IV, p. 55; Senate Journal, Vol. II, p. 78.
42 *Times*, June 12.
43 *Ibid.*, July 2.
44 *World*, July 26.

For several weeks the Frawley committee conducted private investigations in order to lay the groundwork for the public hearings which opened at the Capitol on July 3.[45] The war on the Governor's official family was begun with the summoning of George W. Blake, special commissioner to examine the state prisons. While the ostensible purpose of the committee was to investigate the penal institutions of the state, the hearing resolved itself into an examination of Blake himself, of the circumstances surrounding his appointment, and of the methods employed in his investigation. He was questioned at length about his expense accounts and about the mysterious substitution in the Comptroller's office of a letter allowing him twenty-five dollars a day, in place of the original certificate of appointment which said he was to serve without compensation. He indignantly denied that Sulzer had given him any instructions with regard to the investigation except to " tell the truth," [46] but under the persistent questioning of Richards, acknowledged having in numerous instances changed the testimony of witnesses and having withheld testimony favorable to existing prison conditions. He admitted that he had never seen the original contract for the construction of the Great Meadow Prison, but was " practically certain " he had a true copy.[47] Though admitting that some inaccuracies might have crept into his report, he insisted that his charge that half a million dollars had been lost to the state through carelessness or graft in its construction was substantially correct. Yet he offered little specific evidence to support the accusation, and was finally forced to admit that most of his allegations were based on hearsay and unwarranted assumptions.[48] In order to contradict

45 A verbatim report of the hearings appears in New York Assembly Documents, 136th Session, 1913, Vol. 35, No. 2, pp. 4-240.

46 *Ibid.*, p. 25.

47 *Ibid.*, p. 56.

48 *Ibid.*, pp. 169-205, *passim.* In view of the unsatisfactory character of his testimony before the Frawley committee, Blake issued a public statement on July 26, in which he pleaded for a suspension of judgment as to his honesty

Blake's report, Richards put on the stand Charles A. Sussdorf, Deputy State Architect, who emphatically denied the accuracy of Blake's figures and characterized his charge that bills for inferior work, or for work not done at all, had been passed by his office as " a falsehood." He swore that the work had been uniformly " excellent," done according to specifications, and that not a bill had passed through his hands for which the state did not receive the equivalent.[49]

Richards also sought to discredit Blake's so-called " experts," by exposing them as utterly incompetent and unreliable. One " expert," who had investigated the commissary department in Auburn, Great Meadow, and Sing Sing Prisons, had worked in a small restaurant in New York City ten years before, but had since then been known chiefly as manager of fake circuses and exhibitor of chariot races at county fairs.[50] Another, an " expert " on construction, on whose uncorroborated testimony sweeping charges of graft in the construction of the Great Meadow Prison had been made, admitted he had never done any brick or concrete work and did not even know what the specifications were when he made his report, never having seen the contract.[51] Another investigator employed by Blake admitted that his inspection of the Great Meadow Prison lasted only a day and a half and that his report on the steam-fitting plant there was based on a false set of specifications.[52] Still another qualified as an " expert " on the cost of building materials, because he had at one time been treasurer of an accident insurance company. He had never intended, he said on the stand, that his estimate that the Great Meadow Prison could have been built for half the money be taken as " con-

until all the facts were made known and pending a grand jury investigation. —*Public Papers of Governor Sulzer*, pp. 985-92.

49 Assembly Documents, *op. cit.*, pp. 205-17, *passim*.

50 *Ibid.*, p. 87.

51 *Ibid.*, pp. 81-83.

52 *Ibid.*, pp. 70-76.

clusive," and was only " an off-hand opinion." [53] Obviously
stirred to indignation by the startling testimony, Frawley denounced Blake and his aides as " a pack of scoundrels of the
worst type, going about the State telling falsehoods about
honest and competent public officials." [54]

The Frawley committee subpoenaed Chester C. Platt,[55]
Sulzer's secretary, to furnish Blake's original prison reports as
well as the transcript of all the testimony upon which they
were based, presumably in an effort to ascertain whether they
had been tampered with before being made public. Platt refused
to produce the documents called for on the ground that the
committee had no legal right to papers from the Executive
Chamber.[56] The necessity of taking steps to punish him for
contempt was removed when Sulzer assured the committee that
he was anxious to do all in his power to aid the investigation
and would unhesitatingly submit the records requested.[57]
Despite this explicit pledge of cooperation, Sulzer, a few days
later, curtly informed Senator Frawley that he would send to
the committee only those documents which he deemed " within
the sphere of its legitimate powers " and would communicate
only such facts and information as were "not incompatible
with the public interests." [58] The data withheld included the
original report and testimony on the Great Meadow Prison and
the original letter written by the Governor to the Comptroller,
notifying him of Blake's appointment as special commissioner.
In reply, Frawley pointed out that the documents were not the
private property of the Governor but were public documents
belonging to the state, and that inasmuch as they were per-

53 *Ibid.*, p. 163.

54 *Times*, July 17.

55 The Governor's departure for Gettysburg, to attend a celebration,
prevented the serving of the subpoena on him in person.

56 Assembly Documents, *op. cit.*, p. 23.

57 *Ibid.*, p. 138.

58 *Public Papers of Governor Sulzer*, p. 984.

tinent to the inquiry, the committee was entitled to access.[59] Irritated by the Governor's attitude, he instructed Richards to report the refusal to the Legislature with a view of bringing him to terms.[60]

As a counter-attack on the Frawley committee for attempting to discredit the reports of his investigators, Sulzer initiated grand jury investigations of road contracts in which contractors favored by the Tammany organization were alleged to have been enriched at the expense of the state. His plan was to secure the indictment and prosecution of persons reported by Hennessy to have been involved in the state highways graft exposures in the several counties. Accordingly, he issued an order for a special grand jury to meet in Rockland County, home of Senator Blauvelt, on July 14 to investigate charges of fraud in the construction of state roads under former Superintendent Reel.[61] Two weeks later he summoned the Supreme Courts in Suffolk, Putnam, and Dutchess Counties to meet in extraordinary session in order to try cases growing out of highway construction, and took steps to submit Blake's charge of $500,000 " carelessness or graft " in the building of the Great Meadow Prison to an extraordinary grand jury of the Supreme Court in Washington County.[62] He also proceeded to lay the foundation for new inquiries by appointing Hennessy, his principal adviser on questions of political strategy, as special

59 Assembly Documents, *op. cit.*, p. 85.

60 *Ibid.*, p. 86.

61 *Public Papers of Governor Sulzer*, p. 593. After listening to the evidence of Hennessy and after examining some of the state roads in the county, the grand jury, on August 18, brought in six indictments, one against Bart Dunn, a Tammany leader, and five against corporations, on a charge of conspiracy to defraud. The evidence adduced showed that the highway department was conducted as " a quasi-political organization " rather than as a government agency. It " was more proficient in the dispensation of favors in the form of contracts to contractors having political influence," the presentment found, " than it was in requiring integrity in the execution of such contracts. Incompetency prevailed therein where ability was most necessary."—William Sulzer, *Life and Speeches*, Vol. I, p. 18.

62 *Public Papers of Governor Sulzer*, pp. 594-97.

commissioner with the broad power " to examine and investigate the management and affairs of any department, board, bureau or commission of the State." [63] Simultaneously with his attack on the organization through the courts, Sulzer continued his patronage war by swinging the ax on scores of Tammany men who refused to line up with him.[64] He pruned routine appropriation bills, hitting those bureaus and departments in which Tammany men were employed.[65] Large numbers of Tammany office-holders either found themselves out of employment or suffered cuts in pay.[66] He also showed his open scorn of the Wigwam in his distribution of jobs. He nominated a Republican, Dr. Eugene H. Porter, as State Commissioner of Health,[67] and another Republican, Martin S. Decker, as chairman of the Public Service Commission, second district.[68] Other important posts were filled by independent or Sulzer Democrats.[69]

On July 17 the Frawley committee took up a line of inquiry affecting the official conduct of the Governor himself. A number of Senators and Assemblymen were examined under oath in an attempt to substantiate the charge that Sulzer had used his power of veto to win votes for his direct primary bill at the extraordinary session of the Legislature. No conclusive

63 *Ibid.*, p. 992.

64 *World*, June 4.

65 *Public Papers of Governor Sulzer*, pp. 362-411.

66 At the same time Sulzer showed astonishing generosity toward favored office-holders who might be helpful to him in building up a political machine of his own. He boosted the salaries of some of his commissioners as much as 66 per cent, apart from increases in salaries of their staffs and the creation of a large number of new offices. — See *Times*, April 24, and Brooklyn *Standard-Union*, July 1 and 2.

67 *Public Papers of Governor Sulzer*, p. 1147.

68 *Ibid.*, p. 552.

69 Among his appointees were James M. Clancy, an opponent of Murphy, as warden of Sing Sing Prison, a prize position with Tammany Hall, and John H. Hanify, manager of his direct primary tour, as State Hospital Commissioner.—*World*, July 9 and 10.

evidence was brought out in the testimony that a direct " bargain " had been made between any legislator and the Executive.
The witnesses testified only that when they came to obtain
his support for appropriation or other measures in which they
were interested, he would invariably bring the conversation
around to his own bill. Assemblyman Sweet testified that when
he asked the Governor to approve his bill for a canal bridge
in his district, Sulzer asked him how he had voted on his
direct primaries bill. When informed he had voted against it,
Sulzer remarked, " Remember, I take good care of my
friends." [70] Sulzer vetoed the bill and Sweet concluded that
that was his punishment for not taking the Governor's hint.
Senator Heacock reported a similar experience and quoted
Sulzer as declaring himself a great believer in " reciprocity." [71]
According to Assemblyman Prime, to whom Sulzer expressed
the same sentiment, the way Sulzer put it was, " You for me
and I for you." [72] To all of which Sulzer simply remarked,
" All this blather before the Frawley Committee to the effect
that I used my veto power to promote primary legislation, is
utter rot. There is absolutely no truth in it. I approved or vetoed
every measure that came before me on its merits alone. The
Frawley Committee is just a fishing committee, created as an
instrument for Mr. Murphy who wants to put me out of
office." [73]

On July 23 the Frawley committee submitted a preliminary
report to the Legislature in which it stated that it required
more time to complete its investigation of " many important
matters " that had been brought to its attention. It suggested,
therefore, that instead of adjourning, the extraordinary session
take a recess for a reasonable time so that when it was ready
to report, the legislators would be able " to take such official

70 *Ibid.*, July 18.

71 *Ibid.*

72 *Ibid.*

73 *Times,* July 26.

action as may be advisable." [74] The Legislature complied with the request and adopted a concurrent resolution recessing until August 11.[75]

The decision of the Legislature to take a recess, rather than an ordinary adjournment, was obviously designed not only to await recommendations from the Frawley committee for definite action, but also to block Sulzer in any attempt to remove Tammany office-holders and name their successors as recess appointments.[76] With the continuance of the deadlock resulting from the hostilities between Governor Sulzer and the organization leaders, there was little prospect of material legislative progress. Sulzer took the Legislature to task for its failure to act on his various nominations, still pending in the Senate, or on any of the measures he had recommended for consideration. In a scolding message he urged the members to dispose promptly of pending matters and go home, but the advice went unheeded.[77]

While Sulzer had put no real obstacles in the way of the Frawley probe into the investigations of his agents, he made a determined effort to block the attempt of the committee to pry into his own financial affairs, despite the contention of his friends that there was nothing he sought to conceal. In a long statement issued by his legal adviser, Valentine Taylor, entitled, " Regarding the power of the Frawley Committee to annoy and harass the Governor and other citizens of the State," he challenged the right of the investigators to inquire into his campaign fund.[78] The scope of the authority of the committee, the statement read, was prescribed and defined by the concurrent resolution adopted by the Legislature on May 3, specifically confining its powers to the examination of state supported

74 Assembly Journal, Vol. IV, pp. 88-91.
75 Ibid., p. 92; Senate Journal, Vol. II, p. 123.
76 Times, July 24.
77 Public Papers of Governor Sulzer, pp. 166-73.
78 Reprinted in Sulzer's Life and Speeches.

institutions, and the Thompson resolution, enlarging the powers and functions of the Frawley committee, was " null and void " under the express provision of Article IV, section 4, of the state constitution which provides: " At extraordinary sessions no subject shall be acted upon, except such as the Governor may recommend for consideration." The statement also seriously argued that for either the legislature or the judicial branch of the government to investigate the official conduct of the Governor would be an encroachment upon the executive department and violate " that fundamental theory and maxim of American institutions, known as the tripartite separation of powers." Citizens were advised to pay no attention to Richards' threat that unless they came forward voluntarily to furnish information, a subpoena would be issued compelling them to testify, inasmuch as the subject matter of the inquiry was " without and beyond the jurisdiction and legitimate functions of the Frawley committee." The Governor expressed a willingness to cooperate with the committee if it would give evidence of its sincerity, in its investigation of the 1912 campaign fund, by calling Murphy, Donohue, treasurer of Tammany Hall, and others, whose names he would furnish, and permit them to be examined under oath concerning the contributions they received and for which, he alleged, they had never accounted. Determined, apparently, to prevent the Legislature from taking action on any report that the Frawley committee might make, Taylor also insisted that the Legislature of 1913 had already terminated its legal existence. The reason given was that when the Legislature on July 23 adopted a resolution recessing until August 11, a quorum was lacking in both Assembly and Senate.[79]

79 Sulzer maintained that although the original journals of the respective houses for July 23 showed that 28 Senators and 98 Assemblymen were present at the session, he was " creditably informed " that only 17 Senators and 37 Assemblymen attended, far less than the required majority. Sulzer's assertion that the records had been falsified to show the presence of a quorum was vehemently denied by Lieutenant-Governor Glynn, who, in his indignation,

In official circles the Governor's challenge of the powers of the Frawley committee was construed as an indication that he had received positive confirmation of the report that his impeachment had been decreed by the powers of Tammany Hall.[80] The Frawley committee ignored Sulzer's protest, holding that the opinion of his personal counsel was not binding, and that if any opinion were necessary for its guidance, it would have to come from the Attorney-General.[81]

In order to obtain an official opinion, Sulzer then addressed a letter to Attorney-General Carmody, submitting a series of questions concerning " the scope, authority, jurisdiction and power " of the Frawley committee. He went over the familiar arguments that the committee was without authority to report to the extraordinary Legislature inasmuch as the original resolution, empowering it to investigate state institutions, distinctly stated that it report to the " next session," meaning apparently the new Legislature that would convene in 1914, and that the supplementary resolution of June 25 (the Thompson resolution), authorizing an inquiry into campaign funds and expenditures, was without effect in view of the fact that he had made no recommendation concerning its subject matter. He asked to know whether it was within the appropriate and legitimate functions of the committee or its counsel to demand information concerning campaign contributions and whether a person served with a subpoena was legally obliged to answer questions relating thereto. The letter also requested a formal opinion as to whether the extraordinary session had not ceased to exist when it adopted a concurrent resolution on July 23

likened Sulzer to the most famous liars of history, all of whom, he said, were "tyros in the name of falsehood compared to William Sulzer."— *World*, July 26.

80 About the middle of July, it was said, Murphy and his followers had declared their intention of impeaching Sulzer if he did not come to terms with the Tammany leaders by August 1. Sulzer dismissed the rumor at the time as being all " imagery."—*Tribune*, October 18.

81 *Times*, July 28.

adjourning until August 11, with a quorum lacking in either house, as prescribed by the state constitution.[82] Commenting on Sulzer's contentions, Senator Frawley remarked, " The pitiful thing is that the Governor should try to stand on technicalities to avoid inquiry into his conduct." [83]

In response to the questions submitted to him, Attorney-General Carmody, on August 2, rendered an exhaustive opinion which in almost every respect ran counter to Sulzer's views.[84] Its salient feature was that the extraordinary session of the Legislature had a legal right to vest the Frawley committee with the supplementary powers under which it was investigating Sulzer's campaign fund, that the scope of the inquiry was largely within the discretion of the committee, and that " the motives of its members, whether proper or improper," could not in any way limit or affect its powers.[85] The opinion also upheld the committee's right to subpoena and examine witnesses upon questions pertinent to the inquiry and held that a witness who refused might be committed for contempt.[86]

In answer to Sulzer's query as to whether the attempted legislative recess taken on July 23 was not in effect a dissolution of the extraordinary session, Carmody replied that the Legislature had the power to adjourn to a certain day, that such action did not require the assent or recommendation of the Executive, and that the Legislature could lawfully reconvene at the expiration of the period. In discussing the point

82 Annual Report of the Attorney-General, 1913, Vol. II, pp. 500-02, 508-10.

83 *Herald*, July 30.

84 Annual Report of the Attorney-General, *supra*, pp. 500-19.

85 In holding that the Frawley committee had the power to investigate the Governor's campaign fund, Carmody pointed out that this question was opened by the Governor himself when he recommended to the special session legislation to strengthen the election laws.

86 As precedent for his opinion that a legislative committee had the right to compel witnesses to testify, Carmody cited the Court of Appeals decision in the action begun against William Barnes, Jr., Republican state chairman, on behalf of the Bayne Committee, appointed to investigate conditions in Albany. See *In the Matter of Barnes*, 204 N. Y. 108.

raised by the Governor that less than a quorum of both houses was present when the Legislature ordered its recess, Carmody pointed out that the official journals of the two houses showed that a quorum was present and voted, and that inasmuch as the question of a quorum had not been raised in either house, the journals were " conclusive evidence " of their contents. He pointed out that the Governor himself had recognized the validity of its legislation by having signed three of the bills it passed. In closing, he volunteered the opinion that the investigation undertaken by the committee " should be welcomed by every right thinking citizen," anxious to preserve the purity of the ballot. The adverse character of the Attorney-General's opinion did not weaken Sulzer's determination to block all investigation of his personal conduct before he took office.

The Frawley committee held its first public hearing into the matter of campaign contributions and expenditures on July 30, a subject which it had evidently from the first held in reserve.[87] As shown in the original statement sworn to by him on November 13, 1912 and filed in the office of the Secretary of State, in accordance with the requirements of the so-called Corrupt Practices article of the Election Law,[88] Sulzer acknowledged that as candidate for Governor he had received, during his campaign (from September 23 to November 4 inclusive), a total of $5,460 from sixty-eight contributors and had expended the sum of $7,724.09. Counsel for the committee,

87 A complete transcript of the hearings conducted by the Frawley committee appears in the Assembly Journal, 1913, Vol. IV, Appendix, pp. 310-438.

88 Article 16, section 546. Section 776 of the Penal Law is even more explicit. It requires every candidate for public office in the state, within ten days after election, to file with the Secretary of State an itemized statement " showing in detail all the moneys contributed or expended by him, directly or indirectly, by himself or through any other person, in aid of his election." The statement must give the names of the various persons who received the moneys, the specific nature of each item, and the purpose for which it was expended or contributed. The statement must be accompanied by an affidavit, subscribed and sworn to by the candidate, certifying to its truth.—Consolidated Laws of New York, 1917, (William M. McKinney, ed.), Vol. VII, pp. 282-83.

Eugene L. Richards, immediately put in evidence a cancelled check for $2,500, dated October 14, 1912, from Jacob H. Schiff, prominent New York banker, that had not been included in the sworn statement. In the donor's handwriting, in the upper left corner of the check, was written, " Mr. Schiff's contribution toward William Sulzer's campaign expenses." The check was made out to the order of Louis A. Sarecky, Sulzer's confidential secretary who handled much of his campaign money, and was shown to have gone into the same account in the Mutual Alliance Trust Company, New York City, in which Sarecky was accustomed to deposit other contributions to the Sulzer campaign fund. The failure to account for this gift put a serious aspect upon the charges brought against Sulzer, for the law defined the filing of a false or incomplete statement a misdemeanor.[89]

The most important witness of the day was Sarecky, on whose testimony the committee expected to raise a structure of incriminating evidence against the Governor. He proved balky, however. While admitting to an account in the Mutual Alliance Trust Company, he stubbornly refused to answer any questions relating to Sulzer's accounts or to his campaign fund, unless he were permitted to be represented at the hearing by counsel who, he asserted, would " bring out the whole story and not one side of it " and who would give him an opportunity to explain any items that might appear " doubtful." [90] He admitted he occasionally endorsed checks in Sulzer's name and often made deposits for him. He would give no information, however, concerning any of the contributions to the Governor's campaign fund. On what he said was the advice of counsel, he challenged the authority of the committee to conduct

89 Section 776 of the Penal Law. Section 560 of the Election Law prescribed a fine not exceeding one thousand dollars, or imprisonment of not more than one year, or both, for failure to file a statement or for filing a false or incomplete statement.—Consolidated Laws of New York, op. cit., Vol. III, p. 432.

90 Assembly Journal, Vol. IV, p. 342.

the investigation.[91] Richards suggested that his refusal to testify was at the instance of the Governor, but the witness emphatically denied it. He did acknowledge, though, that he had told him of the subpoena to appear before the committee. The witness' defiant attitude prompted the chairman to advise Richards to take the necessary steps to secure his arrest and punishment for contempt of the Legislature. Another unreported contribution disclosed at the hearing was one for $500 from Abram I. Elkus. The cancelled check, dated October 5, was payable to William Sulzer, and with it was produced a letter from Sulzer acknowledging its receipt. The check had been endorsed by Sulzer and deposited to his personal account in the Farmers' Loan and Trust Company, but like the Schiff contribution, was not included in his sworn statement.

Sulzer's answer to the damaging disclosures was a lengthy statement to the press in which he charged the Frawley committee with conspiring to ruin him and accused Murphy of putting every obstacle in his way of collecting evidence of " gigantic frauds " in order to " shield the thieves." He contemptuously refuted the charge that he had made money by being a candidate for Governor and intimated that Murphy had pocketed unaccounted-for campaign contributions, which had come directly through his " bagman," from contractors, office holders, and special interests.[92] Even such a reticent politician as Murphy refused to sit back to an attack of that sort, and he sent a letter to the Frawley committee the same day, in which

91 In a statement issued the following day, Louis Marshall, Sarecky's counsel, explained that the reason he had advised his client not to submit to any interrogation on the subject of campaign funds was that, in his opinion, the committee was without jurisdiction, inasmuch as its powers, like those of extraordinary sessions of the Legislature, were explicitly limited by the constitution to subjects recommended by the Governor (Article IV, section 4). " The inquisition which this committee has sought to set in motion is not included within any of the recommended subjects," Marshall maintained. " The power of legislative committees is strictly limited and they cannot create for themselves a jurisdiction which is not grounded upon the constitution and the laws."—*Times*, August 1.

92 *Ibid.*

he branded as "untrue" Sulzer's insinuation that he had mis-applied campaign funds. "If Governor Sulzer," he wrote, "has any information as to misconduct on my part relating to campaign contributions I request him to furnish it to your committee, and I will appear for examination at any time." [93] Senator Frawley replied he would be glad to give Murphy an opportunity to testify, and invited Sulzer to appear before the committee to substantiate his charge.[94] The invitation was not accepted.

In numerous public statements made under his own name and in newspaper interviews, Sulzer drew a picture of Murphy as a relentless and cowardly pursuer. He charged him with holding up the business of the state government for vicious purposes, with attempting to force improper appointments upon him, with responsibility for graft in high places, and with baseless assaults upon his own character. He would have had no trouble with the members of the Legislature, he said, if it were not for "outside influences and the dictations of Mr. Murphy." [95] It was his determination "to go after the grafters and crooks" that prompted the investigation into his personal affairs. "The proposition is a simple one," he explained. "I am trying to put the great issue to the front; my enemies are constantly trying to put me to the front. My personality is nothing compared to the issue at stake." [96] His trouble with Murphy, he said, began soon after he took the oath of office, when he made it clear to the Tammany boss that no one could make him "a rubber stamp." [97] "I believe that this fact—that I am after the grafters and am doing everything in my power to bring them to justice—is responsible more than any other

[93] Assembly Journal, Vol. IV, p. 364. This was the first time, so far as was known, that the Tammany chief had ever expressed a willingness to take the stand in a public hearing.

[94] *Ibid.*, p. 365.

[95] *Evening Sun*, July 21.

[96] *Herald*, July 30.

[97] *Evening Sun*, July 21.

factor for the intense hatred of Mr. Murphy and his determination to destroy me at any hazard, even to the extent of impeaching me, if he can." [98] As far back as April 13, when he and Murphy met for the last time, the latter had warned him: " In six weeks I will have you out of office." [99] Because of his eagerness to fight " the people's battle," he rejected all promises of further political preferment. " All I had to do," he wrote, " was to sit tight, do what the boss told me like a nice, good little Governor, and be given the nomination for Governor next year, and the nomination for the Presidency of the United States thereafter." [100]

In an address delivered on August 4 in the Executive Chamber, at a conference which marked the opening of a campaign to secure the nomination and election of Assemblymen pledged to the support of direct primaries, he confided: " My friends, I am carrying a heavy burden. You know something about it, but you do not know all about it. I am doing so simply because I made up my mind when I took the oath of office that I would be the Governor in fact as well as in name. Because I made up my mind that no influence should control me while I was the Governor but the dictates of my own conscience, and my determination to do my duty, day in and day out, come what may. For these reasons, and others, I have been hounded, traduced, vilified, and threatened as no other man has ever been, who occupied this office, in all the history of the State." [101] Sulzer's partisans expressed their " unwavering confidence " in him and adopted a resolution deprecating and denouncing " the unjust and malicious attacks " upon the Governor by his " political traducers." [102]

To all friendly advisers who urged him to make known immediately all the facts in connection with the administration of

98 *Times*, July 26.
99 *American*, July 20.
100 *Ibid*.
101 *Public Papers of Governor Sulzer*, p. 1483.
102 *Times*, August 5.

his campaign fund, Sulzer turned a deaf ear. Instead of making a straightforward explanation or denial of the serious accusations brought against him, in vindication of his personal honor, he simply resorted to hysterical denunciations and sought shelter behind technicalities. Even those who were in accord with his contention that Tammany had set about to wreck his political career because of his assertion of independence, felt that he was injuring his own cause by his delay in refuting the incriminating evidence. If guilty of carelessness or negligence in handling his campaign contributions, he should have frankly said so. If, on the other hand, there was no foundation for the charges, which seemed to be supported by strong prima facie evidence, he should have furnished convincing proof of his innocence, as the people had a right to expect from an elected official. Accusing Murphy of pocketing campaign funds was no answer to the question whether he had falsified his statement of campaign receipts. Governor Sulzer, not Boss Murphy, was on trial. "In a matter of this kind," wrote the editor of a newspaper which had hitherto been sympathetic to the Governor, "the issue cannot be shifted. The Governor cannot vindicate himself by refusing to testify or by accepting a Scotch verdict. Such charges against a Governor are charges that have to be disproved. They are not charges that can rest as unproved." [103] The only pertinent explanation offered by Sulzer regarding the omission of the Schiff and Elkus contributions from his sworn statement was that he had been away from New York campaigning at the time they were received and that they had therefore been attended to by his office.[104] This alibi was easily punctured by Richards, who proved by Sulzer's speaking itinerary, that he did not go on

103 *World*, August 1.

104 Assembly Journal, Vol. IV, p. 367. This explanation was obviously at variance with the statement Sulzer made a few days after his nomination that he had no collector of campaign contributions. See *Times*, October 8, 1912.

his campaign until October 18, several days after the Schiff and Elkus checks were received and deposited.[105]

The Frawley committee resumed its public inquiry into the Sulzer campaign fund on August 6 in the Council Chamber of the New York City Hall. The reason for the shifting of the scene of the investigation from Albany was to facilitate the attendance of witnesses and to place the records of certain banking institutions within the readier reach of the committee.[106] The investigators were greatly strengthened in their course by the opinion of the Attorney-General upholding the legality of the inquiry and by his assertion that witnesses had to answer all questions germane to the investigation. The second hearing not only disclosed additional contributions which Sulzer had failed to report to the Secretary of State but also uncovered evidence that he had diverted large sums contributed to his campaign fund to stock speculation in Wall Street on a margin basis. This amazing revelation came as a distinct shock even to his staunchest supporters.

Among the checks produced by witnesses before the committee and unaccounted for by Sulzer, in addition to the Schiff and Elkus checks previously shown to have been contributed, were one from William F. McCombs, chairman of the Democratic National Committee, for $500, dated October 9, 1912, payable to the order of William Sulzer and deposited by Sarecky in the Mutual Alliance Trust Company; one for $1,000 from Henry Morgenthau, chairman of the Finance Committee of the Democratic National Committee, dated October 5, endorsed and deposited by Sulzer in his personal account in the Farmers' Loan and Trust Company; and a third from John Lynn,[107] for $500, dated October 10, also endorsed by Sulzer himself.

105 Assembly Journal, Vol. IV, p. 367.

106 *Times*, August 1.

107 A brother of H. Gordon Lynn, a member of Sulzer's Committee of Inquiry.

A transcript of the account kept by Sarecky for Sulzer in the Mutual Alliance Trust Company revealed that from October 1 through November 12, 1912 a total of $12,405.93 had been deposited.[108] The bank witness specifically identified the Schiff and McCombs checks. The original deposit slips showed that between nomination and election there had been deposited in this account alone not less than ninety-four checks, besides a considerable sum in cash.[109] That Sulzer knew Sarecky's account contained his campaign contributions was evidenced by a letter to the bank, dated October 12, 1912, in which he authorized his secretary to endorse his name to any checks donated to his campaign fund and to deposit them to his credit. The evidence produced by the Frawley committee also showed that Sulzer, who had always claimed to be a poor man, had deposited to his own account in the Farmers' Loan and Trust Company an aggregate of $24,395.31 between September 1, 1912 and January 1, 1913. His balance on the latter date stood at $22,527.47.[110] Many of the deposits were in substantial amounts of cash, whose source could not easily be traced.

In an effort to link campaign contributions with the purchase of stocks, Richards subpoenaed Arthur L. Fuller, stock broker, member of the New York firm of Fuller and Gray.[111] Sulzer's trading account showed that he had purchased outright 200 shares of the stock of the Big Four R. R. (Cleveland, Chicago, Cincinnati and St. Louis) during the latter part of October, 1912, for which he had paid $11,800, mainly in currency. The account was designated on the books as " number 500," obviously for the purpose of concealment, and the stock, it was

108 Assembly Journal, Vol. IV, p. 371.

109 *Ibid.*, p. 381.

110 *Ibid.*, p. 377.

111 Counsel for the firm entered a formal objection to the subpoena on the ground that the Governor's stock transactions were beyond the scope of the committee's powers, hence should not be made public property, but was overruled by the chairman.

learned, was delivered in devious ways to one, Frederick L. Colwell, alleged speculative agent of Sulzer. When Colwell was summoned before the committee, he admitted knowing Sulzer and having met him several times during the campaign, but refused to say whether Sulzer had a trading account or divulge whether account " number 500 " was Sulzer's under cover. (A clerk formerly in the employ of the company definitely identified Sulzer as sponsor of the account and testified that Colwell was the purchasing agent.) Colwell ignored a summons to appear again before the committee and was consequently cited for contempt of the Legislature.[112]

Further disclosures of Sulzer's speculative activities were made by Melville B. Fuller, of the Stock Exchange firm of Harris and Fuller. The first time he was summoned before the committee, the broker refused to answer any questions bearing on Sulzer's stock transactions on the ground that there was some doubt as to whether the committee had been legally appointed and whether it had the right to inquire into his firm's personal affairs. He denied having conferred with Sulzer, but declined to say whether his unwillingness to give any information was at his instance. Threatened with a contempt charge, he reappeared the following day with a complete transcript of Sulzer's trading account. The Governor, he explained, had authorized him to testify freely. According to the records, Sulzer was heavily involved in stock dealings at the time when he caused to be introduced and subsequently withdrew from the Legislature a bill to double the stock transfer tax, a measure which was bitterly fought by Wall Street. The account, Fuller revealed, was known simply as " number 63," as a precaution that its existence would be kept secret. It showed that on January 1, 1912, when Sulzer was still a member of Congress, he carried on margin 500 shares of Big Four, 200 shares of American Smelters, and 100 shares of Southern Pacific, with

112 Both Colwell and Sarecky were subsequently adjudged guilty of contempt by the Legislature.—Assembly Journal, Vol. IV, pp. 119-20.

a total value of $48,599.38. The only other purchase made
since then had been 100 shares of Big Four on December 5,
1912. Not until Sulzer had been elected to the Governorship,
had any steps been taken to liquidate the indebtedness. Payments for the stock included $10,000 in currency on November
18, 1912, (within two weeks after the election), $6,000 on
December 16, also in currency, and a check for $5,000 on
January 16, 1913. The broker also submitted correspondence
disclosing that when the stock market broke, Sulzer was
repeatedly importuned to make additional margin payments on
his impaired account and had been threatened with being sold
out if he failed to do so. The account was finally closed out on
July 15, 1913, when the stock was taken up and the amount
still due ($26,739.21) paid by Lieutenant Commander Louis
M. Josephthal, a member of Governor Sulzer's military staff.

At subsequent public hearings of the Frawley committee, an
array of witnesses brought to light additional checks representing campaign contributions concealed by Sulzer in his affidavit.
Several of them, bearing Sulzer's endorsement, were shown to
have passed directly through the brokerage firm of Boyer,
Griswold and Company as part payment of railroad securities
purchased by Frederick L. Colwell. The transcript of the latter's
stock transactions disclosed that on October 16, 1912, he
bought outright 200 shares of Big Four for the sum of $12,025.
This amount was paid for with Sulzer's personal check for
$900, certified checks representing a total of $4,000, sent by
contributors to his campaign fund, and the balance, $7,125, in
cash, which at that time flowed freely into the campaign coffers.
There no longer seemed to be any doubt but that money contributed to the Sulzer campaign fund had been used for speculative purposes in Wall Street.

The Frawley committee had met with unhoped-for success.
As the Tammany men followed the Sulzer record, stories at
first vague rapidly developed form. " When our committee
began work," said Senator Frawley, " we had a hunch that
the full account of the Governor's campaign expenditures had

not been published, as the law requires, but it was a surprise to all of us to find that he had used some of the money contributed for his political expenses to try a flyer in Wall Street." [113] The man who had traveled from one end of the state to the other, calling his opponents crooks and grafters, had himself been caught in dishonorable dealings. Not only had it been established that he had received an amount several times over what he had sworn to but had used funds contributed in aid of his election to speculate in securities at a time when he, as Governor, was earnestly pressing legislation affecting the New York Stock Exchange and was solemnly talking about evils of transactions affected by " a gambling taint." [114] The ordinary malefactor could be forgiven, but when evidence showed that a man professing virtue had done the things he blamed others for doing, then came the pillory.

113 *Outlook*, October 18, 1913, Vol. 105, p. 357.
114 *Public Papers of Governor Sulzer*, p. 58.

CHAPTER V

SULZER'S IMPEACHMENT

SULZER'S impeachment, which had been considered a joke when first suggested by Tammany men, was now regarded in a more serious light. After the session of the Frawley committee on August 8 ended, it was certain that some definite step looking to the expulsion of the Governor from office would be taken when the Legislature reconvened. Frawley shared with the other members of the committee and with its counsel the view that incontrovertible evidence had been adduced to prove that Sulzer had knowingly violated the Corrupt Practices Act, and that further disclosures on that point would be merely cumulative. The only question was the procedure that ought to be followed in bringing about his removal. Some members held that the committee should look to the courts for action, urging his indictment on the charge of violating the Corrupt Practices Act, conviction for which would automatically disbar him from holding office. Those who held this view were influenced in a measure by the fear that if the Legislature, controlled as it was by Tammany Hall, should proceed to impeach the Governor, a cry of politics would be raised and a strong public sentiment in Sulzer's favor might thus be aroused. If the aid of the courts were invoked, they maintained, no such contention could then logically be made.[1]

Most of the committee, on the other hand, believed that impeachment by the Legislature, with its heavy Democratic majority and friendly Republican element, afforded the surest and quickest avenue. Should the Governor's case be taken to the courts, they pointed out, there would be opportunity for all sorts of dilatory tactics that would cause a final decision to be deferred until after the Assembly elections in November, in which the Governor's friends might obtain for him a vote

1 *Times*, August 8.

of confidence. Impeachment proceedings could be concluded in a comparatively short time, and from conviction there was no appeal.[2]

Sulzer's failure to utter a single word during the hearings regarding the serious disclosures made and his apparent determination to suppress vital testimony was construed by many, even by those who were kindly disposed toward him, as a confession of guilt. There were signs on all sides that he was losing the support of persons of independent political tendencies, who had applauded the fight he had been making for the direct primary and against Boss Murphy. He had met earlier charges affecting his character with denials that came promptly and emphatically, but turned silent in respect to the graver accusations involving both his honor and honesty. In response to requests from newspaper correspondents for a statement, he sent word that he would have nothing to say until the Frawley committee had completed its investigation and he had had an opportunity to read the official record of the testimony.[3] His sole comment appeared in a statement prepared by his secretary, Chester C. Platt, on August 7, in which he described the testimony before the committee as " fragmentary and garbled." " Some of these charges are false, some are distorted truths, easily explained, and some of these charges are insinuations about which, at present, the Governor is wholly ignorant," he said. " The people understand the motives which actuate the Frawley committee. They know who is behind it, and why the charges against the Governor are being made." [4]

Sulzer's refusal to make any explanation or furnish any reply met with almost universal condemnation. In view of the damning evidence against him, hardly a newspaper in New York, though nearly every one was anti-Tammany, had the hardihood to defend him. " The people of New York do not

2 *Ibid.*
3 *Ibid.*, August 10.
4 *Ibid.*, August 8.

want to believe these shocking things of the Governor of the State," wrote the *Times*, " but if the charges are untrue, why does not Mr. Sulzer deny them at once? If he has any explanation, why does he not make it? To make countercharges against Mr. Murphy and to seek to ferret out wrongful practices, chargeable to the Murphy influence, in the State departments is no answer to the evidence affecting Mr. Sulzer's reputation and honor. Can he be so blind as not to see that his silence will be construed as confession, that any attempt on his part to baffle the committee in its work or to evade a full investigation will also be construed as confession?" His exposure put an irremovable stain on his personal honor. " No denials, no palliations, no imaginable thing he can say will place him where he stood before or regain for him the confidence he has utterly forfeited." [5] The *World* conceded that Sulzer was being exhibited to public disgrace only because he refused to remain subservient to the boss, but pointedly observed that " it was not Murphy who signed William Sulzer's name to a false statement of campaign contributions and expenditures " or diverted personal campaign contributions to carry on Wall Street speculations. It considered his public usefulness at an end no matter what defense he might offer, and called upon him to " spare the State of New York further shame and humiliation " by resigning from office.[6] The *Tribune* felt there was no possibility for the Governor to shift or evade the issue and went on to say: " The prostitution of all the agencies of government to the purposes of a factional fight between the Governor and Murphy has been a sickening fight for all right-minded citizens. It is not half as sickening as to see a Governor who went into office with bright prospects and who had the people's confidence and support while they believed he was honestly fighting corruption, remain silent under disgraceful charges

5 Editorial, August 9.
6 Editorial, August 9.

affecting his personal integrity and his political honor." [7] The *Evening Post*, a friend of neither Sulzer nor Tammany, after ridiculing the Governor's hypocrisy, declared that "the man who has dragged the good name of New York in the dirt should take himself out of its sight." It preferred "a plain, unadulterated Tammany rascal, who stands for what he is, to a political sinner turned saint for a moment and calling for aid to overthrow his quondam pals and bosses in the name of that political justice, decency, and honesty he so long helped to violate." [8] Even Hearst's *American* demanded that the Governor cease quibbling about the legality of the investigation and stop attacking the motives of his accusers. "The undeniable fact that the offenses charged are at variance with Gov. Sulzer's entire career and known character before his nomination does not change the pitiless fact that Gov. Sulzer cannot escape impeachment and removal from office, and possibly conviction of crime, unless he can answer them." [9] Sulzer's denunciation of Tammany and its boss would evidently no longer defend him against the evidence of his own acts, even if dragged to light by men with ulterior motives.

Governor Sulzer finally took heed of the steady alienation of public sympathy induced by his silence, and at one o'clock on the morning of August 11, 1913, at the conclusion of a conference with several of his legal advisers and close political friends, issued a statement categorically denying the ugly charges of the Frawley committee. The statement ran as follows:

"I deny that I used any campaign contributions for personal use.

"I deny that I speculated in Wall Street or used money contributed for campaign purposes to buy stocks either in my own name or otherwise.

7 Editorial, August 9.
8 Editorial, August 9.
9 Editorial, August 9.

" I never had an account with Fuller and Gray or Boyer and Griswold. I never heard of these firms; do not know the members, and knew nothing about the transactions with these firms testified to before the Frawley committee until recently threatened with exposure and the alleged transactions were brought to my attention by the Frawley committee.

" The stock matter with Harris and Fuller was not a speculative account or matter, but a loan made upon stocks as collateral, which stocks had been acquired and paid for years before my nomination for the office of Governor and from other sources than Harris and Fuller.

" Certain checks given to me for campaign purposes were deposited to my personal account, and thereafter I paid the amount of said checks to my Campaign Committee.

" In filing my statement of receipts and disbursements with the Secretary of State I relied on information furnished me by the persons in immediate charge of my campaign, and in whom I had, and have, the most implicit confidence, and I believe the statement furnished by them to be accurate and true." [10]

This belated and sweeping denial, unsupported by any proof, did not constitute a convincing statement of his case and satisfied no one, not even his friends and sympathizers. There were many specifications in the testimony given against him which his denial did not dispose of. If it were true that he had no knowledge of the contributions to his campaign fund not included in his sworn statement until they were brought to his attention through the threats of his enemies, why did he not take instant action and insist upon a thorough investigation, regardless of the extent to which, in so doing, he might have confessed to his faults? When, on the contrary, he sought to hush the matter up by denying the authority of the Frawley committee, he rendered himself guilty of a deplorable blunder. His failure to make known all the facts within his knowledge

10 *Times*, August 11.

or to fix responsibility for the evasion of the publicity law respecting campaign contributions damaged his reputation beyond repair. If his transaction with Harris and Fuller was simply a " loan " and not a speculation in stocks, why did Fuller continually refer to it in his testimony as a margin account? And why should it have appeared on the firm's books under a number and not in his own name? It was also obvious that the stocks used as collateral for this " loan " had not been acquired and paid for " years before " his nomination, as Sulzer alleged. One hundred shares of stock were bought for his account as late as December 5, 1912, which clearly gave the matter the appearance of an open speculative account. Nor did Sulzer attempt to explain how, if he never knew or heard of Boyer and Griswold, campaign checks totalling several thousand dollars went through the hands of these brokers and were deposited in the firm's account in a New York bank. Sulzer's answer was wholly inadequate and some further explanation was manifestly called for.

On the night of August 11 the Legislature reassembled after its long recess in order to receive the Frawley committee's report. It was not until ten o'clock that the gavel fell, the Democratic leaders in the meantime anxiously conferring and counting noses, aware that the slightest tactical error might prove fatal to their plans. A record crowd of curious spectators thronged the galleries of the Assembly, where the impeachment was to be staged. The Governor did not go to the Capitol, as was his custom when the Legislature held night sessions, but remained in constant consultation with his friends regarding ways of staving off impeachment.[11] The first inkling of the Sulzer strength in the lower house came on the motion of the Republican leader, Hinman, to reconsider the vote by which the motion to approve the Journal of July 23 had been adopted.[12]

11 *Ibid.*, August 12.

12 That was the session which ordered the recess taken and which, Sulzer contended, lacked a quorum.

The motion was defeated by a vote of 30 to 66.[13] Hinman's apparent intent to combat the impeachment came as an unpleasant surprise to the Democratic leaders, who had been led to believe by Barnes's attitude that the Republican machine would make common cause with the Governor's opponents.

The formidable report of the Frawley committee reviewed the evidence brought out at the public hearings and concluded that Governor Sulzer had violated the Corrupt Practices Act in making a false statement of campaign contributions; that he had diverted some of those contributions to the purchase of stocks; that he had engaged in stock speculation while advocating anti-exchange legislation; and that he had used the power and patronage of his office to gain support for his favored measures. The committee acknowledged that it had not yet completed the investigation, but urged the Legislature to take immediate action without awaiting a final report. " We submit to the Senate and Assembly," it declared, " that the facts stated are sufficiently serious in character and are so violative of the laws of this State and the rules of fitness for and conduct in high office, that the public interests demand some action in reference thereto whether through the exercise of the powers of the Legislature, or by referring the facts and evidence to other duly constituted officers charged with duties in respect thereof." In closing, the committee worked itself up to a fine peroration. " The questions here involved are vital to clean government. They are above party or partisanship. They are vital to the citizens of the state and call for prompt and well-considered action. They call for an answer from Governor Sulzer, because both his obstructive tactics and his silence warrants the conclusion that the charges can neither be answered nor explained." The report also recommended the punishment of Sarecky and Colwell for contempt of the Legislature.[14]

13 Assembly Journal, Vol. IV, p. 94.

14 The entire report appears in the Assembly Journal, Vol. IV, Appendix, pp. 301-9.

A heated debate in the Assembly followed the presentation of the report. Hinman, convinced that the committee had not made a candid inquiry, opposed any precipitate action. " The lack of impartiality which has characterized the work of this committee brands it as vicious and unfair," he bluntly declared. While the Republicans, he said, wished to remain aloof from the " disgraceful " quarrel in the Democratic party, they nevertheless did insist on preserving the good name of the state.[15] " This malignant attack is made for no good purpose," he concluded. " While Sulzer may not have been a good official, he is entitled to fair treatment. We are not concerned with Sulzer the man, but Sulzer the Governor. We have our own dignity to maintain." [16] A stirring plea for delay " in the name of fair play " was also made by Assemblyman Schaap, leader of the Progressives. " I ask you to look well into your consciences before you adopt without reading recommendations based on this testimony," he pleaded.[17] After several preliminary skirmishes and roll calls, which showed the sentiment to be largely against the Governor, the report was adopted by a vote of sixty-five to thirty-five. The Republicans were divided and but a handful of Democrats voted in the negative.[18]

When the Frawley committee's report was presented to the upper house, Senator Duhamel [19] started a turmoil when he accused the committee of having set out " to crucify " the Governor.[20] This remark brought Frawley to his feet with an indignant denial. After characterizing as " distressing " the prospect of forcing a Governor out of office, particularly of his own party, he loudly protested his friendship for Sulzer. His voice at that point, according to one newspaper correspondent,

15 *World*, August 12.

16 *Times*, August 12.

17 *Ibid.*

18 Assembly Journal, Vol. IV, p. 96.

19 A Hearst follower who was elected on the Democratic and Independence League tickets.

20 *Times*, August 12.

" was drowned out by the loud laughter of the spectators." [21]
Duhamel later explained that he did not intend to imply dishonorable motives to the committee, but simply meant to criti-
cize it for denying witnesses the right of counsel and not awaiting additional evidence before proposing punitive action.[22]
Inasmuch as the Senate was not called upon to adopt the report,
it merely agreed to receive it.[23]

With the adoption of the report of the Frawley committee,
the machinery for the Governor's removal from office was
quickly set into motion. Aaron J. Levy, leader of the Democratic majority in the Assembly, immediately offered a resolution which, after rehearsing the charges contained in the committee's report, called for the impeachment of Sulzer " for
wilful and corrupt conduct in office, and high crimes and misdemeanors." [24] Levy asked that the consideration of the impeachment resolution be set down for the following day. With
only about two-thirds of the members present, any attempt to
force immediate action might have proved disastrous to the
organization's plans. Assemblyman Hinman, supported by
Assemblyman Gibbs, urged at least a week's delay, contending
that the matter was too grave for shorter deliberation. Facing
Levy, Gibbs shouted: " If William Sulzer were the greatest
wretch that ever crawled this earth, you are not giving him a
square deal. I blush for my party and its leadership to have to
say so." [25] Hinman's substitute motion that consideration of the
impeachment resolution be postponed a week was lost, and
Levy's motion carried, 64 to 30.[26] The Assembly then adjourned until eleven o'clock the following morning.

The Assembly convened at the scheduled time but on motion
of the majority leader took another adjournment until 8 : 30

21 *Ibid.*
22 *Ibid.*
23 Senate Journal, Vol. II, p. 132.
24 Assembly Journal, Vol. IV, p. 98.
25 *Times,* August 12.
26 Assembly Journal, Vol. IV, p. 99.

that evening, inasmuch as many members were expected on the late afternoon trains. All day long, by telephone and telegraph, urgent summonses went forth from the party chiefs to absent Democratic Assemblymen to hurry back to Albany. Deputy Sergeants-at-Arms hurried through the capital with orders to compel every member to take his desk on the Assembly floor. The commanders of the impeachment forces took no chance of " going to bat " with the impeachment resolution until enough votes were in sight to pass it.

The evening session attracted vast numbers of spectators. A throng, larger than any that ever stormed the Capitol in the memory of the oldest attendant, poured through the doorways hours before the time set for calling the Assembly to order. The galleries were packed. Hundreds stood outside the railing in the Assembly Chamber. Men and women were reported standing eight feet deep in the corridor leading to the Chamber. Squads of uniformed men from Albany's Police Headquarters were hastily sent to reinforce the Capitol orderlies who were unable to handle the crowd.[27] All day long sensational rumors filled the air with suspense and excitement. One had it that the Governor's friends were planning to barricade the entrance to the Speaker's room, take possession of the rostrum, hold a snap session, and declare the Assembly adjourned *sine die*.[28] Another startling rumor was that the Governor, as Commander-in-Chief, might call out the state militia to break up the impeachment session and retain his office by force.[29] While no one took the belligerent utterances of the Sulzer enthusiasts seriously, unusual precautions nevertheless were taken to frustrate any attempt at violence. In addition to the massing of extra Albany police, the extraordinary rule was established that admission to the Assembly Chamber was to be

27 *Times*, August 13.
28 *Ibid.*
29 *Ibid.*

had only by card bearing the signature of the Speaker and countersigned by another Assemblyman.[30]

Through the tense and exciting hours of debate on the impeachment resolution, the Governor remained in the Executive Mansion, conferring with defense counsel and keeping in constant touch with the proceedings in the Assembly. Personal emissaries hurried between the Governor's Mansion and the Capitol Building, bringing orders for Sulzer's friends to execute and carrying back tidings of the losing fight in which they were engaged. Sulzer was reported to have summoned several Tammany Assemblymen, while the debate was in progress, in a last minute frantic but futile effort to dissuade them from voting for the resolution. Assemblyman James C. Campbell, of New York City, one of the few who answered the call, quoted the Governor as pleading: " I have tried to do what is right. If you have a heart, if you have red blood in your veins, you ought to stand by me." [31] He was also reported to have appealed to Senator Frawley to avert the scandal of impeachment, saying that he had been forced into his fight with the organization by well-meaning but ill-advised counselors.[32] " Jim," Frawley quoted Sulzer as saying, " this has gone too far. I didn't expect anything like this and I know you didn't." But Frawley replied that there was nothing he could do to stop the proceedings. Sulzer was reported as then having remarked, " Let me tell you that if I am impeached there will be a revolution in New York State within twenty-four hours. The people elected me and they won't stand for my being removed this way." [33]

That the Governor made desperate efforts to save himself is evident from the telegrams sent out by his secretary on August 12 to various party leaders throughout the state, urging

30 *Ibid.*

31 *Ibid.*

32 *Ibid.*, August 14.

33 *World*, August 14.

them to bring influence to bear on Assemblymen from their districts to abandon the opposition. A typical telegram was the one addressed to the Buffalo leader: " Will you telephone or telegraph Assemblyman Geoghan [a Buffalo member] immediately? He voted for Frawley report yesterday, but I think if you can reach him you can prevent him from voting for the impeachment. Answer. Can you help with other Assemblymen? You ought to be in Albany." [34] It appears from an examination of the telephone and telegraph bills charged to the state during Sulzer's administration that he was also in communication with Franklin D. Roosevelt and John Purroy Mitchel in a vain attempt to persuade them to intervene in his behalf with President Wilson to save him from the impending impeachment.[35] On the other front, the generalissimo of the Governor's enemies, Charles F. Murphy, sat by the telephone in his home in New York City, receiving periodic bulletins of the progress being made at the Capitol.[36]

At half past eight in the evening, the Assembly reconvened, but the opening was further delayed by the continued round-up of absentee members known to be in the city.[37] Seventy-six, representing a majority of the elected members, were necessary for the passage of the impeachment resolution, but the organization leaders kept sparring for time until they could count on eighty before they could confidently risk the test. In the meantime the Assemblymen smoked, chatted, read the papers, giving no sign in their demeanor that anything serious was at hand. Shortly after ten o'clock the business of vote-gathering ceased. Speaker Alfred E. Smith announced, " The gentlemen in the gallery will kindly stop smoking," and called the house to order.[38] The roll call indicated that the anti-Sulzer forces had

34 *Tribune*, November 2.
35 *Ibid*.
36 *World*, August 13.
37 *Ibid*.
38 *Sun*, August 13.

the necessary number of votes to carry out their program. One hundred and twenty-three members answered to their names: 86 Democrats, 35 Republicans, and 2 Progressives.[39] The Governor's few supporters planned to fight the majority on every technicality and with every parliamentary weapon at their command. Hinman opened the debate with a last plea for delay, repeating his declaration that there was nothing in the Governor's alleged transactions that furnished proper ground for impeachment. The Assembly, he insisted, was without the pale of the constitution in considering impeachment charges at an extraordinary session not expressly summoned for that purpose. Every act of Sulzer's with relation to campaign funds, brought out in the Frawley committee's report, he pointed out, dated back to a period before he took his oath of office, and he quoted legal opinion to support his contention that the Governor could be impeached only for wilful misconduct in office and not for any offense committed before his induction. Several other Republican and Progressive members protested against the haste with which the impeachment was being pushed through, asserting that they had not even had time to read the Frawley committee's report.[40] Assemblyman Gibbs called the proposed impeachment " legislative lynch law," and shouted that Sulzer would not have been made to " walk the plank " had he been an " accommodating " Governor. " Let not these men who have prepared to sacrifice William Sulzer for their own advantage put on a cloak of hypocrisy and shed crocodile tears," he exclaimed, adding bluntly, " Everybody knows that the reason why Sulzer is being demanded as a victim is that he had the manhood to refuse to be tied to the wheels of a certain political chariot." [41] Legislative leaders, on the other hand, declared there was no justification in the law or in the constitution for the contention that there could be

39 Assembly Journal, Vol. IV, p. 101.
40 *World*, August 13.
41 *Times*, August 13.

no impeachment except in cases where malfeasance occurred during the defendant's term of office. The only charge necessary to impeach a public official, they maintained, was that he was unfit to hold his office.[42]

Shortly before two o'clock in the morning, the debate on the impeachment resolution was interrupted by the sensational announcement that Mrs. Sulzer had assumed responsibility for the acts charged to the Governor. According to the story alleged to have been told Senator Abraham J. Palmer, Mrs. Sulzer had, without her husband's knowledge, converted some of the campaign checks for stock trading purposes, hopeful of rehabilitating the family finances and confident of making some quick money. She had not hitherto come forward with her confession, it was said, only because the Governor gallantly refused to allow her to be drawn into the battle.[43] Mrs. Sulzer's " confession " was made the subject of a motion by Hinman that further consideration of the impeachment resolution be postponed, inasmuch as it was in the nature of newly discovered evidence, therefore vital to the Governor's case. Levy gave no credence to the story, characterizing it as simply " an eleventh-hour attempt of a faithful wife to shield her husband." [44] He called attention to the fact that the Governor's speculative operations began years before his marriage and that his correspondence with the brokerage firm of Harris and Fuller belied Mrs. Sulzer's contention.[45] Hinman's motion to defer action was overwhelmingly defeated.[46]

At three o'clock in the morning, Levy began his final appeal on behalf of the impeachment resolution, speaking for two

42 *Ibid.*, August 10.

43 *Ibid.*, August 14.

44 *Ibid.*

45 It was authoritatively stated for a time that Mrs. Sulzer would be a witness at the Governor's trial, but she was never called. News from Albany reported her as having broken down with worry and as being physically unfit to tell her story in court. Mrs. Sulzer soon ceased to figure in the case.

46 Assembly Journal, Vol. IV, pp. 101-2.

hours to a Chamber wearied by the prolonged debate. Audible sounds of deep breathing were heard from some of the members. One observer reported: " In every conceivable attitude of fatigue his fellow Assemblymen lay back in their chairs, most of them with their eyes closed, or their heads sunk forward on their bosoms. Those not assuredly asleep were not discernibly awake, save for the party leaders and their active lieutenants." [47] Levy wound up his speech as the daylight already began to stream through the open windows. A few minutes after five o'clock, the roll call began. Seventy-nine members, three more than necessary, voted " aye," forty-five " no," and William Sulzer, forty-second Governor of New York State, stood the first to be accused of " wilful and corrupt conduct in office, and high crimes and misdemeanors." Of the 79 who voted for impeachment, 72 were Democrats and 7 Republicans. Twenty-six Democrats, 16 Republicans, and 3 Progressives opposed the resolution. [48]

The impeachment machinery was then quickly put into operation. The Speaker of the Assembly appointed a committee of three to go before the Senate and formally impeach the Governor, to inform the Senate that the Assembly would, in due time, exhibit the particular articles of impeachment, and to ask the Senate to order the appearance of William Sulzer to answer to the charges. [49] A committee of five, headed by Aaron J. Levy, was appointed to prepare the articles of impeachment, after which the Assembly recessed for an hour. When the members reconvened, Levy presented the impeachment articles which defined the charges on which the Governor was to be

47 *Times*, August 13.

48 Assembly Journal, Vol. IV, pp. 102-3.

49 *Ibid.*, p. 103. Under the constitutional and statutory provisions governing impeachment proceedings, the Assembly is called upon to draft articles of impeachment to be presented to the Court of Impeachment, which consists of the members of the Senate and judges of the Court of Appeals, the Chief Justice presiding. Thirty days, at least, must elapse from the time the impeachment articles are filed with the President of the Senate and clerk of the Court of Appeals before the trial can be held.

tried.[50] The articles of impeachment, drawn up upon the plan of an indictment, presented eight specifications of wrongdoing, as disclosed by the findings of the Frawley committee, in violation of as many different sections of the Penal Code of the state.

Article I accused Sulzer of "wilfully, knowingly and corruptly" making and filing with the Secretary of State a false statement of campaign receipts and expenditures in connection with his campaign for Governor, "in express violation of the statutes of the state." (Eleven contributions, aggregating $8,500, were specified as having been omitted.)

Article II accused him of "wilful and corrupt perjury" in making oath that his statement of campaign receipts was correct, in violation of section 1620 of the Penal Code.

Article III accused him of "bribing witnesses" and, in violation of section 2440 of the Penal Law, "fraudulently" inducing Louis A. Sarecky, Frederick L. Colwell, and Melville B. Fuller "to withhold true testimony" from the legislative investigating committee.

Article IV accused him of suppressing evidence by "practicing deceit and fraud and using threats and menaces" to prevent the investigating committee to procure the attendance and testimony of those same witnesses, in violation of section 814 of the Penal Law.

Article V accused him of "preventing and dissuading" a witness, Frederick L. Colwell, from answering the subpoena of the said committee, in violation of the statutes of the state and of section 2441 of the Penal Law.

Article VI accused him of larceny, in having converted and appropriated to his own use and to stock speculation eleven checks totalling $8,500 and $32,850 in cash contributed to his campaign fund, in violation of sections 1290 and 1294 of the Penal Law.

50 These are printed in full in the Assembly Journal, Vol. IV, pp. 104-12.

Article VII accused him of improperly using his Executive authority and influence " for the purpose of affecting the vote or political action " of certain members of the Legislature by promising to sign or threatening to veto bills in which they were interested, in violation of section 775 of the Penal Law. (Assemblymen Prime and Sweet were specified as persons to whom such promises or threats were made.)

Article VIII accused him of corruptly using the influence of his office to affect the prices of securities selling on the New York Stock Exchange, in some of which he was at the time speculating, in violation of the statutes of the state and section 775 of the Penal Law.

The impeachment articles were adopted by a vote of 79 to 29 after a brief debate.[51] This done, the Speaker appointed nine " managers " to prosecute the case on behalf of the Assembly before the Court of Impeachment. The committee chosen included Levy (Democrat) of New York, McMahon (Democrat) of Bronx, Greenberg (Democrat) of New York, Gillen (Democrat) of Kings, Ward (Democrat) of New York, Fitzgerald (Democrat) of Erie, Madden (Democrat) of Westchester, T. K. Smith (Republican) of Onondaga, and Schnirel (Republican) of Ontario. They were instructed to convey the articles to the Senate and were authorized to employ counsel and exercise all the powers of a legislative committee.[52] Before adjourning the Assembly showed its contemptuous disregard of Sulzer by repassing, by the overwhelming vote of 108 to 5, the Blauvelt election bill which he had three times refused to sign as a " fraud and a sham." [53]

In the Senate the stage for the trial of the Governor was set without delay. At eleven o'clock, on August 13, the Senate received the committee which formally impeached Sulzer, " in the name of the Assembly and of all the people of the State

51 Assembly Journal, Vol. IV, p. 112.

52 Ibid., p. 115.

53 Ibid., p. 117.

of New York." The Assembly managers then presented the articles of impeachment, after which the President protempore, Robert F. Wagner, announced that the Court of Impeachment would meet at the Capitol on September 18, 1913, at twelve o'clock.[54] After completing action on the impeachment preliminaries, the Senators concurred unanimously in the repassage of the Blauvelt election bill and adjourned until August 19.[55]

The impeachment of Governor Sulzer instantly became a " cause célèbre." Despite the Governor's incriminating silence and the flagrancy of the acts attributed to him, large sections of public opinion expressed their continued confidence and trust in him. Letters to newspapers pleaded Sulzer's services as Governor, his support of reform measures, his exposure of grafters, and his opposition to Tammany, as a presumption of his innocence. His determination to go through with the fight for honest and efficient government, forewarned, long before the Frawley committee set to work to uncover the campaign fund, that he would be accused of all kinds of turpitude unless he yielded to Murphy, was an act so supremely sacrificial, they felt, that it barred the possibility of his being guilty of any wilful wrongdoing. Sulzer was too shrewd and seasoned a politician not to realize that continued opposition to the organization would bring on a relentless effort to discredit and disgrace him. Had he been weak enough to misappropriate campaign funds, he certainly would have given in to avoid exposure. This point of view was well stated by the Philadelphia *Record,* which confessed itself unable " to believe that a man who had the moral courage to defy the powerful boss, with foreknowledge of the consequences, could have been guilty of such mean and dishonorable conduct in the administration of his campaign funds." [56]

54 Senate Journal, Vol. II, p. 144.
55 *Ibid.,* p. 147.
56 Quoted in *Literary Digest,* August 23, 1913, Vol. 47, p. 268.

But assuming even that he had been guilty of indiscretions and improprieties before coming into the governorship, many argued, he was deserving of a full pardon for the courage he revealed when he deliberately chose the road to possible ruin instead of the path to security and higher honors. Sulzer might have sinned in the past, but exhibited such great public virtue in seeking to deliver the state " from the clutches of professional plunderers of the public treasury and the rule of the political bosses " [57] that he had earned the support and gratitude of the people. His chief source of strength, doubtless, was the feeling that the prosecution was begun for purely political reasons, and that whatever truth there might be in the charges, they would never have been brought to light had he been a complaisant servant of Tammany Hall. Sulzer was being exhibited to public shame and disgrace only because of his refusal to take orders from Murphy, and the impeachment was simply the revenge which a corrupt machine was wreaking upon an executive who dared to be independent. It was not for his faults but for his virtues that he was being crucified. His crime, in Tammany eyes, was not that he made false returns of campaign contributions, but that he tried to snatch the leadership of the Democratic party from Murphy's grip. The sight of Tammany Hall, open enemy of political reform, bringing charges of financial irregularities against William Sulzer, avowed advocate of the reform of election methods, impressed the *Outlook* as " artistically grotesque." [58] The Tammany boss ordered the Governor's impeachment " as he would order a beefsteak at Delmonico's and a servile assembly voted the impeachment with more obsequiousness than a self-respecting French waiter would show to a grand duke," observed a Philadelphia editor.[59] Theodore Roosevelt wrote

57 Editorial, Albany *Knickerbocker Press*, August 12, 1913, quoted in Forrest and Malcolm, *op. cit.*, p. 414.

58 August 23, 1913, Vol. 104, p. 886.

59 Editorial, Philadelphia *North American*, August 20, quoted in Forrest and Malcolm, pp. 399-400.

Sulzer: "I have yet to meet a single person who believes, or even pretends to believe, that a single honest motive has animated the proceedings of your antagonists. . . . We have never seen a more startling example of the power of the invisible government under the present system." [60]

A point of view commonly held was that it mattered little whether Sulzer actually did the things charged, since the main issue in the fight was good government and clean politics against Murphyism and all that it stood for. The Philadelphia *Public Ledger* declared, "The real issue at stake is "the integrity of the executive office, not the financial integrity of the executive officer." [61] Sulzer might not be a paragon of virtue but if the indictment were sustained and Sulzer found guilty, Tammany would triumph. One could admit the worst that was alleged against Sulzer, yet consistently support him; for as the *Nation* wrote, "It is not that Sulzer is admired or trusted but that Murphy is detested and feared. In the face of the grave charges against Governor Sulzer, which are so strongly evidenced and which he has not met in a way at all satisfactory, he could hardly have a friend—or, at any rate, a defender—in the state, were it not for one circumstance. That circumstance is named Murphy. Hatred of him almost takes on the guise of love of Sulzer." [62] One up-state newspaper rhetorically asked: "Which do you prefer,—Sulzer, who grievously sinned before he became Governor, but who has been assailing vice in Tammany's citadel ever since that time, or Murphy in absolute control of the government?" [63]

"Whatever his shortcomings of manner or of method," wrote the *Independent,* "Governor Sulzer has proceeded upon the general principle that he represents the people of the state

---

60 From Roosevelt's letter to Sulzer, dated September 2, 1913, reprinted in *Public Papers of Governor Sulzer*, pp. 1487-88.

61 Quoted in *Literary Digest*, August 23, 1913, Vol. 47, p. 269.

62 August 21, 1913, Vol. 97, p. 158.

63 Syracuse *Journal*, quoted in *Literary Digest, supra*, p. 268.

and not the Tammany machine. His independence has brought down upon him the wrath of the gods in the Fourteenth Street Olympus. The nation has before it the edifying spectacle of the administration of a great state hamstrung because its chief executive, the representative of the sovereign people of the state, will not obey the dictates of a political boss." [64] *World's Work* felt that Sulzer's guilt did not "particularly matter." That he had been unfit for the high office of Governor had long been evident, it conceded, but his unfitness was not the reason for his impeachment. The real reason, it said, was "his refusal to hand over the powers of his office to Tammany." [65]

The purpose of the impeachment was stated by the Philadelphia *North American* as being: "First, to wrest from an unexpectedly honest executive State departments controlling vast patronage, the award of huge contracts, and the auditing of expenditures; second, to prevent his forcing the passage of an effective primary law, the enactment of which would be the death warrant of Tammany and its ally, special privilege; and third, to inflict such punishment upon the Governor as would deter future public officials elected by the machine from daring to exhibit like proclivities toward decency and independence." The real controversy, it concluded, was not the regularity of Governor Sulzer's campaign accounts, but whether "corrupt bossism and special privilege shall by 'constitutional' methods strangle popular government in New York State." [66]

Conspicuous among the up-state newspapers which defended Sulzer was the Albany *Knickerbocker Press,* which devoted pages to the printing of the hitherto "untold story" of what it called "the most brazen attempt in the history of the world to overthrow constitutional government without resort to bloodshed." It viewed the impeachment as part of the plan of

64 August 7, 1913, Vol. 75, pp. 293-94.

65 October, 1913, Vol. 26, p. 615.

66 Quoted in *Literary Digest*, August 23, 1913, Vol. 47, p. 268.

the "conspirators" to seize power. "Surely government by the people is a sham if a band of agents of a political boss may by the passage of a frame up resolution remove from office the highest Executive officer of the greatest State in the greatest Republic in the world. . . . Will the people of the State sit idly by and thus have their Chief Executive threatened with political extinction simply because he stood firm in his resolution to expose million dollar grafters?" [67]

From the press outside New York, Democratic as well as Republican, came a storm of protests. The Louisville *Courier-Journal,* for instance, saw in Sulzer's impeachment proof that the people of New York State were " incapable of self-government " and wept over his persecution : " Poor William Sulzer ! What siren voice of honest government could have lured him to battle on the off side of a stream having no bridges, his line of retreat leading through the enemy's country right into the deadly ambuscades and yawning rifle pits of Tammany Hall and Wall Street ? One can well believe he did not wrongfully use a dollar; that the case against him is a ' frame-up '; even that, like the dog in the fable, he was merely caught in bad company." [68] The Norfolk *Virginian-Pilot* wrote : " The whole proceeding smacks of persecution of a retaliatory nature and is therefore to be viewed with extreme suspicion." [69] The Baltimore *Sun,* less guarded, declared that the people of the country,

67 Quoted in New York *Times,* August 17.

The *Knickerbocker Press* also published a series of garish cartoons, drawn by W. K. Starrett, satirizing the impeachment, several of which are reproduced in Forrest and Malcolm, *op. cit.* One cartoon, entitled " Impeaching Sulzer," (p. 134) portrays a Liliputian Al. Smith ensconced in the hand of a colossal Murphy, who cracks the whip over the heads of the terror-stricken Assemblymen. Another, captioned "How Murphy impeached Sulzer," (p. 137) depicts the impeachment session of the Assembly, at which the Tammany members, portrayed according to the traditional concept of a politician, are shown shouting raucously, " We want the graft ! ", " Crucify him to-night ! ", " Murphy is king ! ", " Fire him out ! ", " We want the jobs ! ".

68 Editorial, August 23, reprinted in Thomas, *op. cit.,* 375-77.

69 Quoted in *Current Opinion,* Vol. 55, October, 1913, p. 224.

viewing the impeachment, " see in it what it is—the organized effort of an unscrupulous political machine, which has always stood, and still stands, for all that is worst in politics and business, to maintain its supremacy and to keep the people out of their rights." [70] The Atlantic *Journal* remarked, " Though Sulzer be guilty, the really dangerous criminal is not he, but his hypocritical accuser." [71]

On the other hand, there were many with no love for the Governor's opponents who insisted that Sulzer's wrongdoing was not to be obscured by the motives of his accusers nor by the fact that he had been working in the people's cause. Partisanship or dislike of Tammany and the system it represented should not be permitted to confuse the issue, they maintained. The sole fight was for good government and clean politics; the real enemy was political corruption which, at the time, was personified by Sulzer. The only pertinent question was whether he was guilty of the reprehensible acts alleged against him, and if he was to reinstate himself in public opinion, he must defend himself not by rhetoric, nor by crying out against the political and personal motives behind the charges, but by a frank, clear, and convincing exposition of his conduct in the matters alleged. " Is there no way to combat Tammany save that of condoning all of Sulzer's faults and marching to the fray behind that inspiring leader, brandishing in one hand his Wall Street margin accounts and in the other his incomplete affidavit of campaign receipts and expenditures? Because Murphy is known to be a sinner, must the Sulzer transgressions one and all be overlooked? " inquired the New York *Times*.[72] *Harper's Weekly,* while scorning the " incomparable hypocrisy " of the Tammany politicians in attacking a Governor of their own selection on moral grounds, declared, " Governor Sulzer cannot excuse himself by showing how bad is Tammany Hall. He must stand or fall by his own performances." [73]

70 *Ibid.*   71 *Ibid.*
72 Editorial, August 18.   73 Vol. 58, August 30, 1913, p. 3.

Even Theodore Roosevelt did not allow his dislike of Tammany to excuse the culpable acts charged to Sulzer, and advised him to give a " full and straightforward explanation and answer " to the charges at the " earliest opportunity," saying he owed it to himself and his supporters.[74] " Until the Sulzer case is disposed of," wrote the New York *Evening Sun,* " public attention will be fixt upon the main issue, and the effort to use the highway frauds to bolster up the Governor's case is at once futile and against public interest, because it weakens the effect of disclosures which must otherwise command public attention." [75] The New York *World,* hitherto a strong Sulzer supporter and an outspokenly anti-Tammany paper, while acknowledging the impeachment itself as " the most startling revelation of the degradation of government that New York had ever known," maintained that Tammanyism was not to be overthrown by men of questionable character. By giving the lie to the principles of honesty which he so blatantly professed, Sulzer invited impeachment. " A Governor," it asserted, " is supposed to keep his skirts clear and his hands clean. He is supposed to respect the dignity of his great office and keep himself out of the clutches of political blackmailers. If he violates the law, if he plays fast and loose with his own integrity, if he deceives his supporters and betrays the principles which he pretends to represent, he must take the consequences. He has betrayed the confidence and trust that honest men imposed in him, and that in itself was a form of moral treason." [76] In answer to the flood of letters from its readers disagreeing vehemently with its attitude, it wrote: " Because Sulzer's corruption has been exposed by crooks instead of by virtuous men, Sulzer becomes a hero; because Sulzer has been impeached at

74 *Public Papers of Governor Sulzer,* p. 1488. Sulzer's reply was that his statement of August 10, denying the charges of the Frawley committee, covered the case and that by advice of counsel, he would say nothing further publicly until called on by the impeachment court.—*World,* September 5.

75 Quoted in *Literary Digest,* Vol. 47, August 30, 1913, p. 305.

76 Editorial, August 14.

the dictation of the Assembly's Boss instead of at the dictates of the Assembly's conscience, Sulzer becomes a martyr." [77]

The Governor's stock market operations prompted a newspaper outside New York State to remark, " The country has been shown no such blatant hypocrisy in a public man in many a year. While gambling in stocks with recklessness that financially embarrassed him during his campaign for Governor, he was particularly vociferous about walking ' in the street called straight '; and after his election, this gubernatorial margin speculator became a zealous reformer of stock-exchange practices through legislation. That his fall may be traced to Wall Street gambling seems clear; but the man's brazen deception of the people in his public life makes the ordinary stock market trader seem a saint by comparison." [78]

During the period intervening between the impeachment and the trial, the Frawley committee and Assembly managers occupied themselves with trying to find additional material to supplement the charges previously made against Sulzer, but no real progress was made. The Frawley committee devoted its last meeting, held on September 4, mainly to an examination of the Sulzer direct primary campaign fund. It failed to show, however, that any of the money the Governor's committee received had been misused. Herbert H. Lehman, treasurer of the Direct Primary Campaign Committee, reported the receipt of a total of $17,243.54, of which he personally had advanced $5,500.[79] Other large contributors to the fund, it was revealed, included Henry Morgenthau, Louis F. Josephthal, Ralph Pulitzer, William R. Hearst, George W. Perkins and Vincent Astor, as well as several Sulzer appointees.[80] The only discovery was that in promoting his direct nominations campaign, Sulzer had exceeded by more than $7,000 the appropriation made for

77 Quoted in *Current Opinion*, Vol. 55, October, 1913, p. 223.

78 The Springfield *Republican*, quoted in *Literary Digest*, Vol. 47, August 23, 1913, p. 269.

79 *Evening Post*, September 4.

80 *Ibid.*

printing done by the Executive Department, having charged the printing of his campaign speeches and pamphlets to the state. In the opinion of the committee's counsel, the Governor had violated the state constitution by incurring expenditures in excess of the sum explicitly allowed for that purpose.[81] With this the committee adjourned, subject to the call of the chairman. Richards expressed doubt whether it would go any further in its investigation of the Governor's official conduct, confident that the testimony already adduced would be more than enough to prove his unfitness to hold office.[82] The committee was reported to have uncovered a number of other campaign contributions not listed in the sworn statement, chiefly cumulative in nature, which the attorneys for the prosecution felt would come in to better advantage as evidence before the Court of Impeachment. Frawley and the other Senators, furthermore, recognized the obvious impropriety of their proceeding any further with the investigation of the defendant or of making any comment on the disclosures thus far brought to light.[83]

The Assembly managers of the impeachment took up the investigation of the Governor's campaign fund and related matters where the Frawley committee left off, and held several public hearings with Isidor J. Kresel as counsel, beginning September 12, at their headquarters, 39 Wall Street, New York City. Documentary evidence, supported by oral testimony, was produced, which conflicted with the alleged "confession" of Mrs. Sulzer, assuming responsibility for the stock speculations disclosed by the Frawley committee. The testimony showed that the checks Mrs. Sulzer was supposed to have disposed of had been endorsed by Sulzer himself. Melville Fuller, of the brokerage firm of Harris and Fuller, reviewed in detail the Sulzer account with his firm since it was first opened, in June, 1910, and testified that he had never had any business dealings with

81 *World*, September 5.
82 *Times*, September 5.
83 *Ibid.*

Mrs. Sulzer. An interesting revelation he made was that shortly after the legislative investigating committee had begun to look into Sulzer's stock transactions, the Governor apparently anticipated his wife's " confession." He produced a letter from the Governor, dated July 14, 1913, directing the brokers to turn the stock over to Josephthal, who settled Sulzer's indebtedness, which was signed " William Sulzer. For Mrs. Sulzer." [84] Sulzer's signature, Assemblyman Levy pointed out, showed that even before his stock speculation with campaign funds had been exposed, Sulzer was already preparing to throw the entire blame on his wife.[85]

The Board of Managers uncovered still other campaign contributions not reported by Sulzer, mostly from the brewery interests, and received direct testimony showing that Sulzer had made promises of favor and reward to those who had worked or spent money for his election.[86] Testimony also was given that Sulzer was in debt to the amount of $26,500 to Hugh J. Reilly, the contractor whose claims against the Cuban government Sulzer had handled when he was chairman of the House Committee on Foreign Affairs. Reilly insisted that the money was simply a loan, but his failure to take any security in return led the impeachment managers to believe that it represented still another suppressed campaign contribution.[87] In view of the discovery of new evidence, the Board of Managers at first considered submitting supplementary impeachment articles to the Assembly for adoption. They abandoned the plan, however, after the trial began, deciding to stand on the articles already submitted.

In the meantime tremendous efforts were made by Sulzer's supporters throughout the state to stir up sentiment in his favor. A fund of $100,000 was said to have been raised to

84 *World*, September 13.
85 *Herald*, September 13.
86 *Times*, September 14.
87 *Ibid.*, September 17.

finance a campaign to force the dismissal of the impeachment charges.[88] The Executive Chamber, which had few administrative duties to perform at the time, was busily engaged in an intensive drive to accelerate expressions of public confidence, with the object of bringing outside influence to bear on the Senators, who were to sit as the Governor's judges. The Albany *Knickerbocker Press,* edited by ex-Judge Lynn J. Arnold,[89] a member of Sulzer's " war board," published a series of weekly articles containing an exposé of Murphy's " dastardly attempt to seize the government of the State." Its revelations of fraud were intended to prove " that Aaron Burr was a novice and Tweed a piker." [90] It made wholesale charges of bribery, perjury and corruption, almost unparalleled in American journalism, against legislative leaders. It accused Levy of having accepted a $5,000 "bribe " for aiding in some legislative enactment, claimed to be in possession of evidence " of sufficient weight " to indict Frawley for alleged connection with contract scandals, and declared that indictments for " perjury " would be brought against Wagner and Smith.[91] The accused leaders indignantly denied the " libelous " charges on the floor of the Legislature, attributing the attack to their stand on the Governor's impeachment, and threatened to seek redress through the courts.[92]

John A. Hennessy speeded up his investigation of all Tammany-controlled state departments, despite the fact that the Comptroller's office had cut off his funds.[93] "In more than forty roads examined in twenty-two counties, we have found only

88 *World,* August 19.

89 Arnold's strenuous efforts in Sulzer's behalf were probably prompted not so much by a desire to keep him in the governorship as to keep Glynn out.—*Times,* August 26. Glynn was publisher of a rival newspaper in Albany.

90 From an advertisement in the *World,* August 19.

91 *Times,* August 29.

92 Assembly Journal, Vol. IV, p. 129.

93 *World,* August 19. Private individuals were understood to have provided the means to continue the investigation.—*Ibid.,* August 4.

three that pass muster, and only one that is clean all the way," he wrote in his report to the Governor. " Fraud stands out as clearly as a mountain peak from a valley. All we need is the men and the time to get the legal evidence." In one county (Rockland) he found about seventy per cent of the road building fraudulent.[94] Sworn evidence in his possession, he asserted, led to a " trail of graft " of approximately $5,000,000, implicating prominent government officials and several up-state Murphy lieutenants.[95] " It is a much bigger struggle than the fight against Tweed and against the canal ring," he wrote in the New York *Evening Mail*. " In the entrenchments of the thieves will be found men who have been elevated to high and supposedly virtuous office, and men who have to-day the confidence of their fellow citizens. The trail of graft will run from the Controller's office into the banks and out again. The misuse of the excise department will leave, when exposed, a trail of shame and blacken some of the men now loudly crying for the life of the Governor. When the story of the canal system is told, the highway thefts won't look so big. When the State Election Department is fully investigated, the people will stand aghast in contemplation of the men selected to give them pure elections." [96] But Sulzer's impeachment broke the force of his investigation. Horgan, Delaney, and other witnesses summoned by Hennessy, refused to appear, maintaining that since the impeachment had automatically removed Sulzer from office, Hennessy no longer had the power to conduct investigations as his personal representative.[97]

Sulzer himself sought to win public sympathy by posing as a victim of political vengeance. In a letter sent to a meeting of his supporters, called to protest against the impeachment, he bitterly criticized his enemies and accused them of employing

94 Reprinted in Sulzer's *Life and Speeches*, Vol. I, p. 8.
95 *World*, September 8.
96 Quoted in *Literary Digest*, Vol. 47, August 30, 1913, p. 304.
97 *World*, August 16 and 22.

a band of adventurers and criminals to bring baseless charges against him in an attempt to discredit him in the eyes of the people and to get him out of office. " I am having a terrific struggle to resist the seizure of the State by those who have looted it, and would prostitute its government for private gain," he wrote. " When Mr. Murphy and his allies found out that they could not make a tool of me they attempted to block my every step. They could not, however, stop the machinery of justice which I had set in motion against the criminals throughout the State, who have robbed taxpayers of millions of dollars. There was only one way for my enemies to prevent me from sending these thieves to the penitentiary, and that way was to impeach me and get me out of office." [98]

Sensational reports were circulated in the public press by persons close to Sulzer that in order to block the Court of Impeachment from bringing him to trial, an effort would be made by his " war board," a group of his most trusted lay advisers, to procure the indictment of Alfred E. Smith, Aaron J. Levy, and other legislative leaders on a charge of high treason, for having conspired to coerce certain members of the Assembly to vote for the impeachment resolution, in obedience to Murphy's orders. The action of the Assembly, it would be charged, was part of a criminal plot of the Tammany Boss and his board of strategy to seize control of the government of the state for Tammany Hall.[99] The report persisted for some time despite the vigorous denial of D-Cady Herrick, chief of Sulzer's counsel, that his legal advisers would have anything to do with the plan.[100] Arnold submitted evidence touching this alleged conspiracy to Charles S. Whitman, district attorney of New York County, but failed to convince him of the necessity of instituting criminal proceedings.[101] To the impersonal charge

98 *Times*, September 8.
99 *World*, August 25.
100 *Times*, August 26.
101 *World*, August 29.

that Tammany had influenced the impeachment vote, James C. Garrison, a newspaper man and publicity agent for Sulzer, added a direct one of bribery. " I declare now and positively," he declared in the public press, " that Tammany paid cash for the four votes it needed to pass the impeachment resolution." [102] Garrison was directed to appear before the Assembly Judiciary Committee to substantiate his accusation but persistently refused to answer any questions as to the source of his information. His advice to the committee was to call Murphy, Wagner, Frawley, and others who, he said, could give them " some real information." [103] The Assembly found him guilty of contempt for having offended its " dignity " and " the honor and integrity of its members," and ordered his imprisonment until the adjournment of the Legislature, unless sooner discharged by the Assembly.[104] Garrison was arrested in the Assembly Chamber on September 18 and was kept in the Albany County penitentiary until after the trial, when he was released on a writ of habeas corpus.[105]

During the few weeks between the impeachment and trial, the Legislature met at irregular intervals and attended to little else beyond the details growing out of the impeachment. In compliance with acting Governor Glynn's request, it passed a number of appropriation and deficiency bills, including an appropriation of $75,000 to meet the expenses of the impeachment trial.[106] Concurrent resolutions were passed ordering the arrest of Colwell and Sarecky for contempt of the Legislature in refusing to answer questions before the Frawley com-

102 *Ibid.*, August 16.

103 *Ibid.*, August 29.

104 Assembly Journal, Vol. IV, p. 148.

105 Alfred E. Smith, *Up to Now: an Autobiography*, (New York, 1929), p. 131.

106 Assembly Journal, Vol. IV, p. 134; Senate Journal, Vol. II, pp. 156-58. Supplementary bills were subsequently passed appropriating $121,200 for payment of counsel for the Board of Managers and additional expenses of the trial, and $40,000 as compensation of counsel for Sulzer.—Legislative Record and Index, 1913, Ext. Session, p. 4.

mittee.[107] Aaron J. Levy, chairman of the impeachment Board
of Managers, openly accused Sulzer of hiding Colwell, all
efforts of counsel to locate him either in this country or in
Canada having proven fruitless, so as to prevent his giving
testimony at the trial about his stock transactions.[108]

On the eve of the trial, both sides expressed utmost confidence in the outcome. " I expect a fair trial," declared the
Governor, " and I know that I shall be acquitted." [109] Displaying much of his old-time vigor, he personally directed in a large
measure the collection of testimony which he was sure would
exonerate him. Levy, on the other hand, asserted that the evidence adduced would be so " horrifying and repulsive that the
court could not help but convict." [110] Wagner predicted simply
that the decision would be " in accordance with the evidence,"
and took occasion to add, " I am getting tired of all this talk
that William Sulzer is being persecuted by Tammany Hall.
Neither Tammany Hall nor any other political organization will
sway the result of the impeachment trial. The verdict will be
influenced neither by the sentiment of the Senators nor by
public opinion. Every Senator will feel as fully the responsibility resting upon him as if he were a Judge of the Court of
Appeals." [111] For a time there were rumors that Sulzer's
lawyers were seeking to obtain a postponement of the trial
until after the fall elections, in the belief that a display of anti-
Tammany sentiment at the polls would react in his favor.[112]
Levy also reported that Sulzer had offered to resign if the
impeachment charges were dropped, to spare himself the in-
dignity and humiliation of a trial, but this was emphatically
denied by the Governor's counsel.[113]

107 Assembly Journal, Vol. IV, p. 130.
108 *Times*, September 16.
109 *Ibid.*, September 18.
110 *Ibid.*
111 *Ibid.*
112 *Ibid.*, August 26.
113 *Ibid.*, September 14.

Immediately following the vote of the Assembly to impeach Sulzer, a vital constitutional question arose. Who was to act as Governor in the interim between the filing of the articles of impeachment and the verdict of the Court of Impeachment? The anti-Sulzer forces maintained that the presentation of impeachment charges automatically suspended Sulzer from office and put Lieutenant-Governor Glynn in his place. Their contention was based on Article IV, section 6, of the state constitution which states: " In case of the impeachment of the Governor, or his removal from office, death, inability to discharge the powers and duties of the said office, resignation, or absence from the State, the powers and duties of the office shall devolve upon the Lieutenant-Governor for the residue of the term, or until the disability shall cease." [114] Moreover, it was pointed out, the Code of Criminal Procedure (section 129) provides: " No officer shall exercise his office, after articles of impeachment against him shall have been delivered to the Senate, until he is acquitted." Glynn believed himself entitled at once to exercise all the prerogatives of Chief Executive and in a statement issued on August 13 announced, " I regard myself as acting Governor of New York State and I believe there should be a test as soon as possible to determine this definitely." [115] Sulzer declined, however, to honor his demand to vacate the Executive offices or to surrender the state privy seal or any records relating to the Executive Department.[116] After consultation with his counsel, he wrote Glynn, " I shall continue to exercise and discharge the constitutional duties of the Governor of the State of New York, first, among other things, because I am advised that the Assembly at its present extraordinary session possessed and possesses no power or authority to prefer articles of impeachment, and, secondly, because the Lieutenant-Governor of the State is not authorized

114 Constitution of the State of New York, as amended and in force January 1, 1913. Reprinted in the Legislative Manual, 1913, pp. 65-188.

115 *World*, August 14.

116 *Ibid.*, August 16.

to act as Governor in case of the impeachment of the Governor, unless such impeachment is sustained." [117]

His first contention, that the Assembly had exceeded its constitutional authority in impeaching him at an extraordinary session, was based upon the provision of the state constitution which asserts that " at extraordinary sessions no subject shall be acted upon, except such as the Governor may recommend for consideration." [118] His second assumption, that the powers and duties of the Governor did not devolve upon the Lieutenant-Governor unless the impeachment was sustained, was based upon the supposition that the word " impeachment " in Article IV, section 6, was used in the loose sense of conviction on impeachment charges. To prove that that was the intent of the framers of the constitution, friends of Sulzer called attention to the phraseology of Article VI, section 13, of the constitution, which reads, " Judgment in cases of impeachment shall not extend further than to removal from office, or removal from office and disqualification to hold and enjoy any office of honor, trust or profit under this State; but *the party impeached* shall be liable to indictment and punishment according to law." The words " the party impeached," they maintained, were obviously equivalent to the party punished or convicted under impeachment. The same section prohibits a judicial officer from serving while under impeachment charges until he shall have been acquitted. Inasmuch as the article specifies only judicial officers, the inference might logically be drawn that no other officers should suffer that disability, but should continue to serve even when awaiting trial. This practice would be in accordance with the federal constitution, upon which almost all state constitutions were modelled. Andrew Johnson's authority as President, for example, was not interrupted by his impeachment. That no such prohibition was intended, as respects the Governor, might also be reasonably inferred

117 *Ibid.*
118 Article IV, section 4.

from the injunction in the state constitution, that "on the trial of an impeachment against the Governor or Lieutenant-Governor, the Lieutenant-Governor shall not act as a member of the court." [119] Had the constitution intended that the Lieutenant-Governor could fill the Governor's office from the moment the Assembly preferred charges, then it need not have prohibited him from acting as a judge during the impeachment trial.

Not only did the general provisions of the constitution regarding impeachment imply that the Governor should retain his office, but it would be manifestly against public interest for a bare majority of a single house of the Legislature to be able to suspend him in advance of trial, argued Sulzer's friends. A hostile majority in the Assembly might at any time, by resorting to the impeachment process, depose the state's Chief Executive for months from an office the people gave him, while awaiting trial on any comparatively insignificant and irrelevant charge. A situation like that could hardly have been contemplated by the framers of the constitution, they said.

All these arguments were dismissed by the supporters of Glynn's title to the Governorship as futile and as designed simply to befog the question. The controlling provision of the constitution was Article IV, section 6, of whose meaning there could be no possible doubt. Any attempt to resist its operation would stamp Sulzer as a usurper. In denying the validity of the impeachment, Sulzer's adherents seemed to confuse the function of the Assembly as an impeaching body with its function as a legislative body. Though its legislative acts during an extraordinary session were limited to those recommended by the Governor, its judicial acts were not. Article VI, section 13 of the state constitution specifically says: "The Assembly shall have the power of impeachment, by a vote of a majority of all the members elected." The Assembly, as an inquisitorial body, was not restricted in any way except that it

119 Article VI, section 13.

must act by the vote of a majority of all the members elected. For purposes of impeachment the Assembly might therefore convene and act at any time, during a regular or extraordinary session of the Legislature, or even independently of its convocation by the Governor.

The argument that Sulzer's impeachment would not occur until his conviction after trial betrayed ignorance of an elementary distinction. Impeachment, they maintained, meant accusation by a competent impeaching power and not conviction by the tribunal authorized to try the accused official. This difference was universally recognized in legal terminology and was apparent in the text of the constitution itself. The title of section 13 of Article VI is " Trial of Impeachments," impeachment being obviously something that precedes trial. The same section provides that " the Assembly shall have the power of impeachment," thus clearly distinguishing impeachment from conviction, a power lodged not with the Assembly but with the Senate and Justices of the Court of Appeals.

The disagreement over the meaning of the constitutional provision relating to impeachment thus produced two claimants to the Governorship, each receiving recognition from a substantial following. Inasmuch as he did not recognize the legality of the impeachment proceedings, Sulzer firmly refused to yield his office to Glynn. He did suggest, however, that in order to avoid " any unseemly struggle," the two agree on a test case as a means of submitting the question to the courts for decision.[120] Glynn emphatically rejected the proposal, saying he could not question the functions already imposed on him by the constitution. " It is beyond any power to barter away any of the functions attaching to the office in which I am placed by your impeachment," he wrote Sulzer. " Any attempt on my part to do so or to stipulate a method by which it might be done, would properly place me in the position you now occupy—that of being impeached for malfeasance in office. I

120 *World*, August 16.

cannot and I will not attempt to do it." [121] The entire matter, he pointed out, was already in the hands of the Court of Impeachment, the highest court in the state, and no judgment that any lower court might render would therefore be binding. In closing, he notified his rival that he would perform every function of the office of Governor unless " restrained by your illegal action or by physical force." [122]

Sulzer remained in undisturbed possession of the machinery of the Executive Department, continued to receive mail addressed to the Governor of New York, and to sign official papers.[123] Glynn was satisfied to handle at the Lieutenant-Governor's office such of the state business as came to him. " I am the Governor no matter where I may be transacting business," he declared.[124] Irate Tammany politicians and legislators were said to have urged him to summon the Albany police or to call out a regiment of the National Guard, which was ready to obey his orders, and storm the citadel of his impeached rival, but Glynn announced that no attempt would be made to wrest the Executive offices from Sulzer by force. " I do not intend to enter into any physical contest with Mr. Sulzer over the office of Governor," he said. " As far as I am concerned, there will be no circus or military manoeuvres about occupying the Executive Chamber. The law is supreme." [125] At the same time Herrick issued a reassuring statement on behalf of Sulzer that the Governor " will meet the charges made against him in an orderly and dignified way and will do nothing unbecoming the dignity of the State and will engage in no physical scramble to assert his rights to discharge the functions pertaining to the office of Governor." [126] Nevertheless, Sulzer took no chances

121 *Tribune*, August 16.

122 *World*, August 16.   123 *Ibid.*, August 15.

124 *Ibid.*, August 17. The Attorney-General decided that the seal of the Lieutenant-Governor under existing conditions carried with it the same authority as that of the privy seal of the Chief Executive.—*Ibid.*, August 16.

125 *Ibid.*, August 14.

126 *Ibid.*

and ordered all records of the Executive Department placed under lock and key. The great seal was secured by a steel chain and a new lock was put on the door leading from the Executive Chamber to the Governor's private office.[127] He even stationed a squad of armed guards in the corridor adjoining the Executive Chamber every night.[128]

And so, until the Court of Impeachment met, five weeks later, and decided that the impeachment was legal, there existed the anomalous situation of a divided state, two men claiming to be Governor and exercising such duties of the Chief Executive as came within their reach. The rivalry over the Governorship grew daily more confusing. Sheriffs from other states, seeking the signing of extradition papers, were perplexed as to whom to approach. One West Virginia arm of the law solved the problem by soliciting the signatures of both " Governors." [129] The state departments quickly aligned themselves as partisans in the contest. Officials of anti-Tammany departments and those personally associated with Sulzer continued to look to him for orders, while the Legislature and those whom the Legislature controlled transferred their allegiance to Glynn. The dual system of Governors seriously interfered with the efficiency of the state departments. Department heads hesitated about doing anything, apprehensive of complications that might follow.[130] Local banks held up payroll payments, uncertain as to whose certification to honor.[131] The Highways Commissioner, Carlisle, was unable to get any repair contracts approved by the Tammany-controlled Department of Efficiency and Economy or by the state Comptroller.[132] Few roads were repaired and no new ones were built.[133] Public business at times came almost to a standstill.

The first official pronouncement came from Attorney-General Carmody who, on August 18, in response to an inquiry

127 *Ibid.*, August 16.
128 *Tribune*, August 16.
129 *Ibid.*, August 15.
130 *Times*, August 17.
131 *World*, August 17.
132 *Ibid.*, August 22.
133 *Ibid.*, September 1.

from Mitchell May, Secretary of State, declared Glynn acting Governor, pending the trial and determination of the impeachment charges lodged against Sulzer. " When the Governor is impeached by the Assembly," he stated in his opinion, " all of his powers are automatically suspended until he has been acquitted or the impeachment proceedings dismissed by the court of impeachment. In the meantime the Lieutenant-Governor acts as Governor. This is the plain intent of the Constitution. Any other construction would nullify its express provisions." [134] He justified this conclusion by an exhaustive examination into the history of constitution making in the state. The term " impeachment " was used in the constitution in its ordinary and accepted meaning of presentation of charges and there was nothing to indicate any intention to distort its meaning to " conviction." Ever since 1784, he pointed out, both the organic as well as the statutory law contemplated the suspension of an impeached officer from the exercise of his office until acquitted.[135] The Attorney-General also took occasion to deny the contention of Sulzer's legal advisers that the Assembly was without power to act on the impeachment resolution because the Legislature, of which it formed a part, was convened at the time in extraordinary session for other purposes. The impeachment of the Governor, in his judgment, was a judicial, not a legislative function, hence might properly be taken by the Assembly on its own initiative whenever it chose. " In impeachment proceedings the Assembly acts judicially pursuant to power conferred upon it by the Constitution. This power not being limited in extent nor restricted as to procedure, may be exercised at any time the Assembly may determine upon," he held.[136]

134 Annual Report of the Attorney-General, 1913, Vol. II, p. 550. The entire opinion is printed in *Ibid.*, pp. 538-50.

135 The earlier constitutions made exact provision for the succession of the Lieutenant-Governor to act until the Governor was *acquitted.*

136 This opinion was subsequently sustained by the Impeachment Court. See p. 194.

Sulzer declined to comment on Carmody's opinion but in discussing it privately, declared it would make no difference whatever in his determination to hold on to the Executive office as the "real Governor." [137] He simply proceeded to change the combination of the safe in the Executive offices in which important official documents were kept.[138] The opinion did, nevertheless, fortify the position of Glynn, for it was certain that no head of a state department, no matter what his degree of personal loyalty to Sulzer, would now dare to ignore the ruling of the Attorney-General. Two days after the opinion was rendered, Glynn issued a proclamation in which he summoned the heads of all departments to rally to his support in order that he might bring some order out of the prevailing chaos in the administrative affairs of the state. He disclaimed any intention of using his temporary occupancy of the Governorship to inaugurate any new policies or to make any radical changes in the civil personnel of the state, pending a decision from the High Court of Impeachment. "Under me as acting Governor there will be no political earthquakes and no factional reprisals," was his reassuring statement.[139] Glynn's fortunes steadily improved and he gained by every development in the official business of the state. The Adjutant-General of the National Guard, the Secretary of State, the Trustees of Public Buildings, and others gradually transferred their allegiance to him. His recognition by the Comptroller's office gave him control over the purse-strings of the Executive Department. In New York City, the Corporation Counsel, Archibald R. Watson, advised the Commissioner of Correction not to surrender prisoners on warrants signed by William Sulzer as Governor.[140] On August 27 Glynn was formally recognized by

137 *Times*, August 19.

138 *World*, August 20.

139 *Times*, August 21.

140 In an exhaustive opinion, Watson maintained that the Governor had been constitutionally impeached, the Assembly's power of impeachment being "unrestricted by time, condition, or occasion," and that the mere finding of

the Legislature. The issue was raised in the Assembly in connection with the receipt of a message from the Lieutenant-Governor calling attention to the pressing need of financial legislation to enable the state to meet the interest payments upon its bonds. Assemblyman Schaap objected to the reading of the message on the ground that it had no standing in the Legislature, inasmuch as William Sulzer was still Governor of the state. The Speaker dismissed the point of order, announcing that under the provisions of the constitution, " the Lieutenant-Governor is now acting Governor." [141] The decision of the chair was appealed but was upheld by a vote of 48 to 29.[142] In the Senate, Glynn's authority was not seriously questioned. Senator Wende, of Buffalo, Sulzer's unofficial " floor leader," protested the receipt of Glynn's message but did not press his objections, permitting the reading of the message.[143]

After nearly a month of uncertainty, a test of Sulzer's position was finally made in one of the state courts. Habeas corpus proceedings were instituted designed to compel the warden of a New York City penitentiary to honor the pardon granted by Sulzer as " Governor of the State of New York " to one Joseph G. Robin, a banker imprisoned for financial irregularities.[144] The warden had refused to honor the writ on the ground that Governor Sulzer, having been lawfully impeached, was no longer competent to discharge the powers of the executive office. General Benjamin F. Tracy, volunteer counsel, argued for the validity of the pardon, rehearsing the familiar contentions that the Governor had not been legally impeached, inasmuch as an extraordinary session of the Legislature was powerless to consider any subject on its own initiative, and that the

the articles of impeachment created a legal and constitutional disability to the exercise of official functions until, by acquittal, the disability was removed. The opinion is quoted in full in the *Times* of August 17.

141 Assembly Journal, Vol. IV, p. 123.

142 *Ibid.*   143 *World*, August 28.

144 *The People ex rel. Joseph G. Robin, Relator, v. Patrick Hayes, Warden of New York Penitentiary, Respondent.*

mere adoption of the impeachment charges did not disqualify him from continuing in office, the word impeachment as used in the state constitution contemplating conviction. Of the contention that the Assembly could meet at any time, anywhere, to consider impeachment, he said, " If this be true, then a mere political majority of the Assembly may meet at any time, in Tammany Hall even, without notice and without the presence of the minority, and impeach the Governor and thus suspend him from office until after trial and acquittal." [145] Corporation Counsel Watson argued for the sufficiency of the impeachment, maintaining that its constitutionality could be tested only before the Court of Impeachment itself.

Justice Hasbrouck, presiding at a special term of the Supreme Court in Kingston, ruled the pardon void. Sulzer had been lawfully impeached, and while awaiting trial had no right to exercise any executive functions. The power of the Assembly to impeach was judicial, not legislative, therefore beyond the control of the Governor. The Assembly, he declared, whether in regular or extraordinary session, or whether self-convened, " is the sole impeaching functionary, and, in its exercise of power, it is beyond the let or hindrance of the executive or the courts. It is the exclusive and final judge of the occasion or time it shall select to impeach, and of the acts of the governor it may specify as grounds for impeachment." With reference to the disability of the Governor, he ruled it " perfectly clear " that he was shorn of his power by Article IV, section 6 of the state constitution, " unjustifiable and unreasonable " as the provision might appear. Unlike the federal constitution, he pointed out, the state constitution evaded the fundamental rule that a man is presumed innocent until proved guilty, thereby making the suspension of an impeached executive from office mandatory.[146]

145 *World*, September 9.

146 Miscellaneous Reports, New York, Vol. 82, pp. 165-74. The decision was subsequently upheld in the Appellate Division (163 App. Div. 725-30). An appeal to the Court of Appeals was dismissed (212 N. Y. 603).

Another appeal to the courts was made by Sulzer's friends a few days later, when proceedings were instituted before Supreme Court Justice Alden Chester to restrain the Court of Impeachment from hearing the charges. The application for an absolute writ of prohibition was brought by a taxpayer,[147] on the ground that the Assembly could not legally adopt articles of impeachment at an extraordinary session. In denying the application, Justice Chester laid down the principle that the Supreme Court of the state was powerless to interfere with the prerogatives of a court of higher jurisdiction, and that the Court of Impeachment alone was vested with the authority to inquire into the validity of the impeachment proceedings.[148]

Notwithstanding these adverse decisions, Sulzer did not formally recognize Glynn as acting Governor until the day after the impeachment trial began, when his secretary, Platt, sent a letter to Glynn, transmitting certain papers for his official action. In conceding Glynn's right to exercise the duties of Governor, pending the outcome of the trial, Sulzer made it clear that he was actuated solely by a desire to promote the business of the state government, but that he still denied the Assembly's jurisdiction to impeach.[149] Sulzer continued, of course, to occupy the " people's House " until his removal from office.

147 Samuel A. Fowler, of Rensselaer.
148 *Times*, September 14.
149 *World*, September 20.

CHAPTER VI

THE IMPEACHMENT TRIAL

THE High Court of Impeachment assembled in the Senate Chamber at the Capitol on September 18, 1913, at twelve o'clock noon. It was composed of forty-eight Senators [1] and nine Judges of the Court of Appeals,[2] Chief Judge Edgar M. Cullen, presiding. A formidable battery of counsel were arrayed on both sides. Among those who appeared on behalf of the impeachment managers were Alton B. Parker, former Chief Judge of the Court of Appeals, John P. Stanchfield, Democratic candidate for governor in 1900, Edgar T. Brackett, former Republican leader in the state Senate, Eugene L. Richards, attorney to the Frawley committee, Isidor J. Kresel, former assistant district attorney in New York County, and Hiram C. Todd, prominent Albany attorney. Leading counsel for Governor Sulzer included D-Cady Herrick, former Judge of the State Supreme Court and Democratic candidate for governor in 1904, Irving G. Vann, former Associate Judge of the Court of Appeals, Harvey D. Hinman, former state Senator, Louis Marshall, distinguished constitutional lawyer, and Austen G. Fox, former special district attorney in New York County. With the taking of the constitutional oath by each member of the court to judge the case impartially, and the adoption of rules of procedure to govern the trial, the way was cleared for the great legal battle.[3]

1 Owing to the resignation of Franklin D. Roosevelt to become Assistant Secretary of the Navy, and the imprisonment of Stephen J. Stilwell for attempted extortion, there were two vacancies in the Senate at the time. Senator John C. Fitzgerald was absent on account of illness.

2 Three of these — Justices Hiscock, Chase and Miller — were Supreme Court Judges who had been assigned to the Court of Appeals. One of the seven elected Judges, John Clinton Gray, was absent in Europe.

3 A verbatim report of the trial appears in *Proceedings of the Court for the Trial of Impeachments; the People of the State of New York by the Assembly thereof against William Sulzer, as Governor*, 2 Vols., Albany, 1913. Referred to hereinafter as *Proceedings*.

It was the avowed purpose of Sulzer's counsel to interpose every possible legal and constitutional barrier in the hope of stopping the trial before the stage of taking testimony was reached. The first legal skirmish was precipitated when Herrick challenged the eligibility of Senators Frawley, Ramsperger, Sanner, and Wagner to sit as members of the court. The first three he objected to on the ground that, as members of the Legislative Investigating Committee, they had already formed an opinion as to the Governor's guilt and, if permitted to serve, would be assuming the dual role of prosecutors and judges. Senator Wagner was personally interested in the outcome of the trial, it was contended, because in the event of Sulzer's conviction, he would succeed to the office of Lieutenant-Governor. His challenge, Herrick argued, was based upon the fundamental principle of justice that every accused was entitled to be tried before an impartial tribunal, and in that respect the Court of Impeachment was subject to the same rules of law as applied to other courts. Parker, on behalf of the impeachment managers, contended that neither the constitution nor the statutes of the state gave the court the power to exclude any of its qualified members, on account of interest in the result of the trial or for any other cause, citing numerous precedents in support of his argument.[4] The Presiding Judge agreed that there was no legal ground for the retirement of the Senators in question, declaring that each member of the court had to determine for himself the propriety of his sitting. The court unanimously voted not to entertain the challenge, the four Senators objected to, upon their own request, being excused from voting.

Their first line of attack swept away, counsel for Sulzer next assailed the validity of the impeachment with a motion that the proceedings instituted by the Assembly be dismissed on the ground that they were " without jurisdiction and null,

4 Notably the trial of President Johnson.

void and of no effect." [5] In support of this motion, Marshall delivered a long and scholarly address in which he traversed the history of impeachments from earliest times. His basic proposition was that the Assembly had no power of impeachment except at a regular session, and when convened in extraordinary session, only upon the express recommendation of the Governor. In contradiction to the opinion of the Attorney-General, he maintained that the Assembly, even when acting as an accusing body, was not absolved from the limitations and restraints of the constitution. To permit a bare majority of the Assembly the power to impeach an executive or judicial official anywhere and at any time, he declared, would set " a vicious precedent " and open the door to serious abuses.[6] It would expose every officer of the state to malicious personal and political influences, and threaten the very permanence of our republican institutions.

In replying for the prosecution, Parker asserted that the Assembly's constitutional power of impeachment was " absolute and complete " and might therefore be exercised at any time.[7] From a detailed analysis of the constitution and of the history of impeachment in the state, he concluded that the constitutional limitation that at extraordinary sessions no subject might be acted upon except such as the Governor recommended for consideration, applied only to *legislative* subjects, and not to judicial acts, such as impeachment. In supplementing his associate's argument, Brackett maintained that the public interest demanded that the Governor, and for that matter every official, be at all times subject to restraint and removal. To express his scorn of the Governor's shielding himself behind technicalities, he quoted the remark of Charles Sumner, made at the trial of President Johnson, " Great God, is there any question possible except is this man guilty? " [8] In his rebuttal Marshall force-

5 *Proceedings*, I, p. 57.
6 *Ibid.*, p. 81.
7 *Ibid.*, p. 177.
8 *Ibid.*, p. 188.

fully rejected the opinion that the Assembly's power was plenary, maintaining that the constitutional limitation relating to extraordinary sessions applied to all subjects dealt with by the Legislature, whether executive, legislative or judicial in nature. Commenting on the contention of the prosecution counsel that the Assembly could meet at any time and impeach, and that all it had to do was to present the articles of impeachment to the President of the Senate, he made the significant remark, " Of course articles of impeachment could not be presented to the President of the Senate on 14th Street in the city of New York or at the Throne Room at Delmonico's in that city and make of that an impeachment," (an allusion to the Tammany boss's scenes of activity).[9] Should the Governor be guilty of treasonable conduct during a recess of the Legislature, he pointed out, he could be proceeded against under the Penal Code. With the completion of argument by opposing counsel, the court went into executive session and, by a vote of 51 to 1, denied the motion to dismiss the proceedings.[10] In explaining his vote, Chief Judge Cullen expressed disagreement with the opinion of prosecution counsel that the Assembly had the inherent right to meet at any time and present articles of impeachment, but he did concur in their view that the constitutional limitation relating to extraordinary sessions did not apply to the power of impeachment. Cullen's clear exposition of the law left little doubt on that point.

The next move of the defense was to demand the dismissal of the first, second and sixth articles of impeachment, relating to the Governor's suppression of campaign contributions and his use of funds for speculative purposes, as alleging offenses committed prior to the time he was inaugurated as Governor. Herrick opened the battle against the three articles under attack with an exhaustive argument to the court in which he quoted

9 *Ibid.*, p. 212.

10 The dissenting vote was cast by Senator Wende, a Democrat of Erie County, conspicuous in his allegiance to the accused Governor.

an array of authorities beginning with Jefferson and Hamilton. According to the law of the state, he contended, public officials could be impeached only for wilful and corrupt misconduct while in office; offenses committed prior to the assumption of office were therefore not impeachable. The making of a false statement of campaign contributions and swearing to it were not offenses against the duties of the office of Governor. Unless some limitations were imposed on the power of impeachment, he warned, it might easily be misused for partisan or personal purposes. "If the Assembly," he said, "can impeach for any cause that it sees fit, for acts done by an official during his term of office, as well as for acts done by him when a private citizen before he had become a public official, thereby suspending him indefinitely from discharging the duties of his office, then the door is opened wide to an unscrupulous majority to impeach an official whose conduct in office has been upright and honest, who has stood in the way of graft and corruption, but who, perchance, before coming into office has been guilty of some indiscretion, or worse. To impeach, in fact, not for official misconduct, but because of his refusal to abuse the powers of his office." [11]

Herrick also held that Sulzer had not violated any constitutional or statutory provision by the manner he had adopted in certifying to the contributions made to his campaign fund. The Penal Code [12] and the Corrupt Practices Act,[13] he asserted, required a candidate to file a statement only of campaign contributions made *by* him, not *to* him; nor did the law require an oath. Incorrect statements of facts inserted in an affidavit that was not called for by law consequently did not constitute perjury. Continuing the same line of argument, Fox contended that the terseness of the constitution was not equivalent to a grant of unlimited power, never claimed before in any con-

11 *Proceedings*, I, p. 233.
12 Section 776.
13 Article 16.

stitutional convention nor sustained by any court of law. By impeaching Sulzer for acts committed prior to his term of office, the Assembly had therefore been guilty of grave usurpation of power. Alluding to the political motives animating the impeachment, he declared, " This action of the Assembly is nothing more or less than an attempt to induce the State of New York to trample under foot its own fundamental law, in order that a present advantage may be gained in the restriction and repression of an individual unpopular with certain factions in the State." [14] A careful examination of judicial precedents, he pointed out, failed to disclose a single case, either in New York State or in any other state or under the United States, where an officer had been removed by judicial process for acts done while not in office.[15]

Counsel for the impeachment managers based their refutation on the principle that impeachment might be had for anything in the nature of a crime that demonstrated unfitness to exercise the functions of office. Parker emphasized the fact that each of the state constitutions successively broadened the impeaching power of the Assembly. The constitution of 1777 gave the Assembly the power of impeaching all officers of the state " for mal and corrupt conduct in their respective offices; " the constitution of 1821 added " and for high crimes and misdemeanors," with no limitation as to when committed; the constitution of 1846 removed all limitations, saying simply, " The Assembly shall have the power of impeachment by vote of a majority of all the members elected." That phraseology remained unchanged in subsequent constitutions. In a telling address, replete with condemnatory allusions to Sulzer, Brackett argued the proposition that the offenses charged to Sulzer were vitally connected with his official term, hence im-

14 *Proceedings*, I, p. 387.

15 Officials had been successfully impeached for acts done during a prior term of office, as in the case of Judge George G. Barnard, of the New York State Supreme Court.

peachable. In this connection he quoted former Governor Tilden's opinion that " misconduct wholly outside the functions of an office may be of such a nature as to exercise a reflected influence upon those functions and to disqualify and incapacitate an officer from usefully performing those functions." [16] He described the Corrupt Practices Act as " an official vestibule " to office, linking the position of a candidate legally with that of the official. " Misconduct as a candidate corrupts public duty in office. Wickedness in a candidate is as surely inherited by the official as any hereditary taint by the child from the parent." [17] The making of a false statement of receipts and expenditures, he therefore concluded, was just as much the commission of a crime as the violation of the official oath taken upon induction into office.

In closing the argument for the prosecution, Kresel disputed the contention of defense counsel that the election law did not require a candidate to file a sworn statement of campaign receipts. The whole history of legislation upon the subject of campaign contributions and expenditures, he maintained, showed clearly that the one purpose of the law was to give such contributions and expenditures the widest publicity, and specifically contemplated that a candidate report not only contributions made by him but also those made to him or to his agent.

At the close of the argument as to what constituted impeachable offenses, the Presiding Judge suggested that the objections raised by the defenders of the Governor to articles one, two and six be overruled without opinion, and that the final determination of the motion be deferred until all the testimony had been heard. This procedure would leave the door open to the introduction of every bit of evidence bearing upon the question of Sulzer's guilt or innocence. The court adopted the suggestion by a vote of 49 to 7, all the Judges of the Court of Appeals

16 *Proceedings*, I, p. 305.
17 *Ibid.*, p. 315.

voting with the majority. With this ruling, the last of the preliminary constitutional questions was disposed of, and the way was cleared to the consideration of the case on its merits.

The case proper opened on September 24 with the reading by the clerk of Sulzer's formal answer to the impeachment articles preferred against him. It was a general denial of all allegations. In reply to the first and second articles, however, he added that at the time of making and filing the statement, he believed it to be true and accurate. Richards then delivered the opening address in which he briefly outlined the facts in support of each of the impeachment articles, based largely on the evidence uncovered by the Frawley committee, which the impeachment managers intended to prove. He sounded the keynote of the prosecution in the words: " We shall show that he [Sulzer] was busier in getting money and in trying to get it than he was in getting votes. He went at his campaign for money with system, with cool deliberation and cunning schemes to conceal what he got." [18]

The bulk of the evidence introduced on behalf of the impeachment managers related almost entirely to the first, second, and sixth charges against the Governor, alleging the filing of a false statement of campaign contributions, perjury, and stock market gambling. A steady stream of witnesses, whose generosity Sulzer apparently had reason to conceal, took the stand to testify to Sulzer's solicitation of contributions for which he made no accounting, and a multitude of exhibits in the form of checks and letters were put in evidence. Most of the evidence revealed little more than what had already been disclosed by the Frawley committee, but a number of additional checks for substantial amounts, contributed to Sulzer's campaign fund, were made public for the first time during the trial. In the procession of witnesses were bankers, liquor dealers, lawyers, brewers, merchants, brokers, and politicians. Of the thirty-nine contributions testified to, only four appeared in Sulzer's sworn

18 *Ibid.*, p. 437.

statement of campaign receipts.[19] For the most part the witnesses were manifestly reluctant to testify and acted as if they would have preferred to avoid any public discussion of their contributions to Sulzer's campaign.

A heated verbal battle between opposing counsel arose as to the admissibility of testimony relating to unreported contributions not enumerated in the formal impeachment articles. The defense contended that the court had no right to go beyond the Assembly indictment and that such evidence was therefore immaterial and incompetent. The prosecution, in reply, argued that the board of managers was not limited to the items specified in the charges, but had a perfect right to prove that Sulzer had received and failed to account for other items, as part of a common purpose, namely, to conceal sources of money which might become the subject of criticism. " I concede," was Stanchfield's scathing comment, " that the failure to report one contribution might be an accident; the failure to report two contributions might be a coincidence; the failure to report a hundred is a crime." [20] Convinced that the widest latitude should be given to all testimony that might provide the slightest illumination on the subject under discussion, Chief Justice Cullen ruled that the evidence be admitted, inasmuch as it did not bring in a new and different offense but simply furnished additional proof of an intent to make a false report. The court by unanimous vote sustained the ruling,[21] thus permitting the inquiry to extend to all contributions made to the Governor, whether specified in the articles of impeachment or not. A summary prepared by the prosecution showed that Sulzer had omitted from his sworn statement $12,700 in checks and $47,300 in cash, and that of the total, at least $40,462.50 went to his brokers.[22]

19 A summary of the contributors' testimony appears in *Ibid.*, II, pp. 1470-72.
20 *Ibid.*, I, p. 562.
21 *Ibid.*, p. 566.
22 *Times*, October 13.

That Sulzer never purposed to make a complete report of campaign receipts was disclosed by one of the witnesses,[23] who testified that when he handed Sulzer a check for two hundred dollars shortly before election day, Sulzer remarked to him, " I do not intend to account for this kind of gifts, they must be made to me personally; don't say anything about it; simply between you and myself." [24] To further his plan of concealment, he sought, whenever possible, to obtain cash rather than checks, justifying his preference to contributors on the ground that he needed the money to meet campaign traveling expenses.[25] Much of the money, nevertheless, subsequently showed up in stock brokers' offices. Sulzer's cautiousness in acknowledging contributions was shown by the fact that in none of his replies did he make any direct reference to the amount of money sent him. He always sought refuge in such vague phrases as " thanking you for all you have done for me," or " thanking you for all you have said and done," or " thanking you for your letter and inclosure." In some cases no acknowledgment at all was made.

Almost every witness who testified sought to shield Sulzer from the legal consequences of his failure to comply with the law by characterizing his contribution as a purely personal gift, which presumably would absolve him from having committed a crime. This raised a delicate legal point, and the minds of the donors were searched in the most minute fashion to determine their intent as to how the money given Sulzer was to be used. Jacob H. Schiff admitted that Sulzer had personally solicited a contribution to his campaign fund and that, on his advice, had drawn a check for $2,500 to the order of Louis A. Sarecky, but under cross-examination of defense counsel, avowed that he had placed no conditions upon the use which was to be made of that money. (Q.—" Was anything said in

23 Cornelius S. Pinkney, a lawyer.

24 *Proceedings*, I, p. 902.

25 *Ibid.*, pp. 601, 738.

that conversation as to the use which was to be made of that check or the proceeds of that check by Mr. Sulzer?" A.— "There was nothing said." Q.—"Did you intend that that should be used for any specific purpose?" A.—"I think it was the general intent and purpose of the conversation that Governor Sulzer could use this $2,500 for whatever he would please.")[26] He explained that his memorandum on the face of the check reading, "Mr. Schiff's contribution toward William Sulzer's campaign expenses," had been made at the time he gave it to the Frawley committee for purposes of identification only, not to denote any intention of restricting Sulzer in its use.[27] Henry Morgenthau was equally emphatic in asserting that he had had no desire to limit the use of the thousand dollar check he had given Sulzer, but weakened the defense when he admitted that it was given with the intention of helping him "in his election" and that he would "certainly not" have given Sulzer the money, had he not been a candidate for Governor.[28] Former Judge Conlon similarly testified that four hundred and ten dollars given Sulzer by several members of the Manhattan Club was intended for his personal use, the contributors, he added, believing him to be in an "impecunious condition."[29] Another witness[30] declared that the money was contributed toward Sulzer's "personal expense."[31] They were willing to have Sulzer use the money in any way and for any purpose he saw fit, without any restrictions whatever. Counsel for the impeachment managers objected strenuously to the admission of any testimony bearing on what the donors in-

26 *Ibid.*, pp. 489-90.

27 On being recalled to the stand the following day, Schiff revealed that a few weeks before the trial, Sulzer had offered through his law partner, Frankenstein, to refund the $2,500. Inasmuch as the matter was under investigation, Schiff refused to accept the money.

28 *Proceedings*, I, p. 494.

29 *Ibid.*, p. 673.

30 Richard Croker, Jr.

31 *Proceedings*, I, p. 741.

tended to be done with their contributions as incompetent, but the Presiding Judge overruled the objection. The respondent, in his opinion, had the right to show that whatever the delinquency might be, still he was not guilty of the crime of larceny.[32] The court sustained the ruling by a vote of thirty-three to fourteen.[33]

More important than the rapidly accumulating aggregate of undeclared campaign contributions, and creating an even more unfavorable impression, was the testimony of Morgenthau and Peck that Sulzer had urged them to conceal their gifts by recourse to perjury. During his second appearance on the stand, Morgenthau revealed, under questioning of counsel for the prosecution, that in the early part of September Sulzer called him on the telephone, asking to see him in Albany at once. Morgenthau refused, whereupon Sulzer said, " If you are going to testify, I hope you will be easy with me." And when Morgenthau replied that he " would testify to the facts," Sulzer then requested him to treat the contribution as a " personal " affair between them.[34] Even more damaging was the sensational testimony given by Duncan W. Peck, State Superintendent of Public Works. Its substance was that during Sulzer's campaign he had presented him with a five hundred dollar bill and that when, in July, 1913, he received a letter from the Frawley committee requesting him to state what donation he had made, he showed the letter to Sulzer and asked him what he should do about it. He reported Sulzer as having replied, " Do as I shall; deny it." And when he remonstrated, " I suppose I shall be under oath," Sulzer answered, " That is nothing. Forget

32 *Ibid.*, p. 665.

33 *Ibid.*, p. 734.

34 *Ibid.*, p. 702 ff. How the impeachment managers obtained knowledge of the telephone conversation between Sulzer in Albany and Morgenthau in Port Chester is something of a mystery. Morgenthau himself confesses that he was never able to learn how it was discovered.—*World's Work*, Vol. 42 (September, 1921), p. 479, " What I Learned from Sulzer and Tammany." The only plausible explanation is that the wires were " tapped."

it." [35] Defense counsel tried hard to shake the testimony but failed to do so.

In tracing the money received by Sulzer, counsel for the impeachment managers showed, by the testimony of the banks' employees, that Sulzer deposited to his personal account in the Farmers' Loan and Trust Co. close to $15,000 during the months of September and October, 1912, and that Sarecky's account in the Mutual Alliance Trust Co., from September 5 to December 31, 1912, showed deposits of almost $15,000 more, the account manifesting greatest activity after Sulzer's nomination for office. From the searching examination of the paying teller of the Farmers' Loan and Trust Co., it was apparent that the defense counsel questioned the genuineness of Sulzer's signature appearing on the back of checks given him for political purposes, but the teller, though loath to do so, identified the endorsements as being in the handwriting of the accused Governor.

The court also went into all of Sulzer's alleged stock market operations. Members of the different firms of brokers, with whom he or his agent (Frederick L. Colwell) did business, were called upon to give detailed evidence, most of which had already been paraded before the public view during the investigation of the Frawley committee. The testimony definitely established Sulzer as owner of the accounts appearing on the brokers' books under number, and proved that numerous checks donated to his campaign fund were used to pay for stock purchases. The only evidence possibly linking Sulzer with Colwell's disappearance from the court's jurisdiction was the assertion made by one of the brokers that the last time he met Colwell, which was about the middle of August, Colwell said he was going to Albany to see Sulzer. Melville B. Fuller, also a broker, whose name appeared in the fourth impeachment article as one of the witnesses whom the Governor prevented from testifying before the Frawley committee, admitted on the stand that

Sulzer summoned him to the " People's House " the day after he had been subpoenaed to appear before the committee. He admitted also that Sulzer had told him that he could not legally be compelled to testify, but emphatically denied that he had been advised to withhold any information.

To substantiate article seven, alleging that the Governor had used his veto power for the purpose of coercing legislators to vote for his direct primary bill, the prosecution put Assemblymen Thaddeus C. Sweet and Spencer G. Prime on the witness stand. The testimony offered did not, however, establish incontrovertibly that Sulzer had made any direct requests, and threats of retaliation were, at worst, only implied. Assemblyman Sweet testified that about two weeks after the regular session of the Legislature had adjourned, he went to interview Sulzer in the interest of his bill providing for the construction of a bridge over the Oswego River. The witness: " He [Sulzer] said, ' Assemblyman, how did you vote on my primary bill? ' I said, ' I voted against it.' He then said, ' How are you going to vote in the extraordinary session? ' I said, ' According to the sentiment and in the interest of my district.' He laid his hand on my arm, stroking it, and said, ' See Taylor,[36] smooth him the right way, Assemblyman, and bring your bill to me, but remember, Assemblyman, I take good care of my friends.' " [37] He subsequently saw Taylor, he continued, who in turn referred him to Delaney, Commissioner of Efficiency and Economy. Although the latter submitted a report approving the measure, it was vetoed by the Governor.

According to the testimony of Assemblyman Prime, he visited the Governor in the company of Senator Emerson to induce favorable action on bills providing for the construction of some roads in Essex and Warren Counties at state expense, amounting to about $750,000. Again Sulzer brought up the subject of direct primaries, and after urging the two legis-

36 Sulzer's legal adviser.
37 *Proceedings*, I, pp. 808-9.

lators to read the contents of his bill, he remarked, as they were leaving, " You for me, I for you." [38] The measures were signed. (Assemblyman Prime voted for Sulzer's direct primary bill at the extraordinary session.) The prosecution sought to offer Assemblyman Patrie as an additional witness to sustain the charge of coercion but was prevented from doing so when the Presiding Judge upheld Marshall's objection that his testimony was incompetent, in view of the fact that his name was not specified in article seven.

The only evidence introduced under article eight included Sulzer's messages advocating the passage of legislation for the more stringent regulation of the New York Stock Exchange, the bills proposed, and the laws adopted. But that Sulzer wrongfully speculated in stocks, while such legislation was pending, was purely inferential.

Counsel for the prosecution also made little effort to prove article three of the Assembly indictment, except to attempt to establish that Sarecky's refusal to answer any questions pertaining to Sulzer's campaign fund was instigated by Sulzer himself. Evidence was introduced that about two weeks before Sarecky's appearance before the committee, he was appointed deportation agent for the State Hospital Commission without examination, at a salary of $4,000 a year, this being the first time a layman, not a physician, had been appointed to that position. The secretary of the State Civil Service Commission produced correspondence between the Governor's office and the Commission to show that it was at the instance of the Governor that Sarecky was exempt from competitive examination. The letter of the Hospital Commission praised Sarecky's " peculiar and exceptional qualifications of educational character " to justify the suspension of the rule.[39] This, concluded Stanchfield, presented " the strongest possible circumstantial evidence

38 *Ibid.*, pp. 818-19.
39 *Ibid.*, II, p. 963.

of bribery " for the suppression of testimony.[40] With this, on October 1, the impeachment managers unexpectedly rested their case. More than a dozen other witnesses were held in reserve, it was reported, ready to take the stand should Sulzer testify.[41]

The following day Fox, of defense counsel, made a formal motion that all but the first, second, and sixth articles be dismissed as unsupported by the testimony submitted. The Presiding Judge promptly denied the motion, ruling that it would have to be determined at the close of the trial, as was the earlier motion on the other articles, and the court accepted his view without dissent. An adjournment was then taken until October 6 in order to give the defense time to complete its case.

On October 6 the prosecution asked for and obtained permission to reopen the case for the taking of additional testimony. The newly discovered witness was Allan A. Ryan, son of Thomas F. Ryan, the financier, whose testimony proved to be the most sensational adduced at the trial, and apparently took even Sulzer's own lawyers by surprise.[42] Its substance was that some time during the campaign, Sulzer had telephoned him, asked for the whereabouts of the elder Ryan, and when informed that he was abroad, said: " Tell your father I am the same old Bill." [43] The precise implication of this remark was not explained. The same day, in response to Sulzer's request for a contribution, he sent him $10,000 in currency, which, in common with other large contributions, was not included in his sworn statement. Of even greater significance was Ryan's startling disclosure that during the course of a conversation held about a week before the beginning of the impeachment trial, Sulzer had asked him to go to Washington to see Senator Elihu Root and urge him to use his influence

40 *Ibid.*, p. 950.
41 *World*, October 2.
42 *Times*, October 21.
43 *Proceedings*, II, p. 1041.

with William Barnes, the Republican State Chairman, to induce the Republican Senators to vote the impeachment unconstitutional.[44] This brought Herrick to his feet with a sharp objection that the testimony be expunged from the record as being utterly unrelated to any of the impeachment articles. Judge Cullen, in accordance with a strict interpretation of the rules of evidence, ordered the information given by Ryan struck out. The Republican Senators, led by Elon R. Brown, took issue with the ruling and moved that the testimony be allowed to stand, but the court by a vote of 32 to 18, upheld Judge Cullen's decision. The following day, however, after an executive session, the court reversed itself and permitted Ryan's testimony to remain in the record. Ryan was then recalled to the stand. Supplementing his story about Sulzer's attempted appeal to Barnes, he revealed that although he refused to see Root, he showed Sulzer a memorandum prepared by a " certain party," [45] which contained the information that the Republican organization as such would do nothing for him and that each Republican member of the court would be left to his own judgment. Then, according to the witness, Sulzer made the astounding request that he see De Lancey Nicoll (the elder Ryan's lawyer) and ask him to intercede with the Tammany boss to stop the trial and to place before him his proposition of surrender; namely, that if the impeachment proceedings were called off, he " was willing to do whatever was right." [46] He had never acted upon Sulzer's request, Ryan added. The revelation that the Governor had invoked the powers of the " invisible government," so bitterly and repeatedly condemned by him in public speech,

44 Investigators from the Department of Efficiency and Economy, who examined the records of Sulzer's telephone calls, confirmed the testimony that Sulzer called the Ryan office in New York City on September 8.—*Tribune*, November 2.

45 Ryan did not give the name of his informant at the trial but subsequently revealed that it was a certain Lemuel E. Quigg, an old-time, machine Republican.—*Times*, October 27.

46 *Proceedings*, II, p. 1106.

to save himself from expulsion and disgrace filled even his most loyal friends with consternation.

Harvey D. Hinman made the opening address for the defense. He began with the assertion that the morals or the private life of an officeholder, not affecting the performance of his official duties, did not disqualify him from holding office and could therefore not be made ground for removal. High character and integrity, he argued, were no legal requirements for officeholding. He then took up, charge by charge, each of the articles of impeachment and reviewed the evidence which the prosecution had introduced. Article eight (the Stock Exchange article), he scornfully remarked, was unsupported " by even a scintilla of proof." The evidence showed that Sulzer had stopped his transactions in the stock market after becoming Governor, and that the proposed stock exchange legislation was against his own financial interest, for the effect, if any, would be to lower prices. The defense would therefore not dignify this charge with an answer. Article seven (the " big stick " article) likewise stood " absolutely unproved." None of the things alleged to have been done or said in connection with the bills of Assemblymen Prime and Sweet were covered by, or violated the provisions of, section 775 of the Penal Law. Hence the defense did not feel called upon to furnish any evidence in refutation.

Articles three, four, and five (the " bribery " and " criminal suppression of evidence " articles), he maintained, were devoid of any supporting evidence and were based on " insinuations and innuendoes." There was nothing in the record to show that Sulzer ever communicated with Sarecky concerning the latter's refusal to furnish testimony before the Frawley committee. That Sarecky's appointment to the deportation board had anything to do with his giving or withholding evidence, he contended, was an unwarranted inference. Fuller's testimony, he pointed out, showed that it was he himself who had suggested to Sulzer that he owed it to his customers not to disclose their business affairs except with their consent, and that he subsequently did submit both himself and the books of his firm for examination. As for Colwell, there was nothing to prove Sulzer's connection with his refusal to appear before the Frawley committee. The defense, he concluded, would therefore submit no evidence in relation to any of those three articles, maintaining that there was an utter lack of evidence supporting the charges, or from which any inference against Sulzer could legitimately be drawn.

The allegations contained in articles one, two, and six all concerned acts committed prior to January 1, 1913, when Sulzer was still a private citizen, hence had no bearing upon his right to continue as Governor. Article six, which accused him of " stealing " moneys donated to him during his campaign, he dismissed as altogether absurd, for inasmuch as there was nothing in the evidence to show that they were given to him in trust, there was no element of a criminal offense involved. If any of the contributions were made upon the condition that they were to be used only for campaign purposes, then, Hinman insisted, action to recover could be instituted by the donors alone. " To urge the impeachment of a public official because he did not use money in aid of his election is so unreasonable as to be almost ludicrous," he declared. " We venture the assertion that were it not for political exigencies, such a thing would never have been conceived or even dreamed of." [47] Article two (the " perjury " article), he continued, should be dismissed, because the law did not make it imperative for Sulzer to swear to his statement of campaign receipts and expenditures. Even if he had not acted in good faith, his affidavit was consequently " immaterial." And finally, in extenuation of article one, which charged the Governor with submitting a false statement, he portrayed Sulzer as a man without business experience, proverbially careless and unmethodical in money matters, who had trustingly confided the management of the financial details of his campaign to others.

47 *Ibid.*, pp. 1081-82.

The task of drawing up the report of campaign contributions had been left to his office employees, in whom he had confidence and upon the strength of whose assurance he had signed it. Many of the contributions made by friends and well-wishers were in the nature of gifts and Sulzer had a right to believe that they were intended for himself personally. He admitted that some of the " gifts " had been used in the purchase of stocks, but since there was no attempt at concealment, there was no wrongful intent in connection with those transactions.

What Sulzer did or did not do before he became Governor was of minor importance, declared Hinman. The great question was what he had done after he had taken his official oath of office. And in an eloquent peroration, he urged the court to take into consideration the motives which led to the impeachment. " Was the proceeding instituted because of a desire to accomplish a public good or was it for the purpose of getting rid of a public official who was performing his duty? " he asked. " Was the respondent impeached because, as they say, of ' mal and corrupt conduct in office ', or because of honest conduct in office? Was he impeached, as they say, for ' stealing ' the moneys which his friends gave him, or was it because he was preventing grafters from stealing the moneys of the taxpayers? Was he impeached because, as they say, he made a false oath, or was it because he refused to violate his official oath of office? " [48]

The first witness summoned by the defense was Samuel A. Beardsley, who was prepared to testify that he had offered Sulzer a campaign contribution of $25,000 which was refused. The Presiding Judge excluded the testimony as incompetent, however, on the ground that the witness had no knowledge of any contributions actually given, and the rest of the court sustained his decision. This ruling was a serious setback to the Governor's cause, for the defense hoped to show by several other witnesses that Sulzer had spurned large sums of money

48 *Ibid.*, pp. 1094-95.

offered him by men identified with corporate interests. The next witness was Herbert H. Lehman, New York banker and personal friend of Sulzer, who testified that he had given Sulzer $5,000 in cash prior to his nomination, knowing him to be a man of " straitened circumstances," and that he had spent $6,000 more during his gubernatorial campaign to finance his publicity. The aim of defense counsel, apparently, was to show that Sulzer was well supplied with money in the fall of 1912. Next came Louis M. Josephthal, who had taken up Sulzer's brokerage account with Harris and Fuller. Although the Governor had told him that the stock belonged to Mrs. Sulzer, he testified, he found none of it in her name. In reply to Stanchfield's question, he denied any attempt to influence Sulzer's action on the Stock Exchange legislation, but admitted having made known his opposition to the bill increasing the tax on stock transfers. He had not, he said, contributed to Sulzer's campaign fund; but, following his appointment as naval aide, his firm had retained Sulzer's law partner as counsel.

The star witness was Louis A. Sarecky, the accused Governor's secretary for ten years, whose testimony, though shaken as to details, constituted the only actual defense entered at the trial. With unswerving loyalty, he assumed full responsibility for the transgressions alleged against Sulzer. Calm, self-possessed, and resourceful, he faced the searching cross-examination of Stanchfield without once losing his poise. Under the gentle guidance of Hinman, he testified as to the free and easy manner in which thousands of dollars contributed to the campaign fund were received and disbursed. He described himself as the author of the ambiguous " I thank you for all you have said and done " letters that went out in acknowledgment of campaign contributions, but which made no specific allusion to the receipt of money. Sulzer, he insisted, did not know anything about those letters and had nothing whatever to do with the preparation of the sworn statement of campaign receipts. He testified that he had drawn it up with the help of Matthew Horgan, (then employed in Sulzer's office and later secretary to the Frawley committee), and submitted it to Sulzer who signed it without examining the contents. " Is this all right? " he quoted Sulzer as asking. " This is as accurate as I could get it," was his own reply.[49] The commissioner of deeds who witnessed the instrument, he swore, had never read it to Sulzer before affixing his signature.[50] He testified also that he himself had written and signed the letter purporting to come from Sulzer personally, which requested the Mutual Alliance Trust Co. to accept Sarecky's endorsements on Sulzer's checks. For years, he explained, he had been signing Sulzer's name to checks and correspondence, by virtue of a general power of attorney, and he eagerly gave the court a demonstration of his expertness in imitating his signature.

He frankly acknowledged that the statement did not include all the moneys received and was fully aware of it at the time the statement was prepared. He had compiled it, he said, from his daily memorandum sheets and deposit slips, but when confronted with what the prosecution implied was the deliberate omission of contributions from the liquor interests, Tammany district leaders, and Wall Street financiers, his only explanation was that some of the records might have been missing. He had never, he swore, spoken to the Governor during the progress of the campaign about leaving out of the statement the names of certain large contributors. He had not been in the habit of submitting to Sulzer all campaign checks received, he declared, and had, on his own initiative, used some of the money for other than campaign purposes. The largest amount of cash turned over to him by Sulzer himself at any time during the campaign was $500. He could not remember, he said, whether he had told Sulzer of having been served with a subpoena to appear before the Frawley committee, but when prodded by Stanchfield, admitted he had, but still denied that the Governor

49 *Ibid.*, p. 1160.

50 The commissioner of deeds had previously testified that he read the entire statement to Sulzer before attesting it.

had advised him on his course of conduct. He insisted he had
not conferred with Louis Marshall prior to his appearance
before the committee, and was unable to reconcile that statement with the one made to the committee that Marshall was
the attorney who had advised him not to talk. Asked to produce
correspondence and memoranda bearing on the campaign contributions he took refuge behind the excuse that he had lost,
mislaid, or destroyed them. He declared that shortly after the
Frawley committee began its hearings, he had sent substantially
all evidence relating to campaign contributions, bound into
several volumes, to the Executive Mansion in Albany. He was
not quite clear as to the sources of his salary, nor was he
wholly at ease in describing his successive promotions in the
state service after Sulzer had been elected Governor, first as
clerk in the Adjutant-General's office, then as confidential
stenographer to the Governor, and finally as deportation agent,
for whose duties he conceded he had no special training. But
such admissions as he made hurt himself rather than the
Governor.

The defense also showed that Sulzer had borrowed large
sums of money during his campaign. One witness, Edward P.
Meany, a New York attorney, testified that he had loaned
him ten thousand dollars in cash, without collateral or acknowledgment of any kind. It was not a campaign contribution, he
contended, and involved no obligation on Sulzer's part. Another
was Hugh J. Reilly, whose name had been linked with Sulzer
in the Cienfuegos waterworks contract in Cuba, who told of
having loaned Sulzer a total of $26,500 in cash from August
to November, 1912. In his cross-examination Stanchfield forced
the witness to admit he had never received any security for the
loans and had no written evidence for them. Stanchfield also
sought to show that Reilly and his associates had enlisted the
services of Sulzer in order to secure payment of the contract
from the Cuban government, but Judge Cullen sustained the
objection of defense counsel that that line of interrogation was
wholly immaterial and irrelevant. This ruling thus shut off the

plans of the prosecution to delve into Sulzer's Congressional record.

The last witness put on the stand by the defense was John A. Hennessy, Sulzer's investigator of the Highway Department, who was reported to have brought with him a mass of documents to prove the iniquities of Tammany. His testimony was intended to show first, that Peck, in whose department he had discovered fraud and corruption, had testified as he did in order to save his own job, and secondly, that Sulzer was a good and faithful Governor trying to put the state departments on an honest and efficient basis. But the pretentious plans of the defense were swept away when Judge Cullen held that, under the rules, Sulzer could not discredit the charges against him by attacking the motive that inspired them or the persons behind them. With the dismissal of Hennessy, the court deprived the defense of what it considered its strongest plea. While admitting the logic of the Presiding Judge's ruling in excluding the testimony, some members of the court privately expressed regret that the public had been deprived of the benefit of the disclosures promised by Sulzer, in support of his repeated public declarations of criminal conspiracy on the part of Boss Murphy and his associates in Tammany Hall against the people of the state.[51] Chagrined over the frustration of its proposed attack on Tammanyism, the defense suddenly rested its case.[52]

The abrupt announcement that the case for the defense was closed settled the big question whether Sulzer would appear as a witness and launch from the stand his widely heralded " exposure " of Murphy and the Tammany " plot " to remove him from office. Only a few days after the trial began, he told newspaper men that nothing short of death would prevent him from testifying.[53] He promised " amazing revelations," involving a

51 *World*, October 9.

52 October 1. The subsequent testimony offered by the prosecution in rebuttal was unimportant.

53 *World*, September 22.

score or more of widely known Democratic politicians, confident that in his appearance before the court he would be able
to remove every taint of intentional wrongdoing from his
personal acts and concentrate attention upon the Tammany
organization as the real offender against the public welfare.[54]
" I'll come out of this with flying colors," he predicted, " and
will show the people, who constitute the highest of all courts,
that I am being made a victim of a few little mistakes of mine
which are being made to appear in the light of great crimes.
. . . But when I make my reply and show the real purpose of
this move to get me out of the way, I know the people well
enough to justify the prediction that they will exonerate me
of intentional wrongdoing and will vent their wrath upon
Murphy and the other men from whose clutches I have rescued
the State." [55] He was resolved, according to recurring reports,
to bare his entire record and invite the most searching scrutiny
of his official career, in the belief that any offenses that might
be established against him were inconsequential as compared
with the enormity of the crimes committed by the men now
seeking his removal.[56] He was constantly represented as strain-
ing in his bonds of enforced silence and nearly bursting with
his desire to tell the story of the persecutions that followed
his refusal to go into partnership with Tammany contractors
and state officials in the looting of the public treasury. Two
weeks before the close of the trial, he declared, " I have fully
decided to go on the witness stand. Nothing can prevent me
from going on the stand and telling everything that I know if
the Judges give me the opportunity." [57]

While Sulzer was promising to make an end of Murphy and
lay bare the whole scandalous system of government by blackmail, there was still widespread sympathy for him. Deluded by

54 *Ibid.*
55 *Ibid.*, September 27.
56 *Ibid.*, October 3.
57 *Ibid.*, October 4.

the boastful reports emanating from the Executive Mansion, men in all parts of the state declared themselves on his side. But his change of front regarding the expediency of taking the stand cost him a great many supporters.[58] His sinister silence put the seal of accuracy upon the cumulative testimony of Morgenthau, Peck, and Ryan, and led to a decided change of sentiment even among his most devoted followers. He was apparently content to rest his case, as the *World* pointed out, upon " the unsupported and ridiculous testimony of a scapegoat stenographer." [59] Sulzer's failure to come before the court under oath and make an effort to vindicate himself simply meant that he had no defense to offer, other than that he was not personally responsible for the violation of the Corrupt Practices Act.

The one reason advanced by counsel for Sulzer to explain why he made no personal defense against the charges preferred against him was that he did not want to " drag his wife into the situation." [60] " There would have been no end of condemnation and a well-nigh unanimous demand for his removal if Mr. Sulzer had resorted to such a cowardly act as hiding behind a woman's skirts," said Herrick.[61] This reason sounds implausible when it is considered that no effort was made by Sarecky or by any other witness summoned by the defense to connect Mrs. Sulzer's name with any of the transactions alleged against the Governor. A different reason, given by friends of Sulzer, for his not offering himself as a witness was that the court would not have permitted him to tell anything about his relations with Tammany, as evidenced by its vote to exclude Hennessy's testimony. Sulzer, writes one of his lay advisers, " had an absolute defence to the ' framed-up charges ' of Mr. Murphy. His defence was carefully gone over by his lawyers

58 *Ibid.*, October 10.
59 Editorial, October 9.
60 *World*, October 9.
61 *Times*, October 9.

and they knew that should he take the stand, the revelations he would make would bring about the Governor's complete vindication." But when the "packed" court ruled out the testimony of Hennessy, he goes on to say, it was apparent that it would also do the same to any testimony Sulzer might offer relating to the difficulties he had had with Murphy.[62] The *Times* stated "on excellent authority," however, that there would have been no objection from counsel for the impeachment managers to Sulzer's telling his "human interest" story in order that they might have an opportunity to cross-examine him.[63] They were prepared to make sensational disclosures, hitherto unsuspected, dealing with his private business activities while Governor, in the event that he appeared as a witness,[64] As one of them remarked, "If Sulzer doesn't go on the stand, his failure will be interpreted as a confession; if he does go on, it will be suicide."[65] It seems probable, therefore, that Sulzer was dissuaded from appearing before the court only because, as a witness, he would have exposed himself to a merciless cross-examination. His legal representatives were evidently afraid that he might injure his own case by making himself a target for the prosecution, for every breath of scandal, official or private, that ever touched him would most likely be raked up to attack his credibility. Hence they felt it would be better to rest their case on the ground that the prosecution had failed to prove the charges against their client rather than subject him to that trying ordeal.[66]

Opposing counsel began their closing arguments on October 9. Marshall opened the battle of oratory with an impassioned plea lasting three and a half hours. "We are on the threshold of an event," he began, "which will make a permanent im-

62 Samuel Bell Thomas, *op. cit.*, p. 452.

63 October 21.

64 *Times*, October 21.

65 *World*, October 1.

66 *Ibid.*, October 2.

pression upon the history of our beloved State, which will entail consequences far beyond our ken, which will determine whether or not the reign of law has ceased, and that of passion and prejudice has begun." He then painted a glowing picture of Sulzer's long public career, paid tribute to his manifold legislative achievements, pointed to his ever-increasing popularity, cited his record as Chief Executive in reorganizing state departments and exposing evils and abuses, which absolved him from any suspicion of official misconduct, and asked why a man " who wrought all this " should now be subjected to " this awful degradation." [67] From his appeal for Sulzer the man he swept into his argument for Sulzer the defendant. After canvassing each of the impeachment articles and the prosecution's evidence relating thereto, he held that not one of them had been proved. Articles one and two related to acts committed before Sulzer took office, hence were not impeachable. The Assembly's assumption of an unlimited and arbitrary power of impeachment· was inconsistent with fundamental principles of liberty and justice. The very theory of impeachment, he declared, was that the charges should refer only to acts connected with the public service, and once more submitted proof from the constitutional history of the state and nation that never before had an attempt been made to impeach a public officer for any other cause than official misconduct. The ordinary courts, he pointed out, were provided with ample machinery to deal with crimes which were not acts of official misconduct. An impeachment proceeding was in the nature of a criminal proceeding, he asserted, and was governed by the same rules as were applicable to other criminal prosecutions. Unless, therefore, it had been proved that Sulzer had committed a crime, he could not be held guilty under the articles of impeachment.

He then examined the Corrupt Practices Act in detail and drew the conclusion that the statement required from a candidate had no reference to sums contributed to him. The act,

67 *Proceedings*, II, p. 1316.

furthermore, did not require that the statement submitted by the candidate be accompanied by an oath. Inasmuch as Sulzer's affidavit was voluntary and extra-judicial, it did not come within the definition of perjury. Absence of criminal intent, he argued, was clear from Sarecky's testimony that the making of the affidavit was due entirely to inadvertency. Moreover, according to their own testimony, the donors referred to in articles one and two did not make their gifts to Sulzer specifically as campaign contributions. Sulzer received the moneys with the distinct understanding on his part that he might use them for any purpose he saw fit. In view of the fact that Sulzer did not intend to use the moneys for election purposes, he could not possibly be guilty of the crime of perjury by having omitted them from his statement.

Article three was indefinite, he argued, for it did not indicate how the witnesses were bribed nor what testimony they withheld. Fuller did eventually testify before the Frawley committee, he showed, his earlier refusal being entirely of his own accord. As for Colwell, there was no evidence, oral or written, of any conversation between him and the Governor. The only pertinent testimony was his avowal to one of the witnesses that he was going to Albany to see Sulzer. To conclude that Sulzer bribed him or used any fraudulent means to induce him to withhold any testimony was " a violent conjecture and an ungrounded suspicion." [68] Sarecky, he pointed out, did not refuse to testify before the committee, but simply asked for an opportunity for counsel to be present, a request which was entirely within his rights. There was nothing to indicate that his refusal was based on any instruction from Sulzer. To refute the impeachment managers' contention that Sulzer had " bribed " Sarecky by procuring for him a lucrative appointment, he drew attention to the correspondence between the State Hospital Commission and the Civil Service Commission to establish that they had cooperated in the official action taken.

68 *Ibid.*, p. 1382.

Theirs was the appointment, theirs was the responsibility for determining Sarecky's fitness.

Article four dealt in mere generalities, he held, with no statement as to what deceit or fraud was practiced, what threats were employed, or what facts were concealed. Article five likewise was " a blank record," there being not a word of proof to indicate that Sulzer did anything to prevent or dissuade Colwell from testifying before the Frawley committee. At this point Marshall attacked the truthfulness of Peck's testimony, that he had been asked by the Governor to deny a $500 contribution, as savoring " of a brazen counterfeit and of hypocrisy." [69] He ridiculed his apparent reluctance to testify and his " extraordinary " memory in repeating word for word a conversation that had taken place two months before. He thought it significant also that Peck had never been called before the Frawley committee, though he was supposed to have been summoned. But the principal reason, thought Marshall, why the story could not be accepted at its face value was that Peck had a motive for inventing a conversation such as that to which he had testified. He pointed out that his department had been under investigation and that " irregularities of a very serious nature " [70] had been found which threatened not only his office, but his very liberty. Hence his eagerness to aid in Sulzer's destruction.[71] Taking up Morgenthau's testimony, Marshall considered Sulzer's appeal to be " easy " with him and to treat his contribution as a personal matter perfectly " natural " under the circumstances. Morgenthau himself had testified to the personal nature of the contribution. This testimony, like that of Ryan, was utterly unrelated to any of the impeachment articles,

69 *Ibid.*, p. 1394.

70 *Ibid.*, p. 1395.

71 Peck indignantly characterized Marshall's attack on him as "absolutely false, unjust and inexcusable." His department, he declared, had never been investigated nor had any charges been made against him personally.— *Times*, October 10.

and was injected into the case simply for the purpose of creating distrust of the Governor.

Article six accused Sulzer of grand larceny. But, he argued, there could be no larceny where a candidate had gotten money from his friends as gifts to do with as he liked. Even those witnesses who testified that their contributions were made in connection with the campaign never even suggested that the money was given to him in a fiduciary capacity. Since there had been no agreement that the money was ever to be repaid, nor had any demand been made for its return, nor any complaint made as to the manner in which it was used, there was therefore no basis for a charge of embezzlement. Larceny was a crime against property. But who could say that the title to the moneys given Sulzer remained with the donors? In analyzing article seven, Marshall characterized as "trivial" [72] the testimony of Assemblymen Prime and Sweet, by which the prosecution sought to prove that Governor Sulzer was ready to trade his signature on legislation for support of his direct primary bill. Section 775 of the Penal Law, by which this charge was claimed to be governed, was utterly inapplicable, he contended, and had not the remotest application to the matters alleged in this article. The Governor had a legitimate right to discuss legislation with members of the Legislature and there was nothing improper in urging them to give their support to the direct primary measure. Nor was there any "malign significance" attached to the phrase, "You for me, and I for you." [73] Article eight, Marshall declared, was "if possible, even more contemptible." [74] He could not find the slightest causal relationship between the ownership of stock by the Governor and his advocacy of measures intended to regulate the transaction of securities on the New York Stock Exchange. The contention of the impeachment managers, he pointed out,

72 *Proceedings*, II, p. 1399.
73 *Ibid.*
74 *Ibid.*, p. 1400.

became even more absurd when one considered that the only anticipated effect of the proposed legislation would be to reduce the price of his own investments. Having completed his analysis of each article of impeachment, Marshall bitterly assailed the impeachment managers who, he said, had " lost all sense of proportion " in their efforts to destroy the Governor for daring to assert his independence.[75] His final plea to the court was not to undermine the law or be guided by passion and prejudice. " We are not so much concerned in this case with William Sulzer, the man, or the Governor," he said, " as we are with the supremacy of the law, with the perpetuity of its principles, with the preservation of orderly government. . . . Shall ours be a government of laws, or one of passion and caprice? " [76]

Alton B. Parker followed Marshall for the prosecution in an address which occupied the better part of the afternoon and morning sessions. He confined himself mainly to the constitutional features of the impeachment and the validity of the perjury, false statement, and larceny charges. He began with the sarcastic comment that the defense had failed to answer any of the material facts which had been presented on behalf of the impeachment managers. He then briefly sketched the conditions leading to the passage of the Corrupt Practices Act, which was designed primarily to insure publicity of campaign contributions and expenditures. The accumulation of uncontradicted evidence, he maintained, clearly showed that Sulzer had received in money and checks $37,400 more than he had accounted for. He made much of the fact that Sulzer had failed to appear and deny the damaging testimony given at the trial, but had thrown the burden of carrying the only attempt at defense on the shoulders of " so absolutely worthless a character " as Sarecky.[77] It was impossible, he said, to believe Sarecky's story that Sulzer had trustingly signed the statement

75 *Ibid.*, p. 1402.
76 *Ibid.*, pp. 1403-4.
77 *Ibid.*, p. 1410.

and had had nothing to do with its preparation. Could he have forgotten the contributions from his brewery friends and politicians, or the Schiff contribution which he had personally solicited, or the Ryan money? What was implied in the assurance that he was " the same old Bill," except that he had been serviceable in the past and would continue to be so in the future? Assuming it were true that Sarecky had prepared the statement to the best of his knowledge, as he had testified, still " his master " knew it was a lie when he examined it.[78] Sulzer had wilfully and intentionally violated the law, as charged in article one, he concluded.

In discussing Sulzer's guilt under article two, he refuted Marshall's interpretation of the election law. He held that it plainly called for a sworn statement of all contributions made to a candidate, and so made Sulzer a perjurer. The truth of article six was established, Parker argued, even if he were not a trustee for the contributors. He was still guilty of larceny within the meaning of section 1290 of the Penal Law, which made obtaining money by false pretence larceny. Sulzer secured possession of the moneys with the intention of appropriating them to his own use. The correspondence and testimony of many of the witnesses showed that the contributions were made for campaign purposes or were occasioned by the fact that he was a candidate for Governor. The only reasonable construction that could be put upon the money they gave him was that it would be used to meet the expenses of the campaign, whether specifically stated or implied. Since that was their intention at the time, those campaign contributions did not change because some of the contributors, to save Sulzer from embarrassment, later gave them some other name. Sulzer never informed the contributors that he intended to credit their money to his personal bank account or use it for the purchase of stocks, hence was guilty of fraudulent representation.

[78] *Ibid.*, p. 1411.

He cited once more the provisions of the constitution and other rules of law in support of his contention that an official might be impeached for acts committed prior to his taking office. Impeachment, he asserted, was not and never had been designed as a punishment for crime, but to remove a corrupt and unworthy officer. Inasmuch as impeachment was intended not so much to punish the offender as to secure the state, offenses which were not indictable might still be impeachable. Here he quoted Tilden's opinion to the effect that an officer was impeachable under the constitution and laws of the state for acts committed before, or entirely disconnected with, his office, that the constitution and laws " do not limit the range of impeachable acts . . . but leave the whole judgment as to whether or not the disqualification is produced to the supreme and exclusive jurisdiction of the High Court of Impeachment, which is the ultimate agent of the sovereign people in their supervisory power over public office." [79] An election to office, Parker emphatically declared, was not " a certificate or any guaranty of fitness to hold that office." [80] Sulzer's offenses, he added, were " so closely connected with, and so necessary a condition precedent to his induction into office that it consti- tutes a part of his gubernatorial career." [81]

In conclusion, Parker launched a severe indictment of Sulzer little short of savage. " Every disguise," he declared, " has been torn from his back, from the petticoat in which he trusted for safety to the armor of defiance in which he threatened to attack and expose a political leadership to which we have found him suing later for a merciful obliteration of his misdeeds, and offering the bribe of submission. . . . With this Court, alone, rests the duty of delivering this State from the menace that like the sword of Damocles hangs above it so long as this man

79 *Ibid.*, p. 1439.
80 *Ibid.*, p. 1446.
81 *Ibid.*, p. 1447.

so conclusively demonstrated to be guilty of deliberate and heinous wrongdoing remains in the executive chair." [82]

D-Cady Herrick delivered the concluding arguments against conviction. His address, conciliatory in tone throughout, was an eloquent appeal to reason. He began with a plea to the court to divest itself of all prejudice and do impartial justice solely on the basis of the law and the facts, to lay aside all previously formed opinions, and to disregard all personal or political differences. He addressed himself particularly to the members of the Frawley committee, to members of Tammany Hall, many of whom regarded Sulzer as ungrateful and disloyal, and to those legislators whom he had threatened to drive out of public life. Sulzer, he exclaimed, " is not on trial for disloyalty; he is not on trial for ingratitude. . . . He is not on trial for unfitness for office." [83] His analysis of the evidence in the case added little to what his associate had already said. He ridiculed articles three, four, and five, and condemned the prosecution for seeking to create an atmosphere of suspicion and distrust. He dismissed articles seven and eight as utterly " absurd " and expressed amazement at the " audacity " of the impeachment managers in incorporating them in the articles of impeachment. In dismissing articles one, two, and six, he stressed the point already made by Marshall that the money given Sulzer was for his own particular benefit. Though not defending the ethics, good taste, or morals of a candidate's keeping campaign contributions, a public official, he declared, could not be impeached or removed for low ethical standards. Many notable figures in American public life, he recalled, had received assistance from wealthy friends.

He praised the " fearless " and " frank " testimony of Sarecky and asserted that there was no reason for disbelieving his story of how the statement was prepared or the perfunctory manner in which it was signed. Referring to Peck,

82 *Ibid.*, p. 1449.
83 *Ibid.*, p. 1454.

he observed that "the meanest criminal is the man who turns state's evidence." [84] He justified Sulzer's failure to offer himself as a witness by a vague reference to Mrs. Sulzer. It was to protect her honor and integrity, he declared, that he incurred the risk of his own disgrace by refusing to present any personal defense. Alluding to Ryan's testimony, he condoned Sulzer's efforts to secure the influence of political leaders of both parties to have the impeachment articles declared illegal as perfectly natural and logical in a man with his political education and training. He pleaded the court's indulgence for his client. His term was short and the people could soon eject him if they so desired. And in conclusion he appealed to the Governor's judges to avoid a decision that would bring shame and disgrace upon the state. "The bringing of these impeachment proceedings is lamentable," he exclaimed, "because of the object lesson of what may occur to any man in public life who dares stand and oppose the wishes of those who may know something about his private life and history not known to the general public." [85]

Ex-Senator Brackett, master of courtroom invective, concluded the summing up for the prosecution with an attack upon Sulzer that was couched in the frankest terms of excoriation. From the beginning of the impeachment proceedings, he declared, Sulzer had resorted by "every art known to the demagogue" to terrorize the members of the court and every one associated with the prosecution.[86] He repeatedly referred to the accused Governor as "faithless," "a criminal," "a cringing, miserable craven," "an outcast among men." [87] Having exhausted every dilatory motion and every point of law in an effort to secure the dismissal of the charges, without being called upon to meet the crucial fact as to whether or not he was guilty, Sulzer submitted to the court a general denial of

84 *Ibid.*, p. 1465.
85 *Ibid.*, p. 1492.
86 *Ibid.*, p. 1498.
87 *Ibid.*, pp. 1496-1525, *passim.*

all the charges which, in the light of the uncontradicted testimony, he branded as " an infamous lie." [88] He derided as " sham and pretence " [89] the contention that the money given Sulzer was for his personal benefit. If the Schiff check was a personal gift, why, he asked, should it have been made payable to Sarecky and deposited by the latter in his bank account, along with other contributions? He ridiculed the proposition that after soliciting money from financiers and trust magnates, he became, after assuming the Governorship, a converted man, devoted to the people's welfare. " Oh, but on the first of January, like Saul of Tarsus on his way to Damascus, there came a light. Where, before that moment, he was in gall of bitterness and bondage of sin, although prior to that time he had done nothing but serve the forces of evil, yet from the first day of January when the light came to him, William became a consecrated man and devoted himself thenceforth to the service of God and humanity in the People's House. Oh Saul! Saul! Persecutor of the Saints, but, finally, the greatest of the Apostles, what foolishness has been attempted through the years because of that sudden conversion of yours on the way to Damascus! There is many a man who tries to liken himself to Paul when the only likeness is to that of Saul. . . ." And the courtroom laughed when Brackett shouted this stinging bit of satire: " Can you imagine Paul telephoning to Gamaliel that he was ' the same old Saul,' and ' can't you make it more than $7,500? ' " [90]

He described as of " damning character " Sulzer's request to Morgenthau " to go easy " on him and treat the contribution as personal. " Do criminals," he asked, " find it necessary to solicit witnesses to tell the truth? " [91] In all the denunciation of Peck, an attack which he held to be unjustified and made on

88 *Ibid.*, p. 1501.
89 *Ibid.*, p. 1508.
90 *Ibid.*, pp. 1509-10.
91 *Ibid.*, p. 1515.

grounds outside the record, his testimony remained uncontradicted. If Peck lied, the defense counsel knew how it could have been met. So, too, stood Ryan's testimony, utterly unchallenged. The testimony of these men, he held, proved beyond doubt that Sulzer had urged witnesses to commit perjury. The defense's chief witness, Sarecky, had " sworn himself a criminal," [92] he declared, having confessed to forgery in Sulzer's service. But not only did he go unrebuked by Sulzer, but was rewarded with promotion and public office. If it were true, as Sarecky had sworn, that Sulzer had never told him of any of the omitted contributions, then Sulzer was aware that the one to whom he had entrusted the making up of the statement did not know, and could not know, of the large sums contributed to his campaign. Sarecky's destruction of every item of evidence that might corroborate his story proved that he was simply shielding Sulzer and taking upon himself the blame for any wrongdoing.

With the closing of the arguments, the court adjourned until October 13, the Chief Justice admonishing its members to refrain from discussing the case with outsiders until its final determination. When the court reconvened, the question was raised by Justice Miller whether the testimony of Peck, Morgenthau, and Ryan should be considered as describing acts of misconduct for which the Governor could be held guilty under article four, or, if its scope were insufficient, whether the court had the power to amend the article so as to include such testimony. The court requested opposing counsel to argue the question and, in order to afford them time to prepare their arguments, adjourned until the following day. The article in question charged Sulzer with suppressing evidence before the Frawley committee in violation of section 814 of the Penal Law of the state, in that he had " practised deceit and fraud and used threats and menaces, with intent to prevent said committee and the people of the State from procuring the attend-

92 *Ibid.*, p. 1522.

ance and testimony of certain witnesses, to wit: Louis A. Sarecky, Frederick L. Colwell and Melville B. Fuller, *and all other persons.*" The three points to be decided were: first, whether the article was sufficient to cover the testimony of Peck, Ryan, and Morgenthau, which had not been considered in the preparation of the original indictment against Sulzer; secondly, whether it was within the power of the Court of Impeachment to amend the article by including section 813 of the Penal Code (which declared it a misdemeanor for a person to attempt to commit perjury), so as to embrace their testimony; and thirdly, whether the articles of impeachment had to be returned to the Assembly for revision to supply the deficiency.

Stanchfield, who presented the argument for the effectiveness of article four, took the position that this was not an ordinary criminal trial, and that while the Assembly alone had the power of impeachment, that that did not preclude the court from making the pleading conform to the proof. The testimony in question, he pointed out, had gone into the record without objection by counsel for the defense, who thereby acknowledged it as material and competent evidence. The phrase " and all other persons " in article four, he contended, was adequate to cover the evidence of Morgenthau, Ryan, and Peck, all of whom testified to Sulzer's exercise of unlawful influence to keep them from furnishing evidence. He therefore asked the court to amend article four so as to include the acts testified to, and to read section 814 of the Penal Law in connection with section 813, as being both related to the suppression of testimony and solicitation to commit perjury. He based his request on the thesis that both sections of the law basically related to the same kind of offense, the withholding of testimony and tampering with the administration of justice. The number of the section was not material, the only test being whether the acts alleged in the charge, broadly stated, constituted an offense against the law. In closing, he declared that if, in the light of the change, Sulzer wanted to take the stand in his defense or wanted to produce other testimony to meet the accusation, the managers would raise no objection.

In combating Stanchfield's argument, Herrick and Marshall maintained that this was a criminal trial, governed by the same rules as other criminal trials, and that a defendant could be tried only for the specific offenses brought against him. The evidence of Peck, Morgenthau, and Ryan, they declared, did not cover the offense stipulated in article four, as it stood, and could be considered, if at all, only as bearing upon the general features of the case. Inasmuch as Sulzer's alleged conversations with Morgenthau and Ryan took place after the adoption of the articles of impeachment, they bore no relation to testimony before the Frawley committee, and were therefore automatically eliminated. As to Peck's testimony, there was no evidence, they maintained, that Sulzer had practised fraud or used threats to prevent him from testifying before the Frawley committee, which eliminated it from consideration under section 814 of the Penal Law. The nearest approach to it in the law was section 813 (the perjury offense) which was an absolutely separate and distinct offense. The court, they held, had no power to amend the articles of impeachment, and was restricted to considering only the charges specifically made in the Assembly's indictment.

All matters preliminary to a consideration of the case on its merits having been disposed of, the court went into private consultation. On the afternoon of the following day, the Presiding Judge announced that the court denied the application to amend the articles of impeachment but decided that article four was sufficiently comprehensive to embrace Peck's testimony as substantive proof.[93] With this, the members of the court resumed their deliberations behind closed doors to formulate the views which were to determine their final disposition of the case. The secret session continued through the following day, probably because of the need of instructing the lay members

93 The testimony of Morgenthau and Ryan was considered merely corroborative evidence of the other allegations specified in the charge.

among the Senators as to the legal value of the evidence submitted for and against the Governor. Even the most subservient
of Tammany Senators declared that they would be guided in
their judgment by the views of their judicial colleagues with
respect to the interpretation of the law. " No orders " were
said to have been given by Murphy to influence their judgment.
One Senator, who frankly admitted his allegiance to Murphy,
volunteered the information that " the only suggestion made
by Murphy is that we vote according to the facts and take our
law from the Judges of the Court of Appeals." [94] Though even
his most ardent supporters saw little prospect of his complete
vindication, Sulzer still expressed the belief that the court
would disregard every charge against him, other than those
relating to his alleged acts since his inauguration.[95]

On the afternoon of October 16, the court ended its private
conversations and proceeded to take a public vote on the eight
impeachment articles in turn. A large and distinguished audience filled the galleries, eager to witness the memorable event.[96]
The clerk read the first article, charging Sulzer with filing a
false statement of campaign receipts. Then, as each member
of the court arose in response to the summons of the clerk,
the Presiding Judge put to him the question, in never varying
form, " How say you, is the respondent guilty or not guilty? "
Some replied simply " guilty " or " not guilty," but most members accompanied their vote with a statement of their reasons,
in several instances filing written briefs. Many Senators took
their cue from the Judges of the Court of Appeals and seized
upon their statements to justify their own vote. Those voting
for acquittal did so mainly on the ground that the acts charged,
though actually committed, did not constitute grounds for impeachment under the constitution and laws of the state. Typical
of this viewpoint was the exhaustive and learned opinion read

94 *World*, October 13.
95 *Ibid.*
96 *Ibid.*, October 17.

by Presiding Judge Cullen, whose conduct of the case elicited general praise for its spirit of severe judicial fairness and common sense. Even though he believed the accusation contained in the first article to be true, that the sum actually received by Sulzer was " so grossly in excess " of what he had acknowledged that the error could not have occurred through inadvertence or error,[97] nevertheless he was constrained to vote for acquittal on the strictly legal ground that Sulzer had not committed an impeachable offense. " As has been often expressed," Cullen wrote, " the object of impeachment is to remove a corrupt and unworthy officer. But a corrupt and unworthy officer is an entirely different thing from an officer who has, before his office, been unworthy and corrupt. . . . The rule contended for amounts in reality to an ex post facto disqualification from office for an offense which had no such penalty when committed, without affording opportunity for showing repentance or atonement." [98] Assuming even that falsifying a certificate was technically a crime, he continued, neither disqualification nor forfeiture of office was the prescribed penalty. Three Judges of the Court of Appeals, Bartlett, Chase, and Werner,[99] agreed with Judge Cullen's conclusions. Yet, not one among those voting against conviction made any attempt to condone Sulzer's transgressions. Although there was a division on the question of Sulzer's legal guilt, there was practically no division of opinion about his moral guilt. Judge Chase remarked : " I have no doubt that the respondent is guilty of the immoral acts charged in the first article of impeachment." [100] And Judge Werner asserted even more strongly,

97 The evidence given by Sarecky, he maintained, could not relieve Sulzer of responsibility, for the greater amount of money contributed was received by Sulzer personally.

98 *Proceedings*, II, p. 1625.

99 Unable to reach an opinion with dogmatic certainty as to the legal impeachability of the offense charged, Judge Werner gave Sulzer, as he said, " the benefit of the doubt."—*Ibid.*, p. 1685.

100 *Ibid.*, p. 1603.

" We know that he has committed acts which are so morally indefensible that they can hardly be described in language of judicial air and form." [101] Few of the Senators voting for acquittal volunteered any reasons, content to subscribe to the views of the Appeals Judges.

Those voting for conviction maintained that the constitution conferred upon the Assembly the power of impeachment without any limitation and that the violation of the Corrupt Practices Act did constitute an impeachable offense. While the acts charged to Sulzer were committed prior to his induction into office, it was argued, they were so directly connected with his official life and so intimately related to the discharge of his official duties as to make them inseparable. " A grave offense committed before induction to office may constitute cause for impeachment," wrote Judge Miller, " provided it so touches the office and bears such a relation to the discharge of its duties as to unfit the offender to discharge those duties." [102] There was no precedent for precisely such a case, he pointed out, because the law to secure publicity of campaign contributions was not enacted until 1906. Four Judges of the Court of Appeals shared Judge Miller's views: Hiscock, Collin, Cuddeback, and Hogan. The vote on the first article was: guilty, thirty-nine; not guilty, eighteen, and Sulzer was convicted by one more than the necessary two-thirds. Had the four Senators whose votes were challenged at the beginning of the trial been disqualified, the charge obviously would not have been sustained. Of the thirty-four Senators who voted for conviction, twenty-three were Democrats and eleven were Republicans. Eight Democrats and six Republicans voted to acquit.

The procedure accompanying the vote on the second article, which charged Sulzer with committing perjury in swearing to the correctness of his campaign statement, was similar to that on the first. The balloting followed the reading of the article

101 *Ibid.*, p. 1685.
102 *Ibid.*, p. 1654.

by the clerk. The roll call showed the same division as on the first: guilty, thirty-nine; not guilty, eighteen, the Appeals Judges splitting in precisely the same way as a matter of consistency. Few of the Judges or Senators explained their votes at length, the reasons given, in most instances, not varying from those on the previous article. The only new point was that made by the Chief Judge, who held that legal perjury could not be predicated on falsely swearing to a matter that was not material, inasmuch as the election law did not require that a candidate's statement of contributions received by him be verified by oath. This opinion was challenged by Senator Blauvelt who declared that even if Sulzer were not guilty of legal perjury, his offense, " measured by moral standards," was just as great, since the intent to deceive was there.[103]

On the third article, which alleged bribery on the part of Sulzer in trying to influence witnesses called to appear before the Frawley committee, the vote was unanimous for acquittal. There was no discussion, each member of the court registering his vote as the clerk called his name, the Chief Judge dispensing with the formality of propounding the question to each one individually.

On the fourth article, charging Sulzer with attempting to suppress evidence before the investigating committee by means of threats, he was found guilty by a vote of forty-three to fourteen. Several changes from the preceding vote were recorded. Six members of the Court of Appeals were among those voting to sustain, the only ones casting negative votes being Cullen, Hiscock, and Miller. Judging by the explanatory remarks of the court, Sulzer was convicted on this article chiefly on the basis of Peck's testimony. The position of the dissenting minority was stated by Judge Cullen when he emphatically denied the right of the Court of Impeachment to broaden the scope of the article to include the testimony of Peck and other witnesses, which had not formed the basis of

103 *Ibid.*, p. 1689.

the original indictment. To construe what passed between the respondent and Peck as a threat to remove the latter, he declared with some feeling, " is to substitute suspicion for proof, vagaries of imagination for evidence." [104] Sulzer was being charged with one crime and convicted of another. The majority, however, inclined to the view that the Peck incident was clearly within the purview of section 814 of the Penal Law. " It seems to me to require the narrowest kind of technical reasoning to hold that, because Peck was not mentioned by name in the fourth charge, it must be regarded as insufficient to charge the offense established by his testimony," asserted Judge Werner. A " menace," he added, need not be by word of mouth, "but may be fairly implied when the relations of the parties to such a transaction, as was testified to by Peck, are such that the very request carries with it the menace in case of non-compliance." [105] The importance of Sulzer's conviction on the fourth charge, in a legal sense, lay in the fact that, unlike articles one and two, it applied to conduct while in office.

The vote on the fifth and succeeding articles was taken on October 17, and disposed of in short order. On article five, charging Sulzer with having prevented Colwell from testifying before the Frawley committee, the unanimous verdict was " not guilty." On article six, charging him with grand larceny in converting campaign contributions to his private use, every Judge and Senator likewise recorded his vote in favor of acquittal. The general attitude was that on the evidence adduced, Sulzer had unquestionably taken advantage of his nomination to obtain large sums of money for his own enrichment, but that the misappropriation of campaign contributions could not be regarded as larceny in the legal sense. But there was little to afford comfort to Sulzer and his friends in his acquittal on this article, for all the Judges and Senators who explained their vote took occasion publicly to condemn the moral turpitude of

104 *Ibid.*, p. 1617.
105 *Ibid.*, pp. 1721-22.

Sulzer's offense. Senator Bussey described the acts charged against Sulzer as " panhandling." [106] Senator McClelland characterized the personal solicitation of campaign funds as " candidatial mendicancy." [107] And Chief Judge Cullen, though not considering Sulzer's conduct as illegal or criminal, at the same time stigmatized his acts as displaying " such moral turpitude and delinquency that if they had been committed during the respondent's incumbency of office I think they would require his removal." [108]

On article seven, accusing Sulzer of corrupt use of office in attempting to influence the votes of members of the Legislature, the vote of the court was fifty-six for acquittal, Senator Frawley being excused at his own request. In connection with his vote, Senator Brown made the observation that at least three-fourths of his colleagues felt that the charges made were " matters of such notorious information that they believed them completely," but that they refused to be influenced by knowledge derived from outside sources.[109] On the eighth article, accusing the Governor of using his position to affect the price of securities on the Stock Exchange, he was also unanimously exonerated. While voting not guilty, Senator Foley declared that in seizing upon an issue which was popular, Sulzer was " guilty of hypocrisy and all that may be condemned in the actions of a demagogue." [110]

Having convicted Sulzer on the first, second, and fourth articles of impeachment, the court proceeded to a formal ballot on the question whether he should be removed from office. Forty-three voted " yes," twelve " no," Judge Cullen and Senator Wende, both of whom had consistently declared for acquittal on each of the articles, not voting, and Sulzer stood

106 *Ibid.*, p. 1734.
107 *Ibid.*, p. 1736.
108 *Ibid.*, p. 1621.
109 *Ibid.*, p. 1741.
110 *Ibid.*, p. 1746.

stripped of his official title, the goal of a lifetime of endeavor. Every other Judge of the Court of Appeals voted for Sulzer's deposition. It was a solemn and impressive moment in the courtroom when the verdict, which sent out of office the man who less than a year before had been sworn in as Governor, was announced. Sulzer was spared the crowning humiliation when the court with unanimity, Judge Cullen again not voting, agreed not to disqualify him from ever holding public office again. That question, the members agreed, was one for the people themselves to decide. As the clock reached the noonday hour, the formalities incident to adjournment were complied with, and the only High Court of Impeachment ever convened in New York State to try a Governor went out of existence. The judgment of the court was formally certified by the clerk and Presiding Judge and filed with the Secretary of State. That afternoon the Sergeant-at-Arms of the Senate served a copy on Sulzer, who received the news with surprising calm.[111] Glynn was soon after officially sworn into the Governorship in Judge Cullen's private office.

A few hours after his removal from office Sulzer released to newspaper correspondents at the Executive Mansion the long-deferred and long-heralded statement promised by him at the conclusion of the trial. It proved to be a sweeping profession of innocence and an extended attack on Charles F. Murphy and the Court of Impeachment, but contained no specific allegations concerning his threatened disclosures. " By virtue of a power beyond the present control of our electorate," he began, " I now hand back to the people the commission they gave me, and I hand it back to them untarnished and unsullied." No legal evidence had been adduced at the trial, he said, to disprove the denial of the charges against him that he had made on August 11. He spoke of the impropriety of Senators Wagner, Frawley, Ramsperger, and four others having voted on the impeachment, in view of the fact that they had a personal interest in

111 *Tribune*, October 18.

the outcome of the trial or, as his prosecutors, had condemned him in advance. Had they refrained from voting, he pointed out, he would have been acquitted. " My trial, from beginning to end—so far as the Tammanyized part of the court was concerned—was a farce, a political lynching, the consummation of a deep-laid political conspiracy to oust me from office. I am tired of being calumniated, tired of being hunted and hounded, tired of trying to do my duty and being traduced." All the court's rulings, he maintained, had been against him and well-settled rules of evidence thrown to the winds. " A horse thief, in frontier days, would have received a squarer deal." The Tammany boss had ordered his impeachment, controlled most of the members of the court, dictated its procedure, and wrote its judgment. It was a " star-chamber proceeding," where the enemies of the state could work for his conviction undiscovered. " They called it the high court of impeachment, but history will call it ' Murphy's High Court of Infamy.' The trial was a human shambles, a libel on law, a flagrant abuse of constitutional rights, a disgrace to our civilization, and the verdict overturned the safeguards of liberty, and the precedents of three centuries. The judgment will not stand the test of time. The future historian will do me justice, and posterity will reverse the findings of the court."

Having declined to obey the orders of the boss concerning patronage or stop the further exposure of Tammany graft and corruption, he had been threatened by Murphy with " degradation and removal from office." He had wanted to take the witness stand in his own behalf, he said, to tell the story of his troubles with the boss, to deny the Peck " fabrication," to disprove " the absurd story " of Ryan, and to explain the Morgenthau testimony, but his lawyers had advised against it because, under the rulings of the court excluding the testimony of Hennessy and other of his witnesses, it was apparent that his own story would also be ruled out as incompetent. " Peck lied about me to save his job " was his reply to the testimony of the State Superintendent of Public Works. " Morgenthau was fooled by a clever ruse of an unscrupulous enemy," and Ryan, he said, was kept in Albany several days " under the tutelage of astute counsel to aid the prosecution at the psychological moment in any way desired." He denied that he had ever requested Ryan to intervene in his behalf with Root, Nicoll, Barnes, or Murphy. " The matters were afterthoughts of the prosecution to injure my case with the public, and prejudice my case with the court."

Every dollar given him, he insisted, though deposited to his personal account, had been subsequently turned over either to his campaign committee or to an agent of Murphy. He was still heavily in debt, he said, and poorer than before his election. Had he wanted to make money out of his campaign, he would not have rejected donations of upwards $100,000 or borrowed money from Reilly, Meany, and others. The only admission he made was that he was " careless " about his campaign contributions. " Looking back over it all I am frank to say that I now realize that I should have been more careful in some matters last fall, but I was so busy in the campaign that I gave no heed to details and trusted others, some of whom proved treacherous; but so far as my administration of the Governorship is concerned, I have no regrets, as my conscience is clear and tells me truly that I have done no wrong." [112]

Sulzer's statement was a disappointment even to his friends, who had expected something more definite. In view of his absence from the trial, it lacked whatever force it might otherwise have had. He did not, except in the remotest way, go into the merits of the charges against him. His references to the testimony of Peck and Ryan were suspiciously vague and, in any event, should have been made on the witness stand, under oath and subject to cross-examination. There was no denial of his having sought and received a ten thousand dollar contribution from Ryan. Of the senatorial votes in the impeachment court, some might be attributed to factional hostility, but it is

[112] The entire statement appears in the *Times*, October 18.

safe to assume that the judicial members of the court were swayed by no such considerations. Of the latter, six voted for his conviction on one count and five on two others. To charge his conviction to factional hatred was, therefore, pretty wide of the mark. Even those who voted to acquit him did so only on a point of law. He insisted that he had refrained from taking the stand on the advice of counsel, but Herrick divulged the information that until four days before the close of the trial, counsel for the defense had expected to put him on but decided not to do so *at the suggestion of Sulzer himself.*[113]

For a time there was some talk, emanating from members of Sulzer's " kitchen cabinet," of an appeal to the United States Supreme Court for a writ of prohibition against the judgment of the Court of Impeachment on the ground that the Code of Criminal Procedure limited the cause for removal to corrupt conduct in office.[114] This report was coupled with the intimation that Sulzer would refuse to vacate the Executive Mansion until the highest tribunal in the land had passed on the constitutional aspects of his removal from the Governor's chair.[115] Counsel for the impeachment managers ridiculed the suggestion, pointing out that since an impeachment court had exclusive and final jurisdiction, there could be no review of its proceedings.[116] This view was concurred in by Herrick, who stated there could be no appeal from the verdict.[117] Marshall definitely set the rumors of an appeal to the Supreme Court at rest with a public statement to the effect that his connection with the Sulzer case had ended with the trial.[118]

113 *Times*, October 18.
114 *Ibid.*
115 *World*, October 17.
116 *Ibid.*
117 *Times*, October 18.
118 *Ibid.*

CHAPTER VII
POLITICAL AFTERMATH

THAT the conviction was a just verdict was the prevailing opinion of the New York press. While agreeing with friends of the Governor that political animus inspired the charges of wrongdoing against him, the *Sun* believed that Sulzer's " turpitude and moral unfitness " were clearly demonstrated. " No words of condemnation, of indignation, or of disgust can add a shade of blackness to the picture drawn by the witnesses against him and the self-portrayal by his own course of cowardly, shifty evasion," it wrote.[1] The *Herald* agreed that his " immoral conduct " made him " unfit for high place in the state." [2] The *Evening Post* remarked : " Despite all the reserves one may have about some aspects of the verdict against Sulzer, the final exposure and political extinction of such a man must be thought of as a wholesome thing in our public life. Those who really knew him, knew that he was absolutely unfit to be Governor of New York." [3] The *World* commented : " In Sulzer's downfall the people of New York have a concrete illustration of the fate that overtakes Tammany's office-holders when they waver in their subserviency to Tammany and to Tammany's boss. Had Sulzer continued to take orders from Murphy he would never have been impeached. . . . It was only when he rebelled that they dragged him from his high office to merited shame and disgrace." It concluded quite cogently, " William Sulzer was impeached by Murphy's Assembly not for what he had done but for what he had refused to do. He was convicted by the Court of Impeachment not for what he had refused to do but for what he had done. It is a just verdict. Whatever differences of opinion there may be about certain

1 Editorial, October 17.
2 Quoted in *Literary Digest*, October 25, 1913, Vol. 47, p. 742.
3 Editorial, October 17.

intricate questions of law, there can be no substantial differences of opinion about the facts in the case." [4] The *Times* felt that political and factional motives had nothing to do with the trial. " The Governor's conviction was amply required by the evidence submitted," it declared, " and no man voting for it could be charged with really wronging him." [5] The most charitable view that might be taken was that Sulzer was afflicted with what it described as " moral imbecility " and might not have realized the ignoble nature of his own acts. [6]

The *Tribune* deplored the fact that the court so greatly widened the scope of the impeaching power in treating Sulzer's offenses as impeachable, maintaining that it was a clear departure from constitutional usage to remove a man from office for other than official derelictions. " If a Governor can be removed for doing something as a candidate for office," it remarked, " is he not liable to removal for something he has done as a candidate for nomination, or even years earlier in his business or professional career? Is the impeachment proceeding to be made a drag-net for moral delinquencies running away back to early youth? If this is good law, it conflicts with practical sense." [7] The *World,* on the other hand, regarded the new precedent as " sound and wholesome." What this country needed was more, not fewer, impeachments, it observed, adding, " If the broader powers of impeachment are ever abused, it is for the people to deal with that offense, just as it is for the people to deal with the motives of Sulzer's accusers, which the Court of Impeachment did not and could not take into account." [8]

Up-state newspapers, being almost wholly Republican, showed a disposition to sympathize with Sulzer and to de-

4 Editorial, October 17.
5 Editorial, October 19.
6 Editorial, October 18.
7 Editorial, October 17.
8 Editorial, October 17.

nounce his assailants. " The decree of the Delmonico Directorate has been carried out! The head of William Sulzer has fallen! " declared the Auburn *Citizen*.[9] " He has been recalled because he broke faith with the boss," wrote the Albany *Knickerbocker Press*.[10] The Buffalo *Courier* called his removal " a brutal conspiracy," and went on to say: " No such disgraceful railroading process was ever before known in an impeachment case. It was high-handed, and unworthy of even a Mexico or a Russia." [11] The Rochester *Herald* felt that the Governor stood convicted of " nothing worse than monumental follies and weaknesses. . . . The removal of William Sulzer will be greeted with unconcealed joy by every crooked politician, every grafter in or out of office, and every criminal in or out of jail." [12] The Binghamton *Republican-Herald* was convinced that Sulzer was " put upon the rack and broken " because of his exposure of graft and corruption. " Sulzer sinned morally," it conceded, " but not at a time when his sin attainted his right to the Governorship." [13] The Rochester *Evening Times* saw Murphy " in the saddle " with Sulzer's retirement to private life.[14] " William Sulzer has been punished. Now let the people decide that Murphy and Murphyism shall be punished," advised the Syracuse *Journal*.[15] The Buffalo *Evening News* regarded Sulzer's removal as a revelation of " how Tammany does business," and called for an end to " boss domination." [16] The Elmira *Advertiser* spoke of his conviction as " a great crime of a discredited organization gone mad," adding, " Sulzer undoubtedly brought down the wrath of Tammany upon his

9 Quoted in *Evening Post*, October 21.
10 *Ibid.*
11 Quoted in *Times*, October 19.
12 *Ibid.*
13 Quoted in *Evening Post*, October 21.
14 *Ibid.*
15 *Ibid.*
16 *Ibid.*

head by his decision to break away from the old corrupt organization and to run the State government in the interest of the people. Whatever may have been his faults and his transgressions, we are convinced that this is true, and we give him credit for his good intentions. The State has been disgraced and humiliated." [17] The Utica *Observer* referred to his removal as " this monstrous thing," and declared that it had not in recent years witnessed indications of such deep resentment against a political organization as prevailed against Tammany.[18]

A few up-state newspapers went against the tide of public opinion and refused to permit the motives of his accusers to obscure the question of Sulzer's guilt. The Binghamton *Press,* for example, said : " He made no defense, because he had no defense to make. Only his summary removal from office could wipe out the disgrace he brought on the state." [19] The Poughkeepsie *News-Press* unsparingly condemned his resort to " shifty evasion and cowardly denial." [20] The Buffalo *News* remarked : " That the proceeding had its origin in political feeling is beyond doubt, but the enemies of the Governor could not invent facts, and they did not." [21] The Jamestown *Evening Journal* felt that sympathy on Sulzer was wasted for he was " not of the material of which heroes and martyrs are made." [22] A similar sentiment was expressed by the Rochester *Union and Advertiser,* which found that the deposed Executive's " moral sensibilities " were dulled and that he was lacking in the " fineness " demanded of holders of high office.[23]

Editorials in representative periodicals showed a marked division of opinion. The *Outlook* took the stand that Sulzer's

17 *Ibid.*
18 Quoted in *Times*, October 19.
19 *Ibid.*
20 *Ibid.*
21 *Ibid.*
22 *Ibid.*
23 *Ibid.*

guilt was " secondary in importance to the freedom of a people from selfish, corrupt, and irresponsible rulers." [24] While conceding that Sulzer did all that he was charged with doing, that he was morally culpable and should have been required by his own sense of honor to account for gifts which were obviously intended for campaign purposes, and that the Court of Impeachment was within its rights in recalling from office a man whom it considered unworthy of trust, nevertheless, it contended, " in the light of the facts brought out at the trial, and in the light of the struggle that William Sulzer has had with the Tammany organization, we do not believe that his offenses, though undeniably grave, were of the sort that warrant even so high a court as the High Court of Impeachment to remove him from office." [25] Many men in public life, it pointed out, regarded the Corrupt Practices Act as " mere formal warnings, rather than positive mandates," [26] and were proverbially careless in the handling of campaign funds. Whatever Sulzer's faults might be, he had, during the nine months that he occupied the Governorship, made an excellent record for progressive legislation and, by forcing the invisible government to come into the open, had performed a great public service. " If Mr. Sulzer had been a complaisant servant of Tammany Hall, he would never have been impeached," it remarked. " Not since the days of Tweed has Tammany displayed such confidence in its own power." [27] The *Review of Reviews* took a similar stand. " The trial of Sulzer," it declared, " has been the most shameful proceeding in the history of American administration." [28] It left the Governor's standing as Chief Executive " clear and virtually unassailed." His collection and expenditure of money did not appear in a creditable light, but there

24 October 18, 1913, Vol. 105, p. 360.

25 *Ibid.*, p. 361.

26 *Ibid.*, p. 356.

27 October 25, 1913, Vol. 105, p. 391.

28 November, 1913, Vol. 48, p. 532.

was nothing disclosed at the trial that should have been held as sufficient ground for impeachment. " If Governor Sulzer had been willing to do even a part of the things Mr. Murphy desired, there would have been no thought of impeaching him." [29] The real animus against him was that he tried to be true to his oath of office. Not disgrace, but honor and respect were due him for submitting to exposure rather than " play the game " with Tammany. " It has been Tammany Hall and the Tammany system on trial from the start, with the fate of Mr. Sulzer a mere incident." [30]

The *North American Review,* on the other hand, expressed the belief that Sulzer had never been fit to be Governor and had been nominated wholly as a matter of expediency. " There was never any doubt of his mental incompetency," it observed. " A rattle-brained demagogue he always was and always appeared to be." [31] It called him a " poor, unbalanced egotist " who had been raised to a position of the highest authority, only to wreck his own life and humiliate the whole state. " Whether or not or for what reason Tammany instigated the impeachment of Mr. Sulzer," it concluded, " it was not Tammany, but Mr. Sulzer, who was put on trial." [32] As a matter of public policy, *World's Work* viewed the Sulzer verdict as a real step forward and felt that it established a higher standard of rectitude in public men.[33] The *Nation,* after a careful and objective analysis of the evidence in the case, rendered the following judgment: " In his disgrace and downfall great political lessons are writ large for all the people. We shall not again lightly delude ourselves that the gravest faults of personal character and of public record can be condoned or covered up by patter about ' the people,' as if there were an incantation in the phrase.

29 *Ibid.*

30 *Ibid.*, p. 533.

31 November, 1913. Vol. 198, p. 593.

32 *Ibid.*, p. 595.

33 December, 1913, Vol. 27, pp. 135-37.

Nor shall we be disposed to fancy that the espousal of even good causes by an official unworthy of trust can do anything but weigh them down. Governor Sulzer is removed from office and his power is broken; but the solemn warning of his career will abide." [34]

Though convicted after a fair trial, the ardor of Sulzer's partisans remained undampened. On the eve of his departure from Albany, a group of local admirers arranged a public demonstration for him at the Executive Mansion at which they presented him with a loving cup on which was inscribed: " Presented to Hon. William Sulzer by the Citizens of Albany in Loving Remembrance of Duties well Performed—a Martyr to the Cause of Honest Government." [35] In his brief welcoming address Sulzer expressed his appreciation of the confidence reposed in him, appealed from " Murphy's high court of infamy " to the higher court of public opinion, and announced his determination to continue his fight for the people's rights.[36] He accepted the nomination for member of the Assembly offered him by the Progressives of the Sixth Manhattan District, the candidate already nominated withdrawing voluntarily so as to create the necessary vacancy, as the road to what he hoped would be a political comeback.[37] His return to New York City was like the triumphal entry of a popular war hero. From the moment his train arrived in Grand Central Terminal until he had completed his tour of the lower East Side, he was never deserted by a big crowd of wildly enthusiastic admirers who gave him a tumultuous welcome. Thousands flocked to the sides of his automobile as it swung into the congested thoroughfares of the East Side, blocking its progress. Not only the

34 October 23, 1913, Vol. 97, p. 376.

35 Forrest and Malcolm, *op. cit.*, p. 185. McCabe described Sulzer's visitors as " a collection of the rarest political crackpots I have ever seen."—*Times*, October 19.

36 Forrest and Malcolm, pp. 185-86.

37 *Times*, October 22. Both the county and state chairmen of the Progressive party unsuccessfully opposed Sulzer's nomination.—*Ibid.*, October 21.

streets, but roofs, windows, and even fire escapes were jammed with welcomers, frantically waving, cheering and shouting their acclamation.[38] It was a unique demonstration of the unwavering devotion of those whom he delighted to call " the plain people."

The most detailed statement of " the true and only reasons " for his impeachment and removal made by Sulzer appeared in an interview with James Creelman in the New York *Evening Mail* on October 20, 1913. It was dictated just as soon as the verdict of the Court of Impeachment released him from the " pledge of silence " he said he had given his counsel, and was purported to be based on testimony which he would have given had he appeared at the trial in his own defense. As expected, his story was an arraignment of the Tammany leader. It answered none of the charges on which he was convicted, but was made up almost entirely of his conferences with Murphy, of the humiliating demands made upon him by the Tammany chieftain, and of the threats and insults he had to endure. " I was impeached," he declared, " not because of the offenses with which I was charged, but because I refused to do Charles F. Murphy's bidding, and because, as the records show, I have relentlessly pursued Mr. Murphy's corrupt henchmen in office. . . . This has not been a fight about politics, but a naked fight of dishonesty to crush a governor of the state of New York because he dared to be his own master."

Sulzer revealed how, a few days before taking office, Murphy tried to bind him by offering him " party money " with which to pay his debts. Not wishing " to be tied hard and fast as governor in advance," he declined the offer. He was telling this, he explained, in order to show the people how their elected officials were tempted by the bosses. Nevertheless, he and Murphy continued to have meetings, largely through the instrumentality of Judge Edward E. McCall, in an effort to reach an understanding. The next time they met was at McCall's

38 *World*, October 22.

house in New York City to discuss the appointment of a Public Service Commissioner to replace Willcox. Murphy, he alleged, asked him to appoint a friend of his, John Galvin, to the post. Sulzer, in turn, urged Henry Morgenthau, and finally suggested McCall as a compromise candidate, to which appointment Murphy assented. At this meeting and subsequently, he said, Murphy demanded from him pledges concerning legislation and insisted upon other appointments, some conspicuously unfit. He insisted that George M. Palmer should be named chairman and Patrick E. McCabe a member of the Public Service Commission of the second district. He further insisted upon having " The " McManus for Labor Commissioner, and upon selecting the State Architect, State Hospital Commissioner, and State Highway Commissioner. Following the removal of Reel from the office of Commissioner of Highways, he began to hear " pretty vigorously " from Murphy, who apparently was more determined than ever to secure the place for his friend " Jim " Gaffney. At a meeting in Senator O'Gorman's rooms in the Shoreham Hotel in Washington on the evening of the fifth of March, Murphy again sought assurances that he would appoint Gaffney Commissioner of Highways, as an " organization matter." When Sulzer remained obdurate, repeating his objections to Gaffney, he quoted Murphy as saying, " It will be Gaffney or war."

" I had several talks with Mr. Murphy and in some of these talks I told him I was the governor; that the people elected me to be governor, and that I intended to be governor; that I was not going to be a proxy governor, or a rubber stamp. He laughed at me and rebuked me for this, and said that I might be governor but that he controlled the legislature; that unless I did what he wanted me to regarding legislation and appointments I could not get my nominations confirmed and that he would block everything. I listened to these boasts and threats from Mr. Murphy not once but frequently. It was all disheartening and discouraging, but I tried to be patient, to get along with him, and do my best."

From the beginning of January to April 13, he stated, hardly a day passed that he did not receive peremptory demands from Murphy to do one thing or another. " Some requests were reasonable and I granted them; some were so unreasonable and so much against the people's interest that I refused to consent," for he was determined to make a good record as Governor and do what he believed to be right. On one occasion, during a talk with Murphy, the latter said to him : " Unless you do what I want you to do I will wreck your administration as governor, block all your legislation, and defeat all of your appointments." He warned him also of the things he " had " on him unless he complied. " Stand by the organization and you will be all right. If you go against the organization I will make your administration the laughing stock of the state." Up to the very night the Assembly passed the resolution of impeachment " in obedience to Mr. Murphy's orders," Sulzer said, Murphy's emissaries continued to come to him to demand that he do certain things and to threaten him if he refused. The principal emissary was Edward E. McCall, who usually spoke of Murphy as " the Chief." " I was impeached, not because of any misdoings, but because I declined to recognize Mr. Murphy as ' the Chief '—the invisible and all-powerful ' Chief ' in the government of this state."

Everything that was brought out by the Frawley committee, by the Vermont perjury " fabrication," and by the breach of promise " frame-up " in Philadelphia, he declared, was " used in the secret effort to coerce me into obedience to the boss." His exertions in behalf of truly progressive government were blocked by the refusal of the " Murphy legislature " to let him install in office men capable and willing to work out progress. His attempt to halt " monumental frauds " and " thievery " on the highways and canals was thwarted when the legislators cut off the appropriations necessary for an effective investigation.

His final interview with Murphy took place in the latter's home on the night of April 13, a date, he said, which was marked in his memory for "Murphy's insolence to me and for the sordid brutality of his demands." "We sat in the front parlor and talked over the situation at Albany—appointments, legislation and so on. Mr. Murphy would agree to nothing I wanted, and I didn't agree to anything he wanted. . . . Before we parted that night, I warned Mr. Murphy that he would wreck the party and accomplish his own destruction if he persisted in shielding grafters and violating platform pledges. His angry retort was that I was an ingrate, and that he would disgrace and destroy me." He was reluctant, he admitted, to break with Murphy and anxious to keep on good terms with the organization. "I knew the terrible odds against me in the fight which I courted when I declined to submit to Mr. Murphy's dictation; when I declined to turn my office into an instrument for the corruption of government and the debauching of the state." But it became impossible to avoid a break with Murphy "and not betray my oath of office and forfeit every shred of self-respect." And it was because of his determination to fight that he was marked for "political slaughter."

While Murphy and he quarrelled over patronage and appointments and disagreed on legislation, the real issue was fraud and corruption. "When I discovered through agencies which I set at work the tremendous frauds and overwhelming corruption existing in various departments of the state government, by which a few politicians and contractors were robbing the taxpayers of millions of dollars, I determined as a matter of duty to defy Mr. Murphy, regardless of political or personal consequences. . . . The truth is that if I had been willing to connive at corruption, if I had been willing to act as a pliant and servile tool for the men whose sole conception of politics is plundering the public, there would not have been so much as a breath of attack upon me, or a suggestion of impeachment proceedings." That and his fight for direct primaries severed all relations between the Tammany leader and himself. "It was a matter of self-preservation for Mr. Murphy and his lieutenants." The signal for his destruction was given, he declared, at a meeting between Murphy and several of his aides at Delmonico's on May 20. " The conference lasted many hours and it was finally decreed, after they had gone over everything, that they had to ' get me,' and that I must be removed from office." After that, he continued, every agency known to these " political conspirators " was set in motion. " My life was raked from the time I was born down to the present day by detectives, investigators and various sleuths, with a view of finding out something that would injure me. Criminals and perjurers were utilized to defame me. I was hampered and obstructed in my official duties and privately hounded, denounced and threatened."

Giving his side of the story of the campaign contributions, he took up the case of Samuel A. Beardsley, whose evidence had been ruled out by the Court of Impeachment. During the campaign, he alleged, Beardsley had offered him $25,000 in cash on behalf of Anthony N. Brady. Inasmuch as Brady had interests that might be affected by subsequent legislation, he asserted that he refused the money, and that Beardsley then took it to Murphy, for which the latter never made an accounting in any filed statement of campaign receipts. He had declined to accept more than $100,000 offered him during the campaign. Was it likely, he asked, that a man who turned down such large amounts " would improperly convert to his own use the comparatively petty contributions upon which the Murphy agents in the prosecution laid such great stress? "

Sulzer's story appeared to the *World* as " an astounding revelation of Tammany's system of government by corruption, intimidation and blackmail." [39] But to the *Times* Sulzer appeared to be " self-accusing rather than exculpatory." How did it happen, it inquired, that Sulzer, the champion of the people and eloquent advocate of purity and honesty in public office, found it necessary or expedient to talk over legislation

39 Editorial, October 21.

or appointments with Murphy? " It must have been his incli-
nation, not his duty, that led Sulzer to consult Murphy," it
inferred. After all the insults, threats and humiliations, to
which he himself testified, he nevertheless again conferred
with Murphy as late as April 13. " The conclusion is inevitable," it wrote, " that Mr. Sulzer was very much a Murphy
Governor, a Murphy sort of man. He has never been anything
but a Tammany man, and according to the evidence of his
own statements it appears that he would be a Tammany man
and a Murphy man still but for the fact that his ambition to
be State leader brought him into conflict with the boss." [40]
The *Telegraph* wrote that thinking men would refuse to condemn McCall upon the testimony of a Governor who made
a false affidavit concerning his own campaign expenses, and
concluded: " Sulzer is either an informer who ' snitches ' on his
pals or he is a falsifier of facts. Either horn of the dilemma
leaves him in a sorry plight." [41] The *Commercial* said that
Sulzer's story was all " a matter of inference and innuendo." [42]
The *Sun* found the Sulzer narrative full of inconsistencies,
falsehoods, and admissions of its author's unworthiness. It
recalled his unequivocal statement, issued on February 3, that
Murphy had made no recommendation to him " directly or
indirectly " of any candidate for Public Service Commissioner,
and asked him how he would reconcile that with the one made
in the Creelman interview. That contradiction, it contended,
furnished " an absolute and final test " of Sulzer's right to be
believed in anything he had to say about past political events.
" The direct issue of veracity is between William Sulzer on
February 3, when he had no perceptible motive for misrep-
resentation, and the impeached and disgraced Sulzer on October
20, when every impulse of revenge and every present political

40 Editorial, October 21.

41 Quoted in *Literary Digest*, November 1, 1913, Vol. 47, p. 797.

42 *Ibid.*

interest suggests to his weak and wobbly mind an attempt at falsification." [43]

Answering only for himself, Edward E. McCall professed himself " shocked at the falseness of the utterances " of the deposed Governor and made a categorical denial of Sulzer's statements. Those statements " so far as they refer to me," was his emphatic rejoinder, " have not a word of truth in them, and I have more pity for him than abhorrence of them." He specifically disclaimed ever acting as a go-between for Murphy to the Governor. " I never," he said, " from the time that Governor Sulzer was installed in office down to the present day, took any message of any kind to him." He admitted that the conferences between himself, Sulzer, and Murphy, to which Sulzer referred, took place, but maintained that they were all sought by the Governor himself. Also, he said, every time he visited Albany, it was upon Sulzer's " urgent personal request." [44] He declared that Sulzer repeatedly urged him to become Public Service Commissioner as a duty, a contention borne out by Sulzer's own statement to the press the morning after the appointment was announced, and that Sulzer's reported mention of other names for the position was " pure figments of his imagination." He never, he said, received any intimation from Murphy to call on Sulzer nor did the Tammany leader ever suggest that he recommend anyone for appointment to the Governor. The only names he, McCall, ever suggested to Sulzer were those of two men for Supreme Court vacancies, both of whom were designated.[45] And finally, he said, he had never heard the name of McManus mentioned for an office by anyone except by the Governor himself.[46]

During the municipal campaign that followed, marked by occasional riotous disturbances,[47] Sulzer reiterated his tale of

43 October 22.
44 *Tribune*, October 21.
45 *Post*, October 21.
46 *Tribune*, October 21.
47 *Times*, November 2.

martyrdom and waged a bitter fight on " Murphyism." His removal gave him a grievance which he used to good advantage and he stumped the city in the interests of the Fusion ticket, exposing Tammany corruption in state affairs by employing material that came to his hands during his incumbency as Governor. He played successfully on the emotions of his sympathetic audiences and his speeches were undoubtedly an important factor in the defeat of the Tammany ticket. Among other things, he asserted that he had sent the ten thousand dollars Ryan contributed to his campaign directly to Murphy through Delaney and accused Murphy of failing to account for it. He also stated that it was Murphy who induced him to ask for the money and that the " Chief " continually urged him to solicit contributions from heads of corporations and people identified with special interests, which, of course, he was " very reluctant " to do. In answer to Ryan's testimony before the Court of Impeachment, he denied ever having asked him to tell his father that he was " the same old Bill," nor had he ever asked him to request Root and Nicoll to intervene in his behalf. On the contrary, he declared, it was Ryan himself who, during the early stages of the impeachment, had offered to help him.[48] This drew from Ryan a prompt denial in which he described Sulzer's story as simply another exhibition of his quality of " lying." " Without hesitation," he replied, " I say that Mr. Sulzer is not telling the truth," and repeated substantially the same story he told on the witness stand. He did not volunteer any information at the impeachment trial, he pointed out, and appeared only in response to a subpoena.[49] Probably even more damaging to Tammany were the attacks made by Hennessy during the mayoralty campaign on Murphy and McCall, in which he not only corroborated the ex-Governor's accusations but also gave a mass of details of highway and canal graft that he had un-

48 *Ibid.*, October 26.

49 *Ibid.*, October 27.

earthed during the course of his investigations.[50] His startling disclosures, while they remained to be proved, added fuel to the flames of popular resentment.

In an unusually long statement issued on October 27, Murphy entered a sweeping denial of the series of allegations made against him by Sulzer.[51] " Coming as they do after Mr. Sulzer's conviction for perjury by the highest court in the state, by the significant vote of 43 to 12," he began, " fair-minded and honest men will question the truth of these charges." Why, he asked, if these statements were true, was he afraid to face the High Court of Impeachment and make them under oath on the witness stand? " Up to the very day the court convened he promised to go before the court and expose me. He failed to do so." He scoffed at the suggestion that the verdict was in any way influenced by him. " The fact is," he said, " that the only man responsible for the disgrace and downfall of Governor Sulzer is William Sulzer himself." He branded as " an infamous falsehood " the story that he had offered Sulzer money to pay his debts. " I never offered him a dollar in my life," he declared. He emphatically denied ever sending emissaries to Sulzer to demand that he do certain things or to threaten him if he refused or ever seeking pledges regarding legislation and appointments. He had never asked Sulzer to meet him at any conferences; but it was Sulzer, on the contrary, who asked McCall to invite him. He acknowledged meeting Sulzer and McCall at the latter's home on February 2 and submitting the name of John Galvin for appointment as Public Service Commissioner, but maintained that the Governor opposed the appointment on the ground that " Hearst would not stand for one of Mayor Gaynor's Commissioners," and that then the Governor himself suggested McCall who, after much urging, agreed to accept. Neither at this interview nor at any other was Morgenthau mentioned by Sulzer for that position, he added. He disclaimed threatening the Governor that it would be

50 See especially *World*, October 22, and *Times*, October 25, 28.

51 The entire statement appears in the *Times*, October 28.

" Gaffney or war," contending that the expression was coined by Sulzer himself, and proved from Sulzer's own statement that he was " lying." [52] He had never, he said, endorsed any candidate nor attempted to influence in any way the Governor's appointments to judiciary positions, and had, in fact, advised all to send their applications directly to the Governor. He denied the charge that he had threatened to wreck his administration, to disgrace him, or that he had demanded the calling off of Blake. " This is absolutely false," he declared. " Neither Mr. Blake nor the subject of prisons was mentioned at all. Mr. Blake did not begin his prison investigations until after the meeting referred to." He also branded as " another falsehood " Sulzer's allegation that he had threatened him with impeach- ment unless Hennessy's investigation were called off. With reference to the so-called Delmonico conference of May 20, at which Sulzer's removal from office was supposed to have been decided, he stated: " This is another Sulzer invention. No such conference was held at any time. I was not at Delmonico's at all on May 20." Speaking of the April 13 conference with the Governor in his home, he declared that Sulzer requested the conference over the telephone. " When he [Sulzer] came in," he narrated, " he began at once to assure me he was my best friend, and asked me not to take his speeches seriously. He talked about his direct primary bill, and said it would strengthen and not weaken the organization." There was one statement of Sulzer's that Murphy did not deny altogether. He admitted having received a $25,000 campaign contribution from Beardsley, but maintained that after thinking the matter over, he returned the money to Brady the following day.[53] He denied,

52 In one part of his *Mail* interview Sulzer alleged that Murphy issued the challenge, while in another part he said some one else did. Hennessy thought that the " Gaffney or war " message was brought to Sulzer by a certain William E. Payne, whom he described as a friend of Murphy. — *Times*, October 21.

53 The truth of that cannot be definitely ascertained. Brady died during the summer, but Beardsley issued a statement saying that the money was returned. He did not state, however, who returned it.—*Times*, October 30.

however, the charge that he had received $10,000 as a campaign contribution from Allan A. Ryan, and in conclusion refuted the charge that he had ever told Sulzer to collect money from prominent people or corporations. " Recent events," he remarked sarcastically, " show that he needed no such advice." In view of the direct conflict of testimony, it is not easy from the statements and counter-statements, to reach a definite conclusion. It was simply a case of every one calling every one else a liar.

Sulzer's story that his impeachment was decreed by Murphy and his aides at a conference held in Delmonico's on May 20 was said to be based on information contained in a letter sent to Hennessy by a certain Eugene D. Wood, Albany lobbyist for the public utilities, urging the veto of the Murtaugh hydro-electric bill.[54] If there ever was such a conference, it could hardly have been the one referred to by Wood because his letter, as evidenced by the postmark, was mailed from New York City on May 18![55] The letter, moreover, made no reference whatever to any impeachment; the only subjects taken up at the conference, it said, were the hydro-electric and primary bills.[56] Almost every one of those supposed to have participated

54 Hennessy in the *World*, October 22; also Forrest and Malcolm, *op. cit.,* pp. 76-77.

55 Forrest and Malcolm, *supra*, p. 90.

56 The letter reads as follows :

" My Dear John :—

I hope the Governor is to veto Murtaugh's Hydro Electric Bill. It is surely to his political benefit and advantage to do so. They had a meeting last Wednesday Eve at Delmonico's regarding that Bill and the Primary Bill. Glynn and McCabe were present. So was McCall, McCoohey [McCooey], Wagner and Murphy. It hits many of his enemies by veto—and makes many friends and no enemies by doing so. I wish you would make it strong with the Governor how important it is to him. Of course, I am thinking of how it hurts me. Let me hear if you think I can do anything that will help him to veto the Bill. He can for sure make many friends and get much help by vetoing it, and gain nothing the other way, but help his enemies and give them a club for future use. With best wishes I remain

Yours sincerely,

Eugene D. Wood."

—Forrest and Malcolm, *supra,* pp. 92-93.

in the alleged conference emphatically denied it. Wagner called it " a deliberate falsehood," adding, " I never attended such a meeting." [57] McCall spoke of it as " a pure, unvarnished false-hood." [58] McCabe said it was " a lie from beginning to end." [59] Glynn declared it to be " an absolute and malicious falsehood " and stated, " I never, directly or indirectly, discussed the impeachment of Governor Sulzer with Mr. Murphy at Delmonico's, or with any one else anywhere in the world." [60]

The result of the New York City election cost Tammany four years' control of the government. John Purroy Mitchel, Fusion candidate, rode into the mayoralty on an anti-Tammany wave with more than 120,000 plurality over McCall, carrying every borough.[61] Fusion also swept the Board of Aldermen and won all but one vote in the Board of Estimate.[62] Tammany not only lost control of the municipal government but practically every county and judicial office as well.[63] A severe rebuke was also dealt to the Murphy Democrats up-state, the candidates backed by the organization going down to defeat in every instance. The revolt against " Packy " McCabe's leadership led to the election of a Republican mayor in Albany.[64] Sulzer Democrats also deserted the ticket in Auburn, Amsterdam, Oswego and other up-state cities.[65] The Tammany machine in Erie County was shattered. William Fitzpatrick was deposed as leader when the entire anti-Tammany ticket was elected in Buffalo.[66] Almost all the dispatches to the *Times* of its up-state

57 *World*, October 23.
58 *Times*, October 22.
59 *World*, October 23.
60 *Ibid.*, October 26.
61 *Times*, November 6.
62 *Ibid.*
63 *Ibid.*
64 *Ibid.*, November 5.
65 *Ibid.*
66 *Ibid.*

correspondents expressed the opinion that the feeling aroused by the impeachment of Sulzer was primarily responsible for the reaction against the Democratic organization.[67]

The Democratic party also lost control of the lower branch of the state Legislature, electing only forty-eight members.[68] The Republicans scored heavily even in the old Tammany strongholds. In Kings County, for example, the Democrats elected only six Assemblymen, as compared with twenty-two the year before.[69] In New York County the Democrats elected only eighteen, as compared with thirty-three.[70] In Erie County the Democratic organization succeeded in winning only three of the nine seats, as compared with eight the year before.[71] Of the seventy-nine Assemblymen who had voted for Sulzer's impeachment, only forty-six were renominated, and of those only seventeen were returned by their constituents, all the latter being from Tammany districts in New York, Kings, or Bronx Counties.[72] Sulzer himself, after a spectacular fight, was triumphantly elected to the Assembly, defeating his Republican opponent (who ran ahead of the Democratic candidate) by almost three to one.[73]

The Sulzer impeachment, followed, as it was, by what one newspaper called " the most detailed exposure of the Democratic organization's corruption known since the days of Tweed," [74] was considered by most political commentators a

67 *Ibid.*

68 *Red Book*, 1914, p. 649.

69 Legislative Manual, 1913, pp. 746-50; 1914, pp. 820-23.

70 *Ibid.*, 1913, pp. 752-57; 1914, pp. 825-30.

71 *Ibid.*, 1913, pp. 743-45; *Red Book*, 1914, pp. 693-94.

72 *Times*, November 6. Several Assemblymen in up-state counties, both Republicans and Democrats, who had voted for the impeachment resolution, were refused renomination for that reason alone. See *Current Opinion*, Vol. 55, October, 1913, p. 224.

73 Legislative Manual, 1914, p. 825.

74 St. Louis *Globe Democrat*, quoted in *Literary Digest*, Vol. 47, November 15, 1913, p. 928.

contributory, if not the major, cause of the record-breaking Fusion victory in New York. " The history of William Sulzer, and the incidents, real or apocryphal, ascribed to Tammany rule at Albany," conceded the *Evening Sun,* a McCall supporter, roused " a tremendous and irresistible wave of popular wrath, indignation, destructive fury." [75] Multitudes were convinced that the Governor was a victim of personal and political vengeance, and, so far as Tammany was concerned, was pursued and removed, not because his conduct was illegal or improper, but because he would not take orders from Murphy. Sulzer himself had no doubt that it was his efforts that had brought about the undoing of Tammany. " Murphyism is dead," he cried jubilantly. " I have the satisfaction of knowing that I struck the abhorrent thing and the threatening menace the hardest blow it has received since the days of Tweed." He interpreted the success of the Fusionists as a personal vindication. " The voters have now condemned Mr. Murphy, reversed the judgment of his High Court of Impeachment, and vindicated me by the verdict of the polls, which in the last analysis is the opinion of mankind," he asserted. " My removal from the Governorship by an ignorant, corrupt, and arrogant Boss, whose dictates to do wrong I defied, has been the means of destroying Bossism in the State of New York, and I can console myself with the reflection that I was able to accomplish more out of office than all the Governors in the last decade could accomplish in office. . . . In the theft of the Governorship, Murphy decreed his own destruction." [76]

The removal of Sulzer proved to be a political blunder, for in its efforts to destroy Sulzer, Tammany suffered a débâcle from which it took years to recover. The overwhelming defeat led to open talk of rebellion and freely expressed demands for Murphy's retirement as leader.[77] A former Tammany politician

75 *Ibid.*
76 *Times,* November 5.
77 *Ibid.,* November 6.

bluntly declared that Murphy's " stupid leadership " in forcing
Sulzer's impeachment was directly responsible for splitting the
party in the state and wrecking it in the city.[78] The movement
to depose Murphy was short-lived, however, and he remained
to suffer an even more humiliating defeat in the next state
election.

In January, 1914 District Attorney Charles S. Whitman
began a John Doe inquiry into the graft charges made by
Sulzer during the municipal campaign against Murphy and
others in the Tammany camp before Chief Magistrate McAdoo
and a grand jury. When summoned under subpoena to tell
what he knew about graft conditions in the state, Sulzer again
gave many particulars of his strife with the Tammany leader
and of the latter's repeated threats to wreck his administration
if he persisted in exercising his own judgment.[79] His first difference with Murphy, he said, came in December, 1912, when he
was still Governor-elect. The Tammany boss angrily rebuked
him at the time for " butting in " with regard to some canal
contracts.[80] He quoted Murphy as warning, " If you are going
to begin this way I can see now where you will end as Governor. You do what you are told hereafter and don't take any
action on matters that don't concern you without consulting
me." [81] And when he replied that he intended to be his own
Governor, Murphy retorted, " Like hell you'll be the Governor." [82] His story included the information that when the Im-

78 *Ibid.*, February 3, 1914.

79 *Ibid.*, January 22, 1914.

80 Though not yet Chief Executive, Sulzer had sent a telegram to the
State Canal Board asking its members to defer action on all canal contracts
until he had had a chance to confer with them.—*Tribune*, December 22, 1912.
The explanation given by Sulzer at the hearing for interfering was that
he had learned that the Board was preparing to reject the bid of a certain
contractor, James C. Stewart, even though he was the lowest bidder,
because of his refusal to make a $150,000 campaign contribution to Tammany.
—*Times*, January 22, 1914.

81 *Evening World*, January 22, 1914.

82 *Times*, January 22, 1914.

peachment Court was already in session, Delaney brought him the message that Murphy would obtain enough votes in the court to prevent his removal provided he would halt Hennessy's investigation. " If, up to the very last minute, I had been willing to compromise with corruption, I would not have been removed," he declared.[83] Both Murphy and Delaney assailed Sulzer's testimony. Murphy said it was all " absolutely false " and expressed a readiness to take the stand himself, waiving immunity, and prove Sulzer to be " a perjurer and liar." [84] Delaney asserted that Sulzer's testimony " was made out of whole cloth," that anything concerning him was " false from beginning to end," and likewise asked to be called as a witness in the inquiry in order to be able to refute the testimony under oath.[85] In a second appearance before the grand jury, Sulzer repeated substantially the same story he had told once before and most of his testimony again bore on his war with Murphy that cost him the Governorship.[86] Although he had promised to produce documentary evidence to bolster up his graft charges, he added nothing to what had already been made public. No disclosures were made that warranted criminal action and the John Doe investigation resulted in little more than newspaper headlines.[87]

On February 23, 1914 Sulzer started court action to test the validity of his removal. Mandamus proceedings were entered by his counsel, Alexander S. Bacon, in the Supreme Court of Albany directing the state Comptroller to pay him his salary as Governor from the date of his removal until the end of 1914, when his term would ordinarily have expired.[88] The

83 *Ibid.*, January 23, 1914.   84 *Ibid.*

85 *Ibid.*   86 *Ibid.*, February 27, 1914.

87 When asked by the author why Whitman did not procure any indictments against Murphy or other organization leaders, Sulzer's explanation was that Whitman " sold out " to Tammany for the Governorship.

88 *The People of the State of New York ex rel. William Sulzer v. William Sohmer. as Comptroller of the State of New York.* Attorney-General Carmody appeared in opposition to the petition.

principal contentions raised in the petition were that the Assembly had acted illegally in adopting the resolution of impeachment, being at the time in extraordinary session; that in permitting Justices Hiscock, Chase, and Miller, members of the Court of Appeals only by designation, to sit in its deliberations, the Court of Impeachment was illegally organized; that Wagner and six other Senators should not have been permitted to pass judgment, having, it was alleged, either a pecuniary interest in the proceedings or having openly expressed their hostility to the defendant; and that, in any event, the acts upon which Sulzer had been convicted were not impeachable offenses inasmuch as they had occurred before he took office.[89] On March 9 Justice Alden Chester denied the application for a writ of mandamus as a matter of law and not in the exercise of discretion, taking the position that the Court of Impeachment had already passed on the petitioner's contentions and that its action was conclusive.[90] Without passing on the merits of the case, the Appellate Division of the Supreme Court unanimously affirmed the ruling.[91] The issue was then taken to the Court of Appeals which, in a unanimous opinion, delivered on June 2, sustained the decision. The court held first, that the mandamus proceeding was not a proper or available remedy to try the title to an office already held by another person not a party to the action, and secondly, that by accepting the office of Assemblyman, Sulzer automatically vacated the Governorship.[92] Sulzer's counsel announced his intention of taking the case to the United States Supreme Court for a final determination of the constitutional questions involved, but never did.[93]

89 To the petition were annexed affidavits from three Assemblymen, saying they had no advance notice that the impeachment resolution was to be presented and that if they had been present, they would have voted against its adoption.—*Times*, February 24, 1914.

90 *Ibid.*, March 10, 1914.

91 Reports of the Appellate Division of the Supreme Court of the State of New York, Vol. 162, p. 921.

92 Court of Appeals, State of New York, Vol. 211, pp. 565-66.

93 *Times*, June 3, 1914.

In the Assembly Sulzer attracted little attention.[94] Though elected on the Progressive ticket, he did not identify himself with the Progressive members but labeled himself a Progressive Democrat. He introduced a resolution calling for a sweeping legislative investigation into the affairs of all state departments but the resolution died in committee.[95] On every occasion he assailed " invisible government," continued to speak of graft in large figures and to lay it all on the contractors and politicians working under the agency of Tammany Hall, yet offered no documentary evidence beyond what material he had used in his campaign for election to the Assembly.[96] Despite the fact that he himself had been responsible for the creation of the Department of Efficiency and Economy, he voted with the Republicans and Progressives to abolish it.[97] In an unusually vitriolic speech he called it the " Department of Crooks and Cripples " and described it as the most flagrant example in the country of "waste, graft, and political peculation." [98] This outburst provoked a bitter retort from Alfred E. Smith, who spoke sarcastically of the " broken-down crackpots and ragtag politicians " who hung around the Executive Mansion during his incumbency of the Governorship. He declared Sulzer to be a menace to society whose proper place was in jail.[99] The Citizens Union's estimate of Sulzer's legislative services simply was: " Active. Record of votes good." [100]

Sulzer sought the Progressive nomination for Governor in 1914, but the Progressive leaders, convinced that he was seeking to inject himself into the party solely as a means of furthering his own political interests, contemptuously rejected his

94 *Ibid.*, January 8, 1914.

95 New York Assembly Journal, 137th Session, 1914, Vol. I, pp. 45-46.

96 *Times*, March 1, 1914.

97 *Ibid.*, March 6, 1914.

98 *Ibid.*

99 *Ibid.*

100 *Ibid.*, August 12, 1914.

bid.[101] Members of the Progressive State Committee freely used such epithets as "faker" and "proved crook."[102] Undaunted, he entered the primaries, but was beaten by Frederick M. Davenport, the organization candidate, by a slight margin.[103] Two days before the primaries, Davenport assailed his opponent as "a political and moral bankrupt."[104] Theodore Roosevelt took a similar stand against Sulzer when, in a letter to all enrolled Progressives, he urged them to vote for Davenport, declaring significantly that the party should place in nomination only a man "of character, ability, and a clean record."[105] Sulzer found new political allies, however. After a speech in which he expressed a violent abhorrence of rum, he was nominated for Governor on the Prohibition ticket.[106] He also appeared on the ballot as a candidate of the so-called American party, newly organized by a group of his admirers and independent Democrats, whose emblem was the Liberty Bell and which was dedicated "to God, the people, and the overthrow of the political bosses."[107]

The ensuing campaign was enlivened by Roosevelt's public denunciation of Sulzer. "The trouble with Sulzer," he said, "is that he does not tell the truth." His conduct, he added, was such that no upright and honorable man, after learning the facts, could continue to defend him. "It is useless to expect a public servant to wage war on corruption if his own record is vulnerable."[108] This attack on his integrity drew from Sulzer

101 *Ibid.*, July 10, 1914.

102 *Ibid.*, August 28, 1914.

103 Davenport polled 18,643 votes and Sulzer 14,366. (*Red Book*, 1915, p. 677.)

104 Roscoe C. E. Brown, *op. cit.*, Vol. IV, p. 251.

105 *Times*, September 17, 1914.

106 *Ibid.*, August 16, 1914. Sulzer was, as the *Times* (August 26) pointed out, "a teetotaler of unspecified duration." It is interesting to note that brewers were heavy contributors to his personal campaign fund when he ran for Governor in 1912.

107 *Ibid.*, August 18, 1914.

108 *Ibid.*, October 11, 1914.

an intemperate reply in which he accused the former President of dishonesty in not accounting for his own campaign contributions and of being in alliance with Tammany Hall.[109] Sulzer's avowed purpose in the campaign was to beat Governor Glynn, the Democratic candidate, whom he accused of "plotting" with Murphy "to steal" his office.[110] In this he was successful, for he unquestionably played an important part in the Republican landslide. Charles S. Whitman, candidate for Governor, and the entire Republican state ticket were elected by a large plurality.[111] The Legislature went overwhelmingly Republican. The resentment over the Sulzer impeachment, so strikingly demonstrated in the Fusion victory in New York City in November, 1913, apparently had not yet died down. Sulzer beat Davenport for third place, polling a vote more than twice as large as that of the Bull Moose candidate. Many evidences in the returns showed that large numbers of Democrats, rather than throw their votes away on Sulzer, voted for Whitman, as the most effective way of showing their protest against Sulzer's impeachment.[112] Apart from the Prohibition support and the help of the railroad men, the Sulzer vote was almost entirely one of "sympathy."[113] According to reports from upstate, most of the Sulzer support came from men who still believed that he had been unfairly removed from office and who took this means of rebuking Tammany, whom they held responsible.[114] As one voter said, "I do not think Sulzer is an angel, but after the way he was treated by Tammany I would vote for him if he was the devil."[115] Sulzer saw in Whitman's

109 *Ibid.*, October 13, 1914.

110 *Ibid.*, November 4, 1914.

111 The vote for Governor was Whitman, 686,701; Glynn, 541,269; Sulzer, 126,270; Davenport, 45,586. (*Red Book*, 1915, p. 686.)

112 *Times*, November 7, 1914.

113 Large numbers of railroad employees voted for Sulzer out of gratitude for his signing the full crew bill.

114 *Times*, November 7, 1914.

115 *Ibid.*

election still another " vindication " and " moral victory " for himself.[116]

In 1916 Sulzer was again a candidate, this time for the Presidential nomination on the Prohibition ticket, but was turned down by the national convention.[117] He was offered the nomination by the American party but declined.[118] Politically bankrupt, he retired from the scene and passed into oblivion, with a bitter memory of Tammany which the passage of years could not obliterate.

One may admit the worst about Tammany, yet retain little sympathy for Sulzer. Few men in public office were worse fitted than he for the sort of crusade he undertook. He assumed a part to which he did not measure up. He was new to the role of champion of high principle and official integrity and it did not fit gracefully. For years he had been a loyal henchman of Tammany, in days when it was no better than it was in 1913, and had been as servile to the machine as those whom he now denounced. He was born and bred in Tammany. He had trafficked with Croker and Murphy. He had sought and received political preferment at the hands of the organization. He had been nominated for Governor on the advice of its leaders and elected with their aid. Even after his impeachment he sought to bargain with Tammany for acquittal in consideration of subservience. Blinded either by vanity or ambition, he

116 *Ibid.*, November 15, 1914.

117 *Ibid.*, July 22, 1916.

118 Roscoe C. E. Brown, *op. cit.*, Vol. IV, p. 241. When, the day after election, it seemed Wilson had been defeated by Hughes for President, Sulzer prematurely rushed into print with a statement in which he attributed the Democratic defeat to his impeachment. " Wilson urged me to oust Murphy and clean up conditions in the State, and when I began in earnest to do so and the fight waxed hot Mr. Wilson went over to the impeachers and aided Murphy," he said. " That settled Wilson so far as New York, New Jersey, and a few other necessary States were concerned."—*Times*, November 8, 1916. That was his last significant utterance on politics.

set out to destroy the very agencies that had lifted him to power. But he was not himself acutely sensitive to political misconduct and was incapable of righteous wrath, the first requisite of a crusader.

Sulzer, moreover, did not enter the fight with any singleness of purpose. He saw himself a future President, and, with the lesson of Roosevelt's and Wilson's careers before him, believed that the path to the Presidency lay in championing " the cause of the people." [119] He lacked, however, the necessary courage and conviction and got no further than an unconvincing imitation of their methods. Though declaring his independence from the moment he was elected Governor, he did not consistently maintain it in his conduct. A man of keener perception than he would have foreseen that he was faced with an impossible situation. He was a representative of Tammany, which stood for patronage and the old spoils system, and at the same time of the independent Democrats up-state, who demanded from the administration release from bossism and special privilege. To serve both elements satisfactorily would have been beyond the capacity of a more resourceful statesman than Sulzer. Even his closest associates represent him as trying feebly to compromise with Tammany and as needing the earnest persuasion of his friends to stiffen him in the fight he had undertaken. " When he first went to Albany," says Hennessy, " he was glad to take orders from Murphy." [120] He never ceased playing politics. While he continued to assure the independents that he had been whole-heartedly converted to the cause of reform, he was at the same time assuring his friends in Tammany Hall that he was " the same old Bill." All he did was to go far enough in a surface appearance of independence to rouse the vengeful fury of the Tiger. He had concealed his own corruption so clumsily, that when the Tammany leaders set out to

119 Henry Morgenthau, *op. cit.*, p. 158.
120 *Times*, October 21, 1913.

punish him, evidence of wrongdoing was not hard to get. In the disgrace of William Sulzer future statesmen will find at least one useful lesson—that no man can afford to pit himself against a powerful political organization unless his own record is above reproach.

SELECTIVE BIBLIOGRAPHY

NEWSPAPERS

The files of the New York newspapers furnished a large portion of the material for this thesis. Of greatest value for the author's purpose were the following:

American: 1912-14.
Evening Mail: 1913.
Evening Post: 1912-13.
Evening Sun: 1913.
Evening World: 1912-14.
Herald: 1913-14.
Press: 1913.
Standard-Union (Brooklyn): 1913.
Sun: 1913.
Telegraph: 1913.
Times: 1912-16.
Tribune: 1892-1913.
World: 1893, 1912-13.

PERIODICALS

Century Magazine. Vol. 85 (April, 1913), pp. 951-52, "The Larger Hope against Tammany."

Cosmopolitan. Vol. 53 (July, 1912), pp. 248-49, "William Sulzer—Democrat," by J. T. Graves.

Current Literature. Vol. 53 (November, 1912), pp. 513-16, "Palladium of our Liberties."

Current Opinion. Vol. 55 (September, 1913), pp. 145-47, "Impeachment of Governor Sulzer."

——. Vol. 55 (October, 1913), pp. 223-26, "The Struggle in New York to end the Reign of Terror."

——. Vol. 55 (November, 1913), pp. 301-2, "Historic Trial of Gov. Sulzer ends in Conviction."

——. Vol. 55 (December, 1913), pp. 403-4, "Murphy, the Terrible Ogre of American Politics."

Harper's Weekly. Vol. 56 (October 12, 1912), p. 5, "Sulzer for Governor."

——. Vol. 58 (August 23, 1913), p. 25, "The Dr. Cook of Politics," by Norman Hapgood.

——. Vol. 58 (August 30, 1913), p. 3, "The Limit."

——. Vol. 58 (October 11, 1913), pp. 24-26, "The Tammany Plot," by Norman Hapgood.

——. Vol. 58 (October 18, 1913), pp. 22-23; (October 25), pp. 10-11; (November 1), pp. 25-26, "How Murphy Works," by Edmund R. Terry.

Independent. Vol. 74 (January 2, 1913), pp. 45-46, "New Governor of New York."

——. Vol. 74 (May 22, 1913), pp. 1120-21, " Governor Sulzer's Fight."

——. Vol. 75 (August 7, 1913), pp. 293-94, " The Defeat of Tammany— A National Service."

——. Vol. 75 (August 14, 1913), pp. 359-60, " Fall of Governor Sulzer."

——. Vol. 75 (August 21, 1913), pp. 420-21, " Impeachment of Governor Sulzer."

——. Vol. 75 (August 28, 1913), pp. 474-75, " Partisanship and the Obscuring of Moral Issues."

——. Vol. 76 (October 23, 1913), p. 151, " Twofold Shame of New York "; pp. 154-55, " Governor Sulzer Removed from Office."

——. Vol. 77 (February 2, 1914), p. 153, " Tammany's Boomerang."

Literary Digest. Vol. 45 (September 7, 1912), p. 359, " Organizing Against Tammany."

——. Vol. 45 (November 30, 1912), pp. 1030-31, "A Democratic Democrat."

——. Vol. 46 (May 24, 1913), pp. 1164-65, " Governor Sulzer's Fight on Tammany."

——. Vol. 47 (August 23, 1913), pp. 267-70, " Impeachment of Governor Sulzer."

——. Vol. 47 (August 30, 1913), pp. 303-5, " Struggle in New York."

——. Vol. 47 (October 25, 1913), pp. 742-43, " Removal of Governor Sulzer."

——. Vol. 47 (November 1, 1913), pp. 797-99, " Sulzer and Tammany."

——. Vol. 47 (November 15, 1913), pp. 927-29, " Tammany's Waterloo."

——. Vol. 48 (February 21, 1914), pp. 361-63, " The War on Murphy."

McClure's Magazine. Vol. 39 (October, 1912), pp. 601-13, " Pursuing the President," by George K. Turner and Arthur W. Dunn.

Nation. Vol. 96 (January 9, 1913), pp. 27-28, " New Governor."

——. Vol. 96 (March 20, 1913), p. 276, " Sincerity."

——. Vol. 97 (August 21, 1913), p. 158, " Where it leaves Murphy."

——. Vol. 97 (October 2, 1913), p. 302, " Murphy as Podesta."

——. Vol. 97 (October 23, 1913), pp. 376-77, " End of William Sulzer."

——. Vol. 97 (October 30, 1913), pp. 402-3, " Tammany's Over-played Hand."

——. Vol. 97 (November 13, 1913), pp. 451-52, " Democratic Reorganization in New York."

North American Review. Vol. 198 (November, 1913), pp. 593-95, " Sacrifice of Sulzer," by George Harvey.

Outlook. Vol. 103 (January 11, 1913), p. 51, " Governor Sulzer of New York."

——. Vol. 104 (May 31, 1913), pp. 221-22, " The Sulzer Primary Fight."

——. Vol. 104 (August 23, 1913), pp. 886-87, " Impeachment of William Sulzer."

——. Vol. 105 (September 20, 1913), pp. 106-7, " Sulzer Case in Court."

——. Vol. 105 (October 4, 1913), pp. 239-40, " Impeachment of Governor Sulzer."

——. Vol. 105 (October 11, 1913), p. 287, " Case against Governor Sulzer closed."

——. Vol. 105 (October 18, 1913), pp. 356-61, "Sulzer and the Invisible Government."

——. Vol. 105 (October 25, 1913), pp. 379-80, "Removal of Governor Sulzer"; pp. 391-92, "What are you going to do about it?"

——. Vol. 105 (November 15, 1913), pp. 567-69, "The Significance of the Elections."

Review of Reviews. Vol. 42 (August, 1910), pp. 142-43, "The Governorship and New York Politicians."

——. Vol. 46 (December, 1912), p. 654, "What Happened in New York."

——. Vol. 47 (January, 1913), p. 46, "A Message from the New Governor of New York."

——. Vol. 47 (June, 1913), pp. 682-86, "Gov. Sulzer and the fight for direct primaries."

——. Vol. 48 (September, 1913), pp. 259-72, "Impeachment—an Unusual Process."

——. Vol. 48 (October, 1913), pp. 399-400, "Governor Sulzer and his Assailants."

——. Vol. 48 (November, 1913), pp. 531-33, "Tammany and the Sulzer Case."

Saturday Evening Post. Vol. 186 (March 7, 1914; March 21, 1914; April 4, 1914; April 18, 1914), "The Trail of the Tammany Tiger," by Harry W. Walker.

World's Work. Vol. 26 (August, 1913), pp. 381-82, "Character in Public Men."

——. Vol. 26 (October, 1913), pp. 615-16, "A New Development in the Boss System."

——. Vol. 27 (December, 1913), pp. 135-37, "New Moral Standard for Governors."

——. Vol. 27 (February, 1914), pp. 432-40, "The Twilight of Tammany Hall," by Burton J. Hendrick.

——. Vol. 42 (September, 1921), pp. 465-79, "What I Learned from Sulzer and Tammany," by Henry Morgenthau.

——. Vol. 55 (November, 1927), pp. 27-41, "The Awakening of Al Smith," by Norman Hapgood and Henry Moskowitz.

GOVERNMENT DOCUMENTS

(NEW YORK STATE)

Annual Report of the Attorney-General, 1913, Vol. II.

Assembly Documents, 136th Session, 1913, Vols. 35 and 36.

Assembly Journal, 136th Session, 1913, 4 Vols.

Court of Appeals, Vols. 209 (1913) and 211 (1914).

Court for the Trial of Impeachments—The People of the State of New York against William Sulzer—1913, 2 Vols.

Legislative Manual, 1890-94 (inclusive), 1913, 1914.

Legislative Record and Index, 1913, 1914.

Miscellaneous Reports (cases decided in the Courts of Record other than App. Div. and Court of Appeals), Vol. 81 (1913) and Vol. 82 (1914).

New York Red Book, compiled by Edgar L. Murlin, 1913-15 (inclusive).

Public Papers of Governor William Sulzer, 1913.

Senate Journal, 136th Session, 1913, 2 Vols.

Supreme Court, Appellate Division Reports, Vol. 157 (1913) and Vol. 162 (1914).

GENERAL WORKS

Allen, William H., *Al Smith's Tammany Hall.* New York: Institute for Public Service, 1928.

Blake, E. Vale, *History of the Tammany Society.* New York: Souvenir Publishing Co., 1901.

Blake, George W., *Sulzer's Short Speeches.* New York: J. S. Ogilvie Publishing Co., 1912.

Flick, Alexander C. (editor), *History of the State of New York,* Vol. VII. Columbia University Press, 1935.

Forrest, Jay W. and Malcolm, James, *Tammany's Treason.* Albany: The Fort Orange Press, 1913.

Hapgood, Norman and Moskowitz, Henry, *Up from the City Streets: Alfred E. Smith.* New York: Harcourt, Brace and Co., 1927.

Hennessy, John A., *What's the Matter with New York?* New York: The O'Connell Press, 1916.

Horne, Charles F., *History of the State of New York,* Vol. V. Boston: D. C. Heath & Co., 1916.

Leary, John, *The Safety of the State, who threatens it?* New York, 1913.

Lundberg, Ferdinand, *Imperial Hearst.* New York: Equinox Cooperative Press, 1936.

McGuire, James K., *The Democratic Party of the State of New York,* Vol. III. New York: U. S. History Co., 1905.

Morgenthau, Henry, *All in a Lifetime.* New York: Doubleday, Page & Co., 1922.

Myers, Gustavus, *The History of Tammany Hall.* New York: Boni and Liveright, 1917.

Pringle, Henry F., *Alfred E. Smith, A Critical Study.* New York: Macy-Masius, 1927.

Smith, Alfred E., *Up to Now: an Autobiography.* New York: The Viking Press, 1929.

Smith, Ray B. (editor), *Political and Governmental History of the State of New York,* Vol. III by Willis F. Johnson; Vol. IV by Roscoe C. E. Brown. Syracuse: The Syracuse Press, 1922.

Straus, Oscar S., *Under Four Administrations.* New York: Houghton, Mifflin Co., 1922.

Sullivan, James (editor), *History of New York State,* Vol. V. New York: Lewis Historical Publishing Co., 1927.

Sulzer, William, *Life and Speeches* (a collection of pamphlets comprising speeches by Sulzer, newspaper editorials concerning him, and a sketch of his life by Edgar L. Murlin), 1898-1916. 3 Vols.

——, *Miscellaneous* (a collection of pamphlets consisting of speeches and articles about him), 1879-1917. 2 Vols.

——, *Scrap Books* (compiled by Sulzer during his official life), 1902-6. 7 Vols.

——, *The People's Candidate for Governor* (speeches, editorials, letters, etc. relating to his impeachment). New York: The Truth Publishing Co., 1914.

Thomas, Samuel Bell, *The Boss or the Governor*. New York: The Truth Publishing Co., 1914.

Werner, Morris R., *Tammany Hall*. Garden City, N. Y.: Doubleday, Doran & Co., 1928.

Zink, Harold, *City Bosses in the United States*. Duke University Press, 1930.

In the Cornell University Library are deposited 43 volumes of Sulzer papers containing letters, telegrams, and newspaper clippings. The material is catalogued as follows:

Vol. 1-29—Letters, A-W. Feb. 3, 1906–Jan. 22, 1913.

Vol. 30-33—Telegrams, A-Z. Sept. 4, 1912–Nov. 6, 1913.

Vol. 34-43—Newspaper clippings. March 1, 1912–Jan. 28, 1913.

INDEX